Wise Economies

Other Titles of Interest

The Great Poem of the Earth

A Study of the Poetry of Thomas Hornsby Ferril

Andrew Elkins

Elkins explores Ferril's entire body of work, including his lesser known verses, in which Ferril comes to terms with war, urbanization, and his morality.

230 pp., cloth, 1997, 0-89301-196-7

Loaded Fictions

Social Critique in the Twentieth-Century Western

Scott D. Emmert

A book with a serious scholarly purpose discussing values, character, and freedom in relation to contemporary Westerns.

212 pp., cloth, 1997, 0-89301-194-0

The World of David Wagoner

Ron McFarland

McFarland maps out Wagoner's development as a writer and provides biographical and contextual information of interest and value to the reader.

225 pp., cloth, 1997, 0-89301-200-9

Parallel Expeditions

Charles Darwin and the Art of John Steinbeck

Brian E. Railsback

Railsback demonstrates Steinbeck's careful dramatization of the human as animal.

168 pp., cloth, 1994, 0-89301-177-0

Old West — New West

Centennial Essays

Edited by Barbara Howard Meldrum

Old West—New West offers a contemporary collection of interdisciplinary insights into the character of the West and western literature.

336 pp., 1993, cloth 0-89301-166-5, paper 0-89301-163-3

Wise Economies

Brevity and Storytelling in American Short Stories

Kirk Curnutt

University of Idaho Press
Moscow, Idaho
1997

Published by the University of Idaho Press
Moscow, Idaho 83844-1107
Printed in the United States of America

Library of Congress Cataloging-in-Publication Data

Curnutt, Kirk, 1964–
Wise economies : brevity and storytelling in American short stories / Kirk Curnutt.
p. cm.
Includes bibliographical references and index.
ISBN 0-89301-202-5 (alk. paper)
1. Short stories, American—History and criticism.
2. Narration (Rhetoric). I. Title.
PS374.S5C85 1997 96-50297
813'.0109—dc21 CIP

01 00 99 98 97 5 4 3 2 1

In memory of my father,
Dr. Jerry L. Curnutt
(1942–1992)

Contents

Acknowledgments

A central thesis of this work is that stories make little sense without an audience who listens, shares, and responds. In writing *Wise Economies*, I benefited greatly from the input of colleagues, mentors, and friends, without whom this book would not have assumed the final shape it has. My greatest debt, as personal as professional, is to J. Gerald Kennedy, whose counsel and encouragement can hardly be repaid in a few paltry words. Suffice it to say that without his example, I would have felt neither the inspiration nor the perseverance to tackle such an unruly subject as the short story. After several years of inviting me to participate in various Hemingway Society functions, Susan Beegel was instrumental in introducing my manuscript to the good folks at the University of Idaho Press, whose enthusiasm and interest in the book are deeply appreciated. Linda Wagner-Martin's favorable reading remains a humbling highlight of my career, while Tom Quirk's willingness to critique various drafts when the project's future seemed uncertain is no doubt responsible for its final fruition. James V. Catano, meanwhile, entertained hours of conversation about rhetorical theory; without his insights, the narratological framework of my argument would have suffered greatly.

Others who read portions of the book while in process include Dana D. Nelson, Veronica Makowsky, Dan Fogel, Rick Moreland, Irene DiMaio, and Jesse Gellrich. For friendship and kindness, Sarah Liggett deserves special mention, as do Bob and Jo Clarke. Additionally, my work could not have matured without the aid of Richard Hocks, Robin Roberts, Lan Lipscomb, Scott Peeples,

Eamon Halpin, Russ Pottle, Michelle Massé, Carl Freedman, and Harold R. Mosher, Jr., who published an expanded version of Chapter 4 as "Direct Addresses, Narrative Authority, and Gender in Rebecca Harding Davis's 'Life in the Iron Mill'" in *Style* 28 (summer 1994): 146–68. Stephen Plotkin, curator of the Ernest Hemingway Collection at the John F. Kennedy Library, Boston, Massachusetts, has long served as an invaluable resource and critical sounding board, while Beth Alvarez, Assistant Curator of the Papers of Djuna Barnes at the University of Maryland at College Park, aided my background work during a 1993 visit. Linda Naru of the Center for Research Libraries in Chicago, Illinois, facilitated numerous interlibrary loans of obscure microfilm spools, while the library staff at Troy State University Montgomery—especially Kay Fowler, Elizabeth Heidemann, and Tim Bailey—expedited the paperwork. Glenda McGaha-Curry and Livingston Alexander, President and Vice President for Academic Affairs respectively at Troy State University Montgomery, deserve my thanks for encouraging their faculty's professional development. Dr. Gordon Pickler, Dean of Arts and Sciences at TSUM, has also been very supportive.

Finally, a note to my family, who shared the highs and walked me through the lows: to my mother, Beverly, who endured five years of my anxieties while writing the book; to Kelley, for wanting to be a part of it all; and to Kipley, my son, for his talent as a storyteller. Unfortunately, the person I would have liked most to read *Wise Economies* never will: my father, who died shortly after I completed an early, bloated draft of a chapter in March 1992. It's in his memory that I dedicate this book, for I take satisfaction in knowing the pride and pleasure he would have felt in reading it.

Introduction: Brevity, Storytelling, and the Short Story

"We feed on short stories like living ducks," writes John Barth. "Take a breath, take the plunge, take our tidbit, and soon surface."[1] The simile evokes a variety of sensory impressions, from the tightening of the lungs to the sound of the splash, and the taste of retrieved treasure to the sight of sunlight refracted through lapping water. Perhaps its most impressive quality is compactness, for by suggesting so much in so few words, the economy creates the very experience that the sentences describe. What Barth coyly illustrates here is the fundamental intertwining of brevity and desire, how the condensation of experience inspires a reciprocal longing for its plenitude. Whether a punch or a kiss, what lingers is the sting and the salt, those aftereffects that, by continually kindling memory, inspire unconscious compulsions to repeat and re-imagine experiences. In the case of a story, as Barth suggests, brevity is a particularly profound experience. Because no narrative can absorb all the potential details that might contribute to its significance, some principle of economy must refine it. How a story is minimized in the moment of telling—and what is subsequently left out—is often what tempts the reader to risk another plunge.

The image of a narrative as a tidbit aptly introduces the core question of this study: How do we account for the peculiar element of brevity that, for better or worse, is the sole criterion defining the generic identity of the short story? I mean to enter this long-running debate by approaching this feature not as a spatial concept—not, in other words, as a matter of size, form, or structure—but as a rhetorical tradition whose causes and consequences shift according to cultural temper. More specifically, I believe that by defining brevity in rhetorical terms we are in a better position to understand why two connotations of the word *economy* have consistently attached themselves to the short story. The implications of these connotations will be discussed at length, but for now, I simply outline them. On the one hand, stylistic brevity serves an aesthetic prerogative best captured in the cliché that good fiction must show rather than tell. By presenting information only directly related to the plot, this type of economy is said to create an intensity of effect by immersing the reader in a drama of pure immediacy. Subsequently, one critical point of view argues that short stories "do not 'tell' us things . . . they are things" because their reticence foregrounds images or details at the expense of any distracting reference to context.[2] Yet it is precisely the notion of context to which a second connotation of economy alludes, for the word suggests systems of cultural exchange, narrative exchanges in particular, in which meanings are collaboratively produced by authors and audiences. Thus, another strain of commentary describes the short story in terms of its communicative function, arguing that it is "the artistic form of narrative par excellence" because it is "more self-conscious" than the novel about its status as a circulating fiction.[3]

Traditionally, critics have resolved the mutual exclusiveness of these definitions by claiming that they denote two different types of short fiction: the "dramatized and presentational" plot-driven story that can be traced loosely "from Poe through James to Hemingway" and the more self-reflexive, essayistic form popularized by Irving, Hawthorne, and postmodernists like Barth.[4] My approach, however, is not to suggest that these connotations constitute an either-or proposition, that story writers must choose between one form or the other, but rather to recognize that they progressively operate at cross-purposes. That is, within the space of history that separates antebellum tales from minimalist short stories—the space that separates Washington Irving's "The Legend of Sleepy Hollow" from Raymond Carver's "Where I'm Calling From"—we can examine how stylistic brevity as an evolving aesthetic practice redefined the interpretive demands placed upon readers. Tracing the tensions generated between these connotations of economy through a blend of narrative theory and historical criticism allows us to appreciate more fully the *sui generis* quality of American short stories. What accounts for their uniqueness finally is not any intrinsic feature—not a particular content, shape, or pre-designed effect, as countless critics have argued—but the manner by which these features allow them to assume an ambiguous space between folklore and modernization, between the spoken and written word, between culture and art.

To dramatize the tension between brevity and storytelling evident in the form's development, I have structured this book so that its central argument can be read two ways: (1) from a rhetorical perspective, in which each part examines the interpretive work that a specific narrative device demands within a set of exemplary texts; (2) from a historical perspective, in which each part emphasizes the contextual function of these devices by examining the stories as expressions of the four most prominent narrative styles that developed between the early nineteenth century and the 1980s—romanticism, realism, modernism, and minimalism.

This dual approach represents a departure from traditional genre criticism, which seeks to define the characteristics of the short story within a taxonomy of prose forms.[5] Instead, I am attempting to bridge a methodological fissure splitting the field of short-story criticism. On one side, several histories of the American form are available, from the work of Fred Lewis Pattee and Edward J. O'Brien in the 1920s, to Arthur Voss's 1973 survey, to a recent series edited by William Peden. While the older studies seem rather long in the tooth, they remain required reading, in part because few subsequent efforts have dared to imitate the breadth of their inquiry. More than seventy years after publication, Pattee's *The Development of the American Short Story* (1923)—despite its relentless prejudice against sentimental fiction and its gloomy final chapter, which forecasts the demise of the genre at the hands of textbook formulas—remains the single most exhaustive survey of nineteenth-century short fiction available. As informative as these overviews are, however, they tend not to be *critical* histories because they trace the careers of individual authors in the short-story market and concern themselves only tangentially with definition.

By contrast, a rich and varied body of recent genre theory exists, such as *Short Story Theory at a Crossroads* (1989) and *The New Short Story Theories* (1994), whose titles emphasize the newfound innovation indicative of the field. This energy and excitement can be attributed to interdisciplinary approaches, for whether borrowing from discourse analysis, linguistics, psychoanalysis, structuralism, poststructuralism, or reception theory, short-story theory of the 1980s and 1990s is more multi-dimensional, more sophisticated, and less impressionistic. Most important, its long-term inferiority complex seems to have healed. Indeed, while past commentators lamented the haphazard critical approaches to the short story, describing it as an underrated or neglected art, such disclaimers are no longer necessary.[6] But the major drawback to theoretical approaches is that their definitions are often too inflexible to account for changes in the form over time. While historians perfunctorily address the question of brevity, theoreticians disregard historical context.

Balancing history and theory allows us to redress the generalizations perpetuated by each approach. According to Norman Friedman, theorists formulate inadequate definitions of the short story because they conflate brevity with singularity. Searching for *one* trait, technique, or theme that accounts for the genre's constricted form, they tend to forget that "short stories, [as] common sense tells us, are short in various ways and for various reasons."[7] The reason, I would add, is that theory treats brevity exclusively as a spatial measure. Edgar Allan Poe's definition of the genre, expounded in his 1842 review of Hawthorne's *Twice-told Tales*, is responsible for this tendency. In this review Poe describes the tale as a "short prose narrative" that aims to create "a certain unique or single *effect*" through a "pre-established design." Three interrelated types of brevity are implicit in his definition: *thematic economy*, wherein this single effect is realized at the end of the tale; *structural economy*, wherein the pre-established design expedites this effect without digression; and *temporal economy*, wherein the story can be read in one sitting or in one hour so that, as Poe argues, an author can "carry out his full design without interruption."[8] As Poe's definition has been interpreted, brevity is a product, not a process. It is a function of the size, shape, or structure of the tale, not its style, and can be measured in terms of length, the scope of drama that it contains, or in the plot devices that make it seem abbreviated and condensed. By thinking of brevity only in spatial terms, theorists restrict their purview to the physical dimensions of a text and effectively limit themselves to abstract questions of form.[9]

Short-story historians, by contrast, offer rhetorical rather than spatial definitions of brevity. They also look to Poe for inspiration, but Henry T. Tuckerman provides a better example of their approach. Tuckerman, reviewing Hawthorne in 1851, champions the short story as a "wise economy of resources." "The choicest gems of writing are often the most terse," he writes. "As a perfect lyric or sonnet outweighs in value a mediocre epic or tragedy, so a carefully worked and richly conceived sketch, tale, or essay is worth scores of diffuse novels." While Poe locates brevity in structure, the word *terse* suggests that Tuckerman sees it as a matter of style: "It is a characteristic of standard literature, both ancient and modern, thus to condense the elements of thought and style," he notes. "It gives us the essence, the flower, the vital spirit of mental enterprise." He describes this condensing as both an aesthetic *and* ethical imperative: "All great and true things are remarkable for their simplicity. The direct method is the pledge of sincerity. . . . [T]he perfection of art never dazzles or overpowers, but gradually wins and warms us to an enduring and noble love." Tuckerman declares Hawthorne's style engaging because "he resorts to no tricks of rhetoric or verbal ingenuity" but instead employs language as a "crystal medium" through which we envision clearly "the play of his humor, the glow of his sympathy, and the truth of his observation."[10] Brevity is a commitment to what we might call honest mimeticism: It persuades by appealing to our sense of what is true and good rather than win us over with efflorescent rhetorical shenanigans.

In constructing this tradition of rhetorical brevity, historians draw from commentary by several prominent short-story masters who define shortness as a stylistic rather than formal or structural feature. In the prefaces to the New York Edition of his collected works, Henry James outright rejects spatial measures by renouncing the "rude prescription of brevity at any cost" that the periodical industry forces upon writers. When James began his career editors promoted the "dull view that a 'short story' was a 'short story,' and that was the end of it." Their restrictions made him doubt the value of the genre, for its "shades and differences, varieties and styles, the value above all of the idea happily *developed*, languished, to extinction, under the hard-and-fast rule of the 'from six to eight thousand words.'"[11] Only when Henry Harland invited him to contribute to *The Yellow Book* in 1893 without concern for "arbitrary" length did "the millennium [open up] to the 'short story'" by allowing him to luxuriate in the longer *nouvelle* form mastered by Turgenev, Balzac, and Maupassant.

Elsewhere James argues that brevity results from a writer's arduous effort to restrain his style: "There are not so many quite distinct [themes] in [the artist's] field, I think, as there are sides by which the main masses may be approached," he declares. Whatever topic he or she addresses, a writer must struggle with the fact that its compositional possibilities are endless. The "simplest truth about a human entity, a situation, a relation, an aspect of life, however small," James argues, is that it possesses "space-hunger and space-cunning." The subject matter will always seem insufficiently explained, yet writers must resist succumbing to exposition. Style is the sole device for "foreshortening" the drama because "any real art of representation is . . . a controlled and guarded acceptance, in fact a perfect economic mastery" of the "explosive principle in one's material." This "artful compromise" between content and technique constitutes the only brevity worth discussing, for "the only compactness that has a charm . . . the only spareness that has a force . . . the only simplicity that has a grace" is that which produces "the rich effect" (277–78). By redefining brevity from a formal characteristic (length) to a stylistic technique, James celebrates it as a craft for exploring the "aesthetic moral" that literature embodies.

Hemingway's theory of omission offers another way of defusing a story's explosive potential, for what he calls the "thing left out" refers to an important scene or episode that the writer must delete from the text. One thinks of the suicide that supposedly occurs after the conclusion of "Out of Season," the effects of World War I that underlie Nick Adams's recuperative fishing expedition in "Big Two-Hearted River," or the abortion never explicitly mentioned in "Hills Like White Elephants." Hemingway offered several versions of this theory throughout his career, from tentative, off-hand comments in private correspondence in the 1920s to its first public articulation in *Death in the Afternoon* (1932) to prescriptive declarations in interviews in the 1950s that, significantly, are applied exclusively to the short story. An unpublished 1959 lecture written as a preface to a projected story textbook locates the art of the genre in the omission of structural components: "If you leave out important things or events that you know about, the story is strengthened. If you leave or skip something because you do not know it, the story will be worthless. The test of any story is how very good the stuff is that you, not your editors, omit."[12] To prove it, he details exactly what he left out of his most famous stories, often exaggerating or inventing new information. (The war is not the only thing deleted from "Big Two-Hearted River," he claims: "There were many Indians in the story . . . and none of [them] appeared" [5].) Much as rhetorical brevity allows James to foreshorten the drama, omission, for Hemingway, forces readers to infer pivotal events and conflicts.

Unfortunately, as Paul Smith has shown, manuscript evidence reveals that the theory of omission rarely determined how Hemingway actually shortened his stories.[13] In the case of "The Killers," for example, in which Hemingway claimed to have left "all of Chicago out," the question of why Al and Max want to kill Ole Andreson (motivations explored in the earliest draft of the story) simply lost its relevance as the dramatic potential of symbols like the arc-light in George's diner were discovered and shaped. In the case of "Indian Camp," whose introductory scenes were posthumously published as "Three Shots" in *The Nick Adams Stories* (1972), cutting meant recognizing a superfluous or false start.

Elsewhere, Hemingway could only cultivate a sense of tangible absence by *adding* details during the revision process. Smith traces the development of specific motifs like the "one good trout" that Nick attempts to catch through the multiple manuscripts of "Big Two-Hearted River." He shows how the possibilities of "presentational meaning" were discovered only after the author rejected the original conclusion, a garrulous soliloquy that discourses upon fly fishing, marital relations, and writing. (This piece, too, appears in *Nick Adams* under the title "On Writing.") This uncharacteristic round of extensive revision confirmed for Hemingway the power of narrative reticence captured more intuitively in other early stories. Rather than expound upon Nick's interior traumas, as the original conclusion does, he could evoke them through suggestive connections to the burnt landscape, the nearby swamp, and the river itself. Ultimately, the specific needs that Nick hopes to escape—whether the war, marriage (as "On Writing" suggests), or writing itself—are less important than the effect that their omission ideally inspires, which is a close, attentive reading that attempts to solve the mystery of what is not being said. (Of course, not all audiences are similarly affected; even a sympathetic reader like F. Scott Fitzgerald originally thought "Big Two-Hearted River" was just a fishing story.) Hemingway may have assumed that he was exposing the germinal secrets of his work in "The Art of the Short Story," but the theory of omission outlined is, in many ways, as much a red herring as a good, elusive trout. In his best stories brevity results less from the spatial constriction of his original intent but from his stylistic evocation of a mood of omission.

Flannery O'Connor also defines brevity as rhetorical economy in a lecture that, unlike Hemingway's essay, was actually presented to a conference of story writers. "Fiction writing is very seldom a matter of saying things," she announces, invoking what even then was a fairly hoary cliché, "It is a matter of showing things."[14] The significance of a story lies not in the action portrayed, but in the meaning, "the mystery of existence," that particular events, however bizarre, evoke. An audience should do more than simply observe this mystery; it must experience the events through the author's appeal to the senses, for "no reader who doesn't actually experience, who isn't made to feel the story, is going to believe what the fiction writer merely tells him" (91). Authors fail because they lack the time and patience necessary to write "through the senses." As her terminology suggests, O'Connor's argument applies equally to the novel and the short story. She rejects any notion that brevity can be measured in plot or character and suggests that *short* itself is a misnomer, for a short story "should be long in depth and should give us an experience of meaning. . . . [M]eaning is what keeps the short story from being short" (94–95). Raymond Carver quotes O'Connor in his essay "On Writing," reiterating her notion that storytelling is a process of discovery for author and audience alike, thus implicitly distancing himself from Poe's notion of the pre-established design. As he argues, a successful story offers a "glimpse" of something not quite articulated; it exploits the dramatic tension that arises from "the way the concrete words are linked together to make up [its] visible action" while alluding to the implied "landscape just under the smooth (but sometimes broken and unsettled) surface of things." To achieve this tension, writers must use "clear and specific language, language used so as to bring to life the details that will light up the story. . . . [T]he language must be accurate and precisely given."[15]

Whether we speak of Tuckerman's "crystal medium," James's "rich effect," Hemingway's "thing left out," O'Connor's "mystery," or Carver's "glimpse," rhetorical economy is defined as an artistic imperative, an obligation to engage the sensory perceptions of readers by rendering one's materials in as vivid and immediate a manner as possible. Stylistic brevity is the device by which *mimetic* or imitative arts define themselves as truer and more accurate than *diegetic* or descriptive ones. In all the short-story commentary quoted above, what constitutes the aesthetic quality of stylistic economy is the greater degree of participation it (ostensibly) solicits from the reader. Narrative reticence fosters a sense of immanence, demanding a response deemed more intense and active because the focus is directed toward the fictionalized events rather than the *act* of fictionalizing them. Eudora Welty describes this intensity of engagement when she encourages writers to avoid "talkiness" because those "shafts of argument or preaching" fail to pierce the "poetic world" of suggestion and ambiguity: "The finest story writers seem to be in one sense obstructionists. As if they held back their own best interests. . . . For if we look to the source of the deepest pleasure we receive from a writer, how often do we not find that it seems to be connected with this very obstruction." We find pleasure in obstruction because it allows us "to enter the magical world of pure sense, of evocation," of a beauty arising from "reticence."[16]

Evocation, obviously, is not unique to the short story, so stylistic economy rarely serves as a qualitative distinction between prose genres. Instead, its importance rests in its influence on how the history of the short story has been written because the shift from telling to showing is the force most often identified as driving the development or advancement of the form. Nowhere is this tendency more obvious than in Pattee's survey, which routinely judges nineteenth-century storytellers against "the modern technique" of dramatization. Washington Irving, for example, "retarded" the growth of the tale for at least a generation by disregarding plot and indulging in digressive bouts of emotion: "Lacking sprightly dialogue, [their] movement impeded by description or exposition," his tales are bereft of a "culmination involving all the *dramatis per-*

sonae," and this absence of dramatic resolve accounts for the "general effeminacy and timid softness" in his work (24–25). While few contemporary critics make the mistake of judging romantic tales according to modernist aesthetics, stylistic economy nevertheless continues to exert a powerful influence over perceptions of what the short story is or should be. Indeed, presentational immediacy remains an imperative of both evaluative criticism and teaching, with story handbooks routinely warning writers to avoid the "consequencelessness" of exposition. "Brevity in a story is the art of including appropriate silence," suggests a recent contributor to *The Writer*, a mass-market advice periodical, "of making each phrase, each sentence resonate with implications so that the story is so much more than its length suggests."[17]

Yet not all commentators define rhetorical economy as an aesthetic device. Instead, many link it to vernacular traditions and thus ground their conception of the short story within a second connotation of economy as a storytelling exchange. Perhaps the clearest articulation of this concern is Bret Harte's "The Rise of the Short Story" (1899), which wholesale dismisses Poe and Hawthorne for working with "inherited [i.e., British] literary traditions" and traces the roots of what Harte argues is the truly *American* short story to oral traditions such as the tall tale and joke telling. Obviously, one can take issue with the claim that antebellum story writers perpetuated the "old-fashioned methods" at the expense of native materials, but the argument gains an odd credibility in light of Brander Matthews's comment that this "chatty and somewhat uncritical" article defines "the special kind of Short-story Mr. Harte himself had chosen to write": stories that self-consciously evoke folk culture traditions of oral narrative.[18] However questionable its accuracy, the essay posits an intriguing connection between style and social function. As the "funny story" circulated in informal conversation, it was slowly absorbed into formal events like political stumping, camp meetings, and preaching. While "serious or polite literature" emulated British styles, the oral story became the expression par excellence of American English: "It was a foe to prolixity of any kind, it admitted no fine writing nor affectation of style. It went directly to the point." Because it emerged from the economy of the spoken word, the truly American short story approaches its subject "with no fastidious ignoring of [folk culture's] habitual expression, or the inchoate poetry that may be found even hidden in its slang." Throughout Harte's essay, the two meanings of economy work congruently: Storytelling, as a popular form for circulating shared experiences, must avoid the prejudices of more elitist, literary styles. Rhetorical brevity is not the product of aesthetic reticence but of devotion to the "naturalness" of American language.

Harte's argument is by no means without precedent. As early as 1744, *The American Magazine and Historical Chronicle* pontificated on "The Art of Story-telling" in decidedly proto-nationalistic terms, for to speak "not a Word too much, or too little" necessitates a brisk, economical language, something unfortunately not possessed by the French, who tend to tell "little or nothing in a great number of words." John Neal's "Story-Telling" (1835) likewise foreshadows "The Rise of the Short Story" by claiming that a good story cares little for the literary affectations of style but draws its authority from the voice of "real life." Whether discovered in "a steamboat or a stage-coach . . . a bar-room or a barber's shop," its drama arises less from the cleverness of its presentation than its *whapper* quality, the necessary "straightforwardness and simplicity" of expression, "which are irresistibly impressive." One could cite as well Mark Twain's "How to Tell a Story" (1895), which educates would-be storytellers on the mechanics of constructing an effective persona grounded in feigned naïveté, casual indifference to the punch line or *snapper*, and a smart use of pauses. Twain may claim that the advice is valuable only for those seeking to tell a tale "by word of mouth," yet the techniques outlined are so characteristic of his tales, whether "The Notorious Jumping Frog of Calaveras County" or "The Man that Corrupted Hadleyburg" that medium is ultimately a moot point.[19]

Such essays are concerned with aesthetics, but not *literary* aesthetics. Rather, by associating the short story with what Walter Benjamin in his luminous essay "The Storyteller" (1936) calls "the realm of living speech," Harte, Neal, and Twain define a different sort of engagement than James, Hemingway, O'Connor, and Carver. The latter claim that stylistic economy demands a more intense reader response because it renders events more vivid and immediate, while the former agree with Benjamin that stories are social events through which a storyteller "takes what he tells from experience—his own or that reported by others. . . . And he in turn makes it the experience of those who are listening to his tale."[20] It is the act of exchanging stories and the profound cultural ramifications of that act that are foregrounded in these essays. What they outline is a type of brevity that, rather than requiring us to grapple with the unfolding of an aesthetic form, invites participation in a community. Benjamin's somber meditation on the dying art of storytelling in the industrial age specifies how the brevity of the vernacular tradition functions. The heaping on of "psychological analysis" and "shading" whose "prime requirement is that it appear 'understandable in itself'" fails to invite readers to assimilate the story within their world view. "The more natural the process by which the storyteller foregoes psychological shading," Benjamin writes, "the greater becomes the story's claim to a place in the memory of the listener, the more completely is it integrated into his own experience, the greater will be his inclination to repeat it to someone else someday, sooner or later." Such repetition is vital because "storytelling is always the art of repeating stories" (89–90). By speaking of brevity as the exclusion of facts and details so "the narrative achieves an amplitude that information lacks" (89), he defines short stories (at least those that evoke oral traditions) as the broken bread of experience. Though passed from lip to lip, they are never fully consumed but always replenish themselves through the solemn, social gesture of sharing.

Again, short-story historians traditionally account for differences between these traditions of rhetorical brevity by claiming that they distinguish different types of short fiction. The problem with categorizing texts in this manner is that their segregation implies that stylistic economy and storytelling are mutually exclusive issues. "Dual-tradition" arguments enable the notion that narration is less relevant to a Hemingway text simply because it is less obvious, or worse, that an Irving tale is somehow less artistic because it foregrounds its performative context, as Pattee insists. Historical criticism can benefit from an application of narrative theory, for a more productive form of analysis would recognize that in any given text, brevity and storytelling operate in a certain concomitance or ratio that creates interpretive demands particular to that story. Hemingway's "The Killers" offers a convenient illustration of how even an extreme economy of presentation nevertheless reveals itself as a story told to an audience. While the style is so pared down, so dependent on dialogue that many critics describe it as a story without a storyteller, certain clues do indeed imply that our access to events passes through an intermediary perception. A simple sentence like "In their tight overcoats and derby hats [the killers] looked like a vaudeville team" reveals an evaluative consciousness texturing the story since someone must be responsible for this analogy. As Susan Snaider Lanser remarks, the fact that "asides" like this do not break the overall tone of reticence implies the presence of an "invisible eyewitness" rather than a "wholly effaced recorder of words and deeds."[21]

In such a case, the quotient of stylistic brevity to storytelling provides a device for challenging the commonplaces of historical and theoretical approaches to the short story. Because historians often betray aesthetic prejudices by describing the genre's development as an *evolution* from primitive telling to sophisticated showing, we can explore how readers might compensate for presentational immediacy and retain a sense of the storytelling exchange. And because theorists tend to measure brevity in spatial terms without reference to historical context, we examine the devices that evoke the storytelling exchange as products of the short story's various periods. In this approach, brevity is not fixed within a formal or structural feature but serves instead as a relative measure, a sort of sliding scale, of the signs of address that convey to us just how we should assimilate a story. Obviously, the specific narrative devices I examine (storytelling frames in romantic tales, direct addresses in realistic short stories, attributional devices in modernism, and the present tense in minimalism) are not the only ones by which a scale of rhetorical economy can be constructed. Nevertheless, they allow us to trace the exchange between storytellers and audiences as we survey the protean forms that storytelling has assumed over the last two centuries. Doing so, we recognize that brevity in American short stories need not be measured according to size, shape, or form but according to the rhetorical acts that define its shifting social function.

Part 1

Getting the Point: Storytelling Frames and Narrative Purpose in Romantic Tales

Prologue

In an 1847 review of Hawthorne's short fiction, Poe attacks prevailing attitudes toward brevity by calling into question the "fatal and unfounded [critical] prejudice, which it will be the office of this age to overthrow—the idea that the mere bulk of a work must enter largely into our estimate of its merit." While even the most superficial critic likely recognizes that "size or mass," when "abstractly considered," bears little relation to quality, Poe complains that reviewers nonetheless equate artistic accomplishment with the "sustained effort" necessary to produce more expansive works, especially the epic. "Let us . . . admire the effort," he declares, but not "the epic on the effort's account." Confusing the labor of literary production with its fruit is fallacious, for "perseverance is one thing and genius quite another." As proof of the foolishness of this prejudice, he quotes from a *North American Review* attack on William Gilmore Simms's story collection *The Wigwam and the Cabin* (1846) that smugly claims to have "little opinion of the mere tale." "The honesty of the avowal," Poe responds in a clever put-down, "is in no slight degree guaranteed by the fact that this Review has never yet been known to put forth an opinion which was *not* a very little one indeed."[1]

While perhaps not as small-minded as Poe claims, reviewers in the antebellum era were hardly circumspect when expressing their indifference toward the "mere" tale. Fred Lewis Pattee's *Development of the American Short Story* excerpts several *bon mots* that confirm the persistence with which perseverance was equated with genius: "We should advise the accomplished writer to try her hand at a more elaborate and sustained effort," reads one unattributed quotation, employing the very phraseology that Poe singled out for disdain. The brevity of form rendered short fiction a journeyman or apprentice practice; at best, it provided a "literary toy" by which "our young men" might "prove their powers and . . . prepare them[selves] for future and nobler exertions . . . to be worked up in more enduring materials."[2] As "enduring" implies, prejudice against brevity was not reserved for diminutive size alone but addressed as well the genre's physical ephemeralness, its material dependence on the periodicals, gift books, and annuals popular in the mid-1820s and 1830s. Always embedded within a larger design, surrounded either by magazine articles or other short fictions compiled in a collection, the tale was incapable of standing alone and presenting itself as an *objet d'art*.

This prejudice haunts the genre throughout its history, of course, but it seems particularly entrenched at a time when the sustained effort of literary production was emphasized—dramatized even—by publisher packaging. The popular multivolume format for novels enhanced their market value by investing in them a material opulence; even works that were too short to bind profitably by halves or thirds were published with multiple title pages, as if to foster the illusion of greater mass. Given this stress upon physical dimension, the tale was doomed to appear anemic or frail by comparison. Indeed, for many publishers, the form's lack of autonomy raised severe doubts about its commercial viability. In the mid-1830s, Poe's prospective story collection *Tales of the Folio Club* was rejected by two publishers who recommended that he sell them piecemeal on the periodical market where they were more likely to turn a profit. Before the appearance of *Twice-told Tales* in 1837, Hawthorne's earliest attempts to gather his work in book form met a similar fate when three different story collections failed to interest publishers, leaving individual pieces to be printed in the periodical press.

Obviously, Poe was not the only critic who attempted to legitimate the tale as a viable form of literary expression. Like Henry T. Tuckerman, who described the genre as a "wise economy of resources" whose reticence allowed meanings to be "shadow[ed] forth" rather than declaimed, Rufus Griswold sought to change negative attitudes toward brevity in an early celebration of national literature entitled *The Prose Writers of America* (1847). Producing the three-volume novel may demand "more application," more "time and toil," Griswold conceded, but the shortness of the tale necessitates the "finer genius" of knowing what to leave out, an art more noble than any aptitude for padding that expansive works might display. Similar comments appear with increasing frequency throughout the 1850s as periodical editors liberally borrow from Poe's reviews of Hawthorne—sometimes acknowledging his influence, sometimes not—as they trumpet the greater unity and intensity of effect that brevity affords.[3] And just as detractors did not restrict their suspicions of the tale's merit to questions of form, not all defenders defined shortness in aesthetic terms.

Indeed, a comparatively neglected body of commentary is devoted to advancing a cultural function for brevity instead of advocating its artistic merit. In an 1838 editorial supporting the need for an international copyright law, *The American Monthly Magazine* claimed that what critics derided as "minor literature," including tales and sketches (as well as essays and reviews), was actually "the highest species of writing" because the magazines in which they appeared afforded them "a mode of reaching the public mind more direct than the writing of a book." Few readers, the editorial claims, enjoy the leisure time necessary to luxuriate in thick folios:

> This is too busy and active a time for the older forms of literature. . . . [Instead,] the age requires condensation, vigor, point. Modern literature is miscellaneous in its character; it has no less influence than the old, but it is exerted in a different way. It gains and conquers by repeated blows.[4]

The shift from "condensation" to "miscellaneous" is so swift that one can easily glide over the connection established here. As an inexorable condition of the age, brevity demands a simplicity of presentation that makes these "minor" literary forms accessible to an audience beyond the "quiet old gentlemen living on retired entailed estates" who have time to bury themselves in big books. Because periodical literature reaches more people, it functions as an agent of diversity by linking disparate audiences. By speaking to the varied interests and desires that characterize a broad readership, shorter prose forms "giv[e] a general cast to society," a representative picture of the differences contained within similarity.

As Kristie Hamilton notes, a similar argument can be found in the prefaces to several story miscellanies. From Washington Irving to Nathaniel Parker Willis to Fanny Fern, sketch and tale writers excused the diminutiveness of individual selections by claiming that brevity accommodated a variety of temperaments and expectations. Audiences might not be satisfied by the overall performance, but every reader could find at least one appealing element. The result of this emphasis on the part instead of the whole, as Hamilton demonstrates, was to portray reading as a uniquely private form of pleasure, an experience determined by "distinct individual preference—there is something for everyone but everyone has different tastes."[5]

I introduce these definitions of brevity largely by way of justifying why I will not be speaking more formally about them, for I want to explore here the narrative implications of this link between condensation, vigor, point, and miscellaneity. That is, I want to examine how the communicative structures of the tale encourage the "distinct individual preferences" of its readership by framing audience expectations and inviting participation in the storytelling exchange. Because this invitational function is abbreviated throughout the genre's history (and not its size, form, or structure), this part of the book sets the scale against which subsequent sections are measured. Privileging explicit narrative forms is a strategic maneuver on my part, for although the tale has long been distinguished from the later short story according to the prominence of its "enunciative posture" and "interested language," which "suggest how the reader is to take things," genre critics until recently described this convention as a primitive trait that the form wisely shed as it evolved.[6]

Traditionally, the tale's narrative self-consciousness is defined thematically (as opposed to functionally) in the context of Romantic poetics. "Interested language" either underscores artists' intrigue with the pathetic appeal of poetic language or, because it dramatizes the power of fancy, celebrates the higher morality of imaginative literature. More recently, gender-oriented approaches have read the tale's relative garrulity as an extension of the sex roles assumed by literary personae. Storytelling frames may provide the ironic masks by which male writers assumed the ethos of "teases" and "loiterers," deceptively practicing the art of self-deprecation in order to hide their "self-congratulatory manifesto of irresponsibility," as Ann Douglas describes the bachelor narrators populating

Irving's *The Sketch Book of Geoffrey Crayon, Gent.* (1819–20), Willis's *Pencillings by the Way* (1844), Ik Marvel's *Reveries of a Bachelor* (1850), and George Curtis's *Pru and I* (1856). Or they may afford women authors earnest, empathetic voices by which they dramatize the values of interdependence and mutuality in stories constructed around the daily rituals and customs of village life, as Sandra A. Zagarell labels works like Mary Russell Mitford's *Our Village* (1824–32), Leslie Sigourney's *Sketch of Connecticut, Forty Years Since* (1824), and Caroline Kirkland's *A New Home—Who'll Follow?* (1839).[7]

What has not been discussed, however, is how the tale's narrative framing expedites the central function of storytelling: engaging audiences in acts of evaluative response. Only when we approach stories as processes of social interaction rather than aesthetic artifacts can we recognize the importance of the evaluative component of narration, which literary criticism often ignores in favor of more formalized dramatic elements like plot, theme, and characterization. Yet a narrative is more than a recitation of an event; it must justify its existence by revealing to its audience why it is worth hearing or reading. Every story must, in other words, define its purpose or point. As William Labov writes, "Every good narrator is continually warding off this question [of purpose]; when his narrative is over, it must be unthinkable for a by-stander to say, 'So what?'" Ross Chambers explains that for readers, getting the point requires decoding a tale's "situational self-reflexivity," the interpretive context embedded in the work that "specif[ies] the conditions—the necessary understandings between text and reader—for [stories] to be successful acts of literary communication."[8] Examining how Romantic storytellers stage their purpose is integral to understanding how they imagine the belief systems determining their readers' responses—and how they either accommodate those values or compensate for them. Because the appeal to readers determines continued circulation of a good story, the narrative strategies that frame a story govern the nature of the interpretive work in which readers are asked to engage.

Subsequent sections will explore the function of internal or embedded evaluative devices that lend a subjective coloring to otherwise undramatized narration, from modals and attributional devices to tense. In the case of the Romantic tale, I want to focus on the way storytelling frames comment upon the medium of transmission, because a striking characteristic of this period's short fiction is the frequency of thematic and stylistic juxtapositions of the spoken and printed word. Within these juxtapositions the link between brevity and miscellaneity can be examined, for evocations of orality and writing offer readers two different value systems within which they might evaluate the point. On the one hand, orality creates the illusion of a homogeneous "folk paradise" by inscribing into the text the immediacy of an audience bound together by mutual interests. As Alessandro Portelli writes, "these imaginary traits [of mutuality] offer a pleasant contrast to the urban, typographic experience, represented by the discrete articulation of the alphabet and the press and the strife and discontent of pluralistic politics." Storytelling frames do not resolve the clash between the idealized values of orality and the frenzy of modern print culture; rather, they fashion a "*cordon sanitaire,* a 'literary picket fence' that separates . . . vernacular orality from the observer's stance of detached writing."[9] The mingling of media is an ambivalent gesture, an attempt to maintain a sense of contact with a familiar, identifiable constituency while reserving the right to distinguish oneself from that crowd.

The richest example of the interfolding of orality and print in the Romantic period is Irving's *The Sketch Book.* The author's sentimental amanuensis Geoffrey Crayon foreshadows the nostalgia of Benjamin's "The Storyteller" as he laments the loss of community fostered by oral narration and associates "the art of book-making" with impersonal commerce. Throughout the collection books are caricatured as the province of the pedantic political elite that manipulates print to maintain its self-serving authority, while speech is the medium of honest human contact, conveying intimacy and fellow feeling. In one selection, Crayon is ejected from the British Museum's reading room for not carrying an admission card: "At first I did not comprehend . . . but I soon found that the library was a kind of literary 'preserve,' subject to game laws, and that no one must presume to hunt there without special license and permission."[10] Elsewhere, he complains to a musty old Renaissance quarto (which has mysteriously come to life) that "the inventions of paper and the press . . . have made every one a writer . . . the stream of literature has swoln into a torrent—augmented into a river—expanded into a sea" (105). The smug quarto, speaking in "intolerably antiquated terms," confirms Crayon's suspicion that print cannot accommodate the changes that time subjects upon language. In "The Legend of Sleepy Hollow" (putatively narrated by Diedrich Knickerbocker, the persona Irving first employed in his 1809 burlesque, *A History of New York*), the supernatural tales of Tarry Town residents are contrasted to witchcraft stories that Ichabod Crane recites from an edition of Cotton Mather. While the villagers enjoy the legends as entertainment, Crane assumes that his ghost stories must be true if they have been printed, his credulity allowing the Headless Horseman to scare him from the valley. Significantly, Crane disappears from Tarry Town without his books, which his landlord promptly burns because "he never knew any good come of this same reading and writing" (295).

Upon closer inspection, however, Irving's style in "Sleepy Hollow" would seem to oppose this theme, for while parodic allusions, lavish descriptive passages, and epic catalogues allude to the oral tradition of the tale, the narrative voice is far from vernacular. In what minimal dialogue there is, characters speak the same impeccable Addisonian prose as the storyteller, without the dialectical variation or regional neologisms ("Americanisms" as they were called) with which Irving's contemporaries hoped to establish a national language distinct from British English. To acknowledge this seeming contradiction, we need not be familiar with Irving's reputation as an imitator of old-world prose models, nor with the disdain for colloquial language that surfaces in his notebooks.[11] We need only contrast the Crayon/Knickerbocker voice to the narrators of Poe's "The Tell-Tale Heart" or "The Black Cat" (in which ellipses and dashes evoke extemporaneous speech) to recognize that orality is more of a thematic than stylistic issue in *The Sketch Book.*

As such, the editorial frames surrounding the story rationalize its writtenness: A brief parenthesis, presumably affixed by Crayon in the act of copying the tale into his sketchbook, notes that the legend was "found among the papers of the late Diedrich Knickerbocker," followed again by the signature of Crayon, who introduces selections with a fragment of poetry. A postscript also "found in the handwriting of Mr. Knickerbocker" describes how the historian first heard of Crane: "The preceding Tale is given, almost in the precise words in which I heard it related at a corporation meeting of the ancient city of Manhattoes. . . . The narrator was a pleasant, shabby, gentlemanly old fellow . . . whom I strongly suspected of being poor, he made such efforts to be entertaining" (296). Simply put, "Sleepy Hollow" is a *thrice*-told tale. Casting it as a verbal performance transcribed into print, Irving implicitly justifies the absence of orality in his style.

Because the concluding note inscribes into "Sleepy Hollow" its own writing down, the passage from speech to print, however fictional, raises the question of what stylistic changes have been wrought to accommodate the change in medium. If we think of print in admittedly clichéd terms such as dispassionate and rational, we might expect this retelling to formalize what was originally extemporaneous, to set straight any digressions, and to foreground clearly the purpose or point. Yet within the postscript, such expectations are ridiculed outright when the "pleasant, shabby, gentlemanly old fellow" from whom Knickerbocker first hears the tale is confronted by a heckler who demands to know "the moral of the story, and what it went to prove." The storyteller at first offers a syllogism that "most logically" explicates his intention, but when the protestor complains that the tale is still "a little on the extravagant," the shabby gentleman denies believing the story himself (297). Not to belabor the joke here, but Irving employs a print convention to satirize the mediating function that it typically serves. Within Knickerbocker's postscript, the expectations for a statement of purpose that the editorial device should gratify are rejected as superfluous. The result here is what Chambers calls an "antimodel" of reader response that tells us how not to interpret the tale. This sort of satire did not originate with Irving, of course, but, the implications of storytelling frames are more complex than the irony that a fictional editorial preface brings to, say, a *Moll Flanders*. Framing in "Sleepy Hollow" does not just undermine the difference between fact and fiction. Rather, the editorial device superimposes a written scene of storytelling upon an oral one, and, in so doing, precludes our attributing the narrative "I" to one specific narrator. Even while it passes from speech to print, the story refuses to be "authored" by a single storyteller, emphasizing instead the selfless, communal voice of oral traditions.

How this juxtaposition of orality and print solicits evaluative responses can be illustrated through a scale of narrative framing borrowed from short-story critic Ian Reid. "The Legend of Sleepy Hollow" offers an example of intertextual framing, by which "a text signals how its very structure of meanings depends on both its similarity to and its difference from certain other texts or text types."[12] Irving defines the purpose of his narrative by contrasting content-minded readers, including Ichabod Crane, to oral audiences who discover the significance of fiction *through* the narrative event, not *from* it. Nathaniel Hawthorne's "Wakefield," by contrast, defines its point through extratextual framing: The storyteller claims to tell his tale with a moral purpose in mind, a boast realized by a series of pseudo-sermonic narrative interjections and a concluding moral. However, these devices seem to misinterpret the story, thus challenging readers to evaluate the story's sincerity. Doing so, as Reid suggests, we recognize that the stance assumed by a narrator—be it sincere, ironic, or even parodic—is "not so much a quality inherent in a text as an extratextual frame through which a reader construes or subdues the other framing elements" (308).

Finally, Herman Melville's "Bartleby, the Scrivener" utilizes a pattern of intratextual framing. Here the temporal distance that separates the story from its subsequent telling hints at the significance of curious shifts in the narrator's style from parodic passages of legalistic prose to more spontaneous, emotional outbursts. Regardless of how each tale makes its point, these strategies of narrative framing serve a similar purpose, for by dramatizing the necessity of audience involvement in a story, they vividly illustrate the community-creating function of storytelling.

1 Washington Irving: Intertextual Framing and Oral Tradition in "The Legend of Sleepy Hollow"

"I fancy much of what I value myself upon in writing, escapes the observation of the great mass of my readers, who are intent more upon the story than the way in which it is told," Irving complained to his friend Henry Brevoort in 1824. "For my part, I consider the story merely as a frame on which to stretch my materials" (29: 90). Although "frame" is a synonym for plot and not an anticipation of Chambers' concept of "situational self-reflexivity," the quote nevertheless conveys Irving's habitual fear that his audience misread his work by focusing exclusively on moral import. Given the immense popularity of *The Sketch Book* in the early 1820s (more than 5,000 American readers paid the exorbitant price of $5.37 for the seven pamphlets in which the tales appeared), such concern may seem gratuitous if not unfounded—until we happen upon a response like that of a *Western Review and Miscellaneous Magazine* contributor, who confessed that, while enjoying "Rip Van Winkle," he could not "conjecture how the story can be reconciled with reason or common sense."[13]

For those first introduced to "Rip" or "The Legend of Sleepy Hollow" as exemplary Americana—exquisite folklore retold in theatrical adaptations, children's books, and animated films—any attempt to establish their reasonableness undoubtedly seems absurd, on a par with trying to track down John Henry's death certificate or conjecturing on the size and color of Paul Bunyan's ox. But in complaining that Irving fails to offer an explanation for Rip's twenty-year nap, this reviewer questions not merely the story's verisimilitude but its *raison d'être*: "If . . . it were intended as a satire upon the credulity and superstition of the ancient Dutch inhabitants of New-York, we ought surely to have been furnished with some solution of the mystery." Without the explicit resolution that we "naturally look for," however, the "pleasure that ["Rip"] would otherwise afford" is "very much diminish[ed]." For this reader, the tale's sole defect can be attributed to Irving's unwillingness to reveal the point of the story.

Although the *Western Review* is comparatively obscure, variations of its criticism can be traced throughout nineteenth-century commentary on Irving. In one of the first reviews of American short fiction, William H. Prescott identifies the lack of "direct moral tendency," "direct moral purpose," and "direct moral aim" as the glaring failure of *The Sketch Book*. Of course, by insisting that a text's reason for being be defined in terms of moral utility, Prescott reveals that his evaluative responses are shaped by different reading expectations than those of the *Western Review* critic. Instead of wondering how "extravagance" can be reconciled with "common sense," Prescott acknowledges that Irving's "principal object [is] to delight" but rejects the idea that mere pleasure is a proper end of reading. He insists that encouraging audiences to luxuriate in "deep feeling and sentiment" promotes a "disrelish" for "less stimulating compositions" that sharpen rational thought. One may be tempted to dismiss this argument as indicative of the compulsory didacticism to which early American authors were expected to ascribe, but equally important here is the emphasis placed upon the word "direct," for Irving is again accused of not sufficiently guiding the reader's response. Thirty years later, Horace Binney Wallace recast this charge in aesthetic rather than moral terms: "The attractiveness of [Irving's] tales does not depend upon their material, upon their construction, upon the novelty, variety, or impressiveness of their incidents, upon an anxious crisis or a brilliant denouement" but upon a style that "delight[s] us into a forgetfulness of purpose or want of purpose." Despite their varied expectations, all three readers object to the absence of "some definite end" in the tales.[14] The frequency of the complaint raises a basic narrative issue: What is the point?

The answer may seem obvious to twentieth-century critics for whom the significance of "Rip Van Winkle" and "Sleepy Hollow" has been determined largely through biographical readings.

R. Jackson Wilson summarizes the critical consensus arrived at by Terence Martin, Daniel Hoffman, William L. Hedges, Haskell Springer, and Jeffrey Rubin-Dorsky (among many others) when he describes the tales as allegories of frustrated authorship addressing "the difficult situation of the man of intellect and imagination, in a world that barely tolerates his presence."[15] Both Rip and Ichabod Crane are inveterate storytellers, their comically marginal status in their respective communities is symbolic of Irving's own sense of exile from a nation in which, as he complained as early as 1813, "literary leisure is confounded with idleness" and "the man of letters is almost an insulated being, with few to understand, less to value, and scarcely any to encourage his pursuits" (28: 52). It is important to stress, however, that Irving's earliest audience did not read his tales biographically. Although one can find intimations of this interpretation in Evert Duyckinck's entry on Irving in the *Cyclopaedia of American Literature* (1855), the depth of his professional anxieties did not become public knowledge until the appearance of nephew Pierre M. Irving's *Life and Letters of Washington Irving* in the decade following his 1859 death. If antebellum readers lacked the extratextual resources that have since determined modern readings of these stories, we should turn toward the internal evaluative devices that might have engaged their responses.

Perhaps the most obvious of these devices are the plots themselves, for "Rip" and "Sleepy Hollow" are stories that talk a great deal about the role stories play in a particular community. Even if we do not identify their main characters with their author, narration is such an obvious theme that these works offer casebook examples of how, in Chambers' words, "stories produce by textual means their own narrative situation" (22). These means include dramatized scenes of storytelling, intertextual references to works that must be judged models or antimodels of reader response, and allusions to contemporary interpretive strategies. Unifying these devices is an extended contrast between oral and print discourse, for both "Rip" and "Sleepy Hollow" assert a cultural function for narration by illustrating its proper effects within the context of an oral performance. Even though they have been transcribed and packaged within editorial frames that present them as history, neither story claims that its factuality makes it worth telling. Rather, the tales emphasize their oral origins, retaining an open-endedness characteristic of folklore, in order to cultivate the reader's awareness that narrative significance is produced through the act of exchange.

Although I am primarily interested in "Sleepy Hollow," the function of storytelling set forth in "Rip" is worth sketching briefly because it offers a less complicated example of how the contrast between print and orality assists in framing the story's point. Having napped through the American Revolution, Rip returns to a village unfamiliar to him, yet the dramatic moment in which his identity crisis is intensely felt ("I'm not myself.—I'm somebody else") is resolved with surprising rapidity when he discovers that he has a story to tell. His neighbors at first doubt whether he truly encountered the legendary Dutch explorer Hendrick Hudson and the crew of the *Half Moon* playing nine pins in the mountains. Foremost among these doubters is one "self important man," a stock target of Irving's ridicule, who finds so little humor in the tale that he scours and stomps back to his field rather than tolerate the tomfoolery.

Yet the villagers' incredulity relaxes when their elder, Peter Vanderdonk, "corroborate[s] his story in the most satisfactory manner." It is the old man's cultural authority, not the credibility of Rip's claim, that persuades them: "[Peter's] ancestor the historian" taught him "that the Kaatskill mountains had always been haunted by strange beings." His father, furthermore, once encountered the Dutch spirits just like Rip, and Peter has heard them at play in the hills. Satisfied, the villagers "almost universally" accept Rip's story. Despite some variation in its details—"He was observed at first to vary at some points, every time he told it, which was doubtless owing to his having so recently awaked," reports Diedrich Knickerbocker in the concluding paragraph—it becomes, through repetition and circulation, an integral text of village history, for "not a man woman or child in the neighbourhood but knew it by heart" (40–41). Rip thus becomes the community patriarch by assuming the role of village storyteller. Significantly, his adventure is not the only tale he tells, for the gossip and "endless sleepy stories" that he once traded with his "junto" at the door of Nicholaus Vedder's inn become an imaginative link by which the village, despite its newfound "busy, disputatious tone," can maintain contact with its prerevolutionary past.

The storytelling scene in "Rip Van Winkle" suggests that fictions are neither true nor false but rather a creation of cultural reality woven from community fabric. Narration is a device not for documenting experience but for making sense of it. By endorsing the credibility of Rip's story through a "fact handed down," Vanderdonk reconciles it with a body of folkloric knowledge, a cultural belief system, that defines the village norms of truthfulness. As Rubin-Dorsky suggests, the story is told

> precisely because there is a quality about experience that must be conveyed—call it magic, mystery, incomprehensibility, or whatever—and we as readers, as important an audience as Rip's pals, realize that common sense is unnecessary. The story prevails on a level far removed from such logic. It is true, even if it never happened.[16]

Yet it is the literal truth of events that the surrounding editorial apparatus attempts to substantiate through the stamp of approval of various paper authorities, including Knickerbocker himself. Just as Vanderdonk preserves the legends of the village, Knickerbocker, as the introductory note tells us, is a historian whose "scrupulous accuracy" has been "completely established." Their source of authority differs, however: Vanderdonk has earned his status through family ties and old age, but Knickerbocker's "unquestionable authority" is conferred as his book is admitted into "historical collections." This "old gentleman" symbolizes the transitional stage between oral and print cultures, for his life's work is drawn from elderly burghers and their wives who are especially "rich in that legendary lore so invaluable to true history"—as opposed to history *books*, which are exactly what Knickerbocker produces. The folklorist even regards his subjects "as a little clasped volume of black letter" to be studied "with the zeal of a book-worm."[17]

Whereas Vanderdonk needs no supplementary proof of the reasonableness of Rip's story, Knickerbocker calls upon the authority of writing for authentication. In a postscript, he reports having "seen a certificate on the subject taken before a country justice and signed with a cross in the justice's own hand writing. The story therefore is beyond the possibility of doubt" (41). The justice's role in this case is not all that far removed from Knickerbocker's, for both record spoken testimony to preserve it, and both validate the texts by signing them. Yet substituting a cross for his signature hints that the judge may be illiterate and further impugns the random power of paper authority to certify truth through textual markers. Neither the historian nor the judge, the conclusion implies, can claim greater authority over the truth than Vanderdonk. The printed word is simply a device in *our* cultural belief system that functions analogously to the handing down of facts in the Dutch village.

"Rip Van Winkle" can thus be read on at least two levels. The tale itself dramatizes the vital role that oral storytelling plays in a community when an audience is willing to participate in the exchange and not simply dismiss it as an idle, unprofitable craft.[18] And the note and postscript project a vision of textual authorities so befuddled and blinded by their duty to regulate truth that they become unconscious conspirators in the proliferation of what they would otherwise dismiss as highly fanciful stories. In "Rip," imagination is validated as a cultural resource, for the titular hero emerges as an important figure in his society. But according to critics, the same cannot be said for "Sleepy Hollow." As Wilson writes, Ichabod Crane is initially "what Rip becomes in the end: a man whose calling is to ideas, notions, and tales" (110). While Rip's storytelling gains him status in the community, Ichabod's narrative fancy renders him a perpetual dupe. The "unfortunate pedagogue" succeeds only by "escap[ing] *from* his comic status as a man of letters to become a self-made man" in the tradition of Benjamin Franklin. Upon departing Sleepy Hollow, he is said to return to a career in the bureaucracy that paper authority creates, first as a lawyer, then as a journalist, and finally as a justice in the small-claims court—"careers," according to Wilson, "that anyone with Irving's experience would have recognized at once as a sure path to fame and fortune in the new Republic" (112). What Crane learns from his encounter with the Headless Horseman, according to Terence Martin, represents "a victory for common sense and hard-headed practicality over imaginative indulgence," a "basic pattern" of Irving's "most characteristic fiction."[19] The fantasy of acceptance that "Rip" represents is thus worlds away from the inevitable routing of imagination that "Sleepy Hollow" predicts. Why is storytelling as a cultural practice validated in one tale and disparaged in the other?

The answer is somewhat obscured by the fact that "Rip" underscores its contrast between orality and print by juxtaposing the story and its surrounding frame, while the satire of paper authority permeates both textual spaces in "Sleepy Hollow." Yet it is obvious enough that Rip and Ichabod are different types of storytellers who establish vastly different relationships with their audiences. While the Catskill daydreamer is an oral storyteller, the Yankee sent to the Hudson Valley as a "pioneer of the mind" is associated with metaphors of print. If Rip becomes a living archive of village history, Crane symbolizes the dangers of an imagination isolated by reading. Alone, he studies Mather's supernatural lore "until the dusk of evening made the printed page a mere mist before his eyes." Even while participating in local storytelling sessions, recounting his "anecdotes of witchcraft," he is distinguished by metaphors of textuality. The villagers think of him as a "traveling gazette," a local newspaper, "carrying the whole budget of local gossip from house to house." He memorizes epitaphs from the local tombstones to woo the county damsels, scribbles romantic verse on foolscap, and even repeats Franklinian maxims like "spare the rod and spoil the child" to his students. He mixes "direful omens" with science, terrifying the villagers with "speculations upon comets and shooting stars, and with the alarming fact that the world did absolutely turn around, and they were half the time topsy-turvy!" (277). What makes Crane susceptible to the Headless Horseman legend is his belief that stories never lie. As a reader, he trusts Mather's status as a historian to the point that, though described as "a perfect master" of the text, he is in fact mastered *by* it. When Brom Bones and his gang of rough riders break into his elaborately secured schoolhouse, he never wonders whether he is the victim of a practical joke. Crane simply concludes that "all the witches in the country held their meetings there" (283).

Crane's slavish devotion to these "direful tales" is the most obvious antimodel by which the text suggests its interpretive expectations. The references to Mather function as intertextual frames that ask readers, in Chambers' words, "to *situate* [Irving's] text in terms of a literary or discursive context that serves as the interpretant, or criterion of relevance, and determines the selective process of reading" (31). This is an evaluative judgment that we undoubtedly feel less pressured to make than an 1820s audience would, because the truthfulness of Mather's "anecdotes" has been rendered a moot point for most of us because we first experience them as cultural myths. That is, Irving's erosion of the generic distinction between the history of *maleficium* and the folklore spun by the Dutch villagers affects us less immediately than it would a reader living in an age in which Mather's credibility as a historian was hotly contested.

Two aspects of Irving's allusions to Mather suggest how the "selective process" of reading might be influenced. On the one hand, the humor of Crane's gullibility necessitates our recognizing that his heightened imagination parallels Mather's Puritan habit of interpreting natural phenomena as a demonic manifestation, as Satan appearing "in diverse shapes." Crane's "firm" and "potent" belief in the truthfulness of what he reads distinguishes him from his neighbors, for whom (as we shall see) truth is a more figurative process arrived at *through* stories, not *from* them. At the same time, there is an ironic assertion of generic status here, because Mather never titled a book the *History of New England Witchcraft*. Instead, readers encounter a misnomer for one (or perhaps all three) of the Puritan minister's major texts on the supernatural. The use of a fictional title to refer to a historical document is typical of the story's evaluative strategies, which collapse distinctions between truth and fiction.

But equally important as *what* Crane reads is *how* he reads: The reference to his conning—an archaic word at once meaning to examine carefully and to memorize—suggests that he is "intent more upon the story than the way in which it is told," as Irving would later characterize the majority of his own readership. Ichabod preaches what he practices, too, for an earlier reference to the "low murmur of his pupils' conning over their lessons" implies that he educates his students by having them recite their daily exercises. As a schoolmaster, Crane subscribes to the dominant pedagogy of the post-colonial era in which literacy was achieved through oral recitation, a strategy focused on articulation rather than interpretation. By enunciating the words on a page according to set oratorical principles, a student demonstrated apprehension of meaning that was fixed and predetermined on the printed page. As a contemporary primer recommended, "Try to read as if you were telling a story to your mother or talking to some of your playmates. *Reading is talking from a book.*"[20]

In "Sleepy Hollow," conning symbolizes more than Crane's pedanticism; it also reveals the self-consciousness with which he tells and receives stories, which helps explain why they affect him more than his neighbors. As Benjamin argues, the "germinative power" of stories arises from their ability to commend themselves to our memory. To do so, however, we must absorb them in a "state of relaxation" that allows us to assimilate more than the surface meaning, more than "the essence of the thing." What expedites this loss of self-consciousness are rituals like weaving and spinning whose work-like rhythms "seize [us] . . . in a way that the gift of retelling [tales] comes to [us] all by itself." Conning is a more intent form of memorization, one in which the "essence" is consumed as it is internalized *en toto*. Tales agitate Ichabod's "excited imagination" because he has nothing functional to do with them. While the Dutch wives trade their tales "spinning by the fire," he sits "snugly cuddling in the chimney corner," eagerly indulging in the "fearful pleasure" that he associates with storytelling.

Crane is more than a one-dimensional dupe, for another metaphor of reception reveals a darker side of his internalized imagination. Throughout the story, his "appetite for the marvellous" is dramatized through extended metaphors of consumption: "No tale was too gross or monstrous for his capacious swallow" (277). The image is by no means original, of course, for eating as a metaphor for reading dates back at least to the Scriptures. In nineteenth-century America the trope often served a specific pedagogical function, for consuming books meant that the moral was taken in, absorbed, and digested. Irving attempted to appropriate and revise its didacticism in the preface to his third story collection, *Tales of a Traveller* (1824), in which Crayon claims to have "hid [his] moral from sight, and disguised it as much as possible by sweets and spices, so that while the simple reader is listening with open mouth to a ghost story or a love story, he may have a bolus of sound morality popped down his throat, and be never the wiser for the fraud" (10: 4).[21] The metaphor of eating links consumption with reading and greed as Crane begins to resemble the modern reader that Benjamin describes as "seizing upon his material more jealously than anyone else . . . ready to make it completely his own, to devour it . . . to swallow [it] up . . . as the fire devours logs in the fireplace" (100).

Nowhere is Crane's alienation better demonstrated than at the "merry making," the communal feast hosted by Baltus Van Tassel. While the Dutch squire welcomes his guests with a loud, boisterous laugh, Ichabod keeps his greedy giggles to himself, "chuckling with the possibility that he might one day be lord of all this scene of almost unimaginable luxury and splendour" (291). His rival for Katrina's affections also exudes communal mirth and gamesmanship—Brom Bones has "more mischief than ill will in his composition; and with all his overbearing roughness, there was a strong dash of waggish good humour at bottom" (284). Critics often describe Brom as a symbol of the practical American masculinity that crushes the effeminacy of Crane's imagination, yet it should be noted that the rival is a consummate storyteller, able to deliver a "thrice marvellous adventure." As in "Rip Van Winkle," the storytelling scene dramatizes the function that stories serve in a community. While Crane's hunger for fiction is linked to print, villagers come to life through analogies to oral discourse. They "gossip" about the past, "drawling out long stories," freely tailoring their narratives to suit the whims of the moment. "Just sufficient time had elapsed [since the Revolutionary War, which provides the setting for most of the stories] to enable each story teller to dress up his tale with a little becoming fiction, and in the indistinctness of his recollections, to make himself the hero of every exploit" (287). "Becoming fiction" is a clever pun here, for by dressing up the tales to engage the interest of the audience, the villagers transform their narratives, putting them through the process of becoming stories. However self-aggrandizing, the narratives draw upon a communal belief system preserved through exchange.

At first glance, the storytelling scene in the postscript might seem designed to articulate the interpretive expectations dramatized through the contrast between Crane and the villagers. The ideal audience is represented here by the deputy aldermen, who can enjoy the misadventures of the schoolmaster despite dozing through large portions of them—an extreme but nonetheless efficacious example of the Benjaminian "self-forgetfulness" necessary to assimilate the point of a story. The overly intent listener is the incredulous old man who puts a halt to the "laughter and approbation" by challenging the original storyteller to account for its morality. The old man listens intently as he "look[s] down upon the floor, as if turning a doubt over in his mind" (296). He symbolizes yet another reader wrongfully absorbed with the story instead of the experience of its telling, a reader not unlike the self-important man in "Rip," or even Ichabod Crane himself. (Indeed, at least one critic has suggested that this doubtful old gentleman might just *be* Crane.)[22] By ridiculing the old man's demand that he account for the more "extravagant" parts of his narrative—a demand not dissimilar from the *Western Review* critic's response to "Rip Van Winkle"—the storyteller could not articulate any less directly how one should receive the tale. "I don't believe it one half myself" is a sign that, as Chambers suggests of similar stories, "the text's claim to power can lie only in its being *recognized* by the reader, and treated as, fiction." To do so is to relinquish the expectation that the story has some direct purpose, that its point, in the words of the old man, is "to prove" some moral truth. Instead, readers must recognize that it "has only the *latent* power of relating in a meaningful way to [our] pragmatic experience" (Chambers 37–38).

But if this self-definition was the only consequence of the scene, the postscript would be a mere addendum. Instead, the connection between the story and the editorial device raises two implications concerning how the medium models the story's "situational self-reflexivity." The first of these has to do with the identity of these "Manhattoe" aldermen, who appreciate imaginative literature as much as the Dutch villagers. Irving's original nineteenth-century audience should have been struck by the sight of New York City municipal officials trading tales, for there is a rich history that portrays them as humorless, greedy, and uneducated—the type of audience who would regard storytelling as a waste of time. Irving had already characterized such aldermen in his early work *Salmagundi* as "tinkers" who bend the law to their own advantage by proliferating an endless variety of self-serving statutes.[23] By portraying their appreciation of tales, he transforms them into an ideal readership. Their characterization is yet another example of Irving's eroding the boundaries between fact and fiction.

More complexly, the presence of this sympathetic audience, rather than being limited to the postscript, is dispersed throughout the text by virtue of the ambiguity of the Knickerbocker/Crayon framing device. Because the "authentic historian" transcribes the story "almost in the precise words" in which he heard it told, readers technically have no way of determining the identity of the narrating "I." Critics routinely attribute the narration to Knickerbocker, arguing that Crayon merely "includes" the tale in his portfolio, while completely ignoring the presence of the oral storyteller. Such assertions overlook the fact that, as William L. Hedges has remarked, the narrative voice just does not sound like the Knickerbocker of *A History of New York*, for the "essential quality" of the "old historian . . . the rather desperate need to inflate limp subjects with a flourish of rhetoric, is quite lacking."[24] The frame creates an insoluble interpretive problem when it comes to attribution because the "I" who announces that "many years have elapsed since I trod down the drowsy shades of Sleepy Hollow" *might* be Knickerbocker, but it just as easily *might* be Knickerbocker transcribing the exact words of the oral storyteller. "Sleepy Hollow" must be read as a story that simultaneously addresses at least two distinct audiences: the "determinate" group of aldermen and Knickerbocker's (and Crayon's) "indeterminate" mass readership. This elaborate narrative framing dramatizes what Benjamin describes as the "slow piling one on top of the other of [the] thin, transparent layerings" of tellings and retellings (93).

But if "Rip" and "Sleepy Hollow" model their interpretive ideals by contrasting orality and print, Irving's original readers—or his reviewers, at least—missed the point. The absence of any discussion of Knickerbocker's editorial mediation suggests that the storytelling medium was a non-issue for them. Only in the commentary of the *Western Review* on "Rip" are readers' expectations addressed, and the critic assumes that the assertion of the tale's status as "absolute fact" satirizes the "credulity and superstition" of the Dutch, not the authenticating function of print (248). By judging it according to standards of "reason and common sense," this reader resists accepting the story as it presents itself—as a fiction that specifically defers the application of those faculties. Because this type of response again corresponds to Irving's description of how his tales were misread, it seems fair to ask what influences dissuaded critics from recognizing the story as "merely . . . a frame" upon which the author could "stretch [his] materials."

The most obvious contextual explanation, voiced by didactic critics like Prescott, who define purpose exclusively in moralistic terms, is that what Irving felt valuable in his writing—"the play of thought, and sentiment and language . . . the half concealed vein of humor that is often playing through the whole"—were insufficient ends of narration as public discourse (29: 90). For Irving to claim through framing devices that neither "Rip" nor "Sleepy Hollow" were really "about" anything, that their point was not to be found in their content but in the pleasure of experiencing them, was to cater first to the individual reader's evaluation rather than responses that could be defined as publicly useful. Critics argue that soliciting personal judgment is not only inevitable but fundamentally imperative to the function of storytelling—readers must constantly engage in acts of evaluation in order to determine the story's purpose. The story asks readers to reconcile their responses with those of other audience members, thus effecting community.

This function is realized in the multitude of responses that an oral storytelling context may inspire. For example, when the shabby gentleman in "Sleepy Hollow" answers the old man's doubts about the story's purpose with the satiric syllogism, he effectively informs this stubborn respondent that his expectations are out of synch with the other aldermen's. Negotiating audience expectations is more abstract in a printed text, however. Not only are speakers distanced from their audience, but the medium itself projects the illusion that meaning is manifest within a physical artifact that can be endlessly reproduced. In other words, the immanence of print can presuppose community responses, thus discouraging readers from recognizing their subjective roles in the creation of meanings. The degree to which Irving's intertextual framing empowers readers by insisting that they articulate their responses in terms of enjoyment explains why as late as the 1850s (long after didactic criticism had been supplanted by aesthetic criticism) reviewers like Horace Binney Wallace complained that Irving's tales "communicate pleasure," allowing themselves to be "more enjoyed than eulogized."

But there is a broader explanation for why readers pass over the frames of self-reflexive, open-ended works like "The Legend of Sleepy Hollow" and deem them tangential or even inconsequential. If, as Benjamin argues, storytelling is the art of inspiring the retelling of a tale, it seems fair to reason that "self-situating" evaluative devices render themselves obsolete. That is, as stories attempt to frame our responses and encourage us to accept the fiction in the terms that it presents itself, they serve their function. By ensuring the passing on of a tale, they allow themselves to be substituted with a new set of frames particular to the new narrative situation. Such a process can be inferred in the reception history of both "Rip" and "Sleepy Hollow." I speak now not of the critical reception history, but of its cultural assimilation into American folklore, for throughout the countless adaptations of both tales Irving's notes and postscripts are almost universally deleted from their retellings.

Scattered commentary helps explain why. In his autobiography, Joseph Jefferson, whose stage version of "Rip" was one of the longest-running theatrical productions of the nineteenth century, describes the challenges of transforming a story that "was purely a narrative" into a visual event. With an "interesting, but not dramatic" theme, the tale seemed too "descriptive" for the stage. "The character of *Rip* does not speak ten lines," Jefferson complains. "What could be done with so simple a sketch?" His adaptation reveals how he answered the question: He re-wrote the story, cutting the frame and doing away with Knickerbocker as well as Vanderdonk, thus creating a *different* story, despite the essential sameness of plot. A similar process is implied by John Kerr's less successful 1824 adaptation of "Sleepy Hollow," which ignores the Manhattoe aldermen frame, as do a number of the children's books based on the tale. Thomas M. Leitch suggests why oft-told tales like Irving's are infinitely adaptable: "Our appetite for what we usually consider different versions of the same story is based on the expectation that each version will display not simply a given situation or plot or state of affairs but different aspects or implications of that situation."[25] Throughout these numerous retellings, different aspects of Irving's tales are brought forth and formally realized. In the process, "Sleepy Hollow" and "Rip" become stories of American identity, ghost stories, and comedies of manners—but not stories about the function of storytelling. These adaptations offer metaphors for the process of interpretation itself. In reading the stories, we (knowingly or not) respond to the self-situating devices in the text by re-framing them according to our own purposes.

For this reason one last retelling of "The Legend of Sleepy Hollow," written by Irving nearly twenty years after first publishing the tale, deserves mention. Significantly, the long-neglected sketch "Sleepy Hollow," published in the *Knickerbocker Magazine* in May 1839, revises the story's original narrative situation, not the plot, in a way that further illuminates Irving's opinion that readers were focused upon plot. Here Geoffrey Crayon recalls traveling to Tarry Town with Knickerbocker and hearing, for the first time, the legend in a "goblin-looking mill" from an "African sage" and an old woman at a spinning wheel, both of whom possessed "that invaluable kind of information, never to be acquired from books." He said, "I verily believe it was to his conference with [them] that we are indebted for the surprising though true history of 'Ichabod Crane and the Headless Horseman,' which has since astounded and edified the world" (29: 110). Neither the shabby gentleman nor the Manhattoe aldermen of the original postscript is mentioned; the situational self-reflexivity of the story is also revised, for whereas the original storyteller dismisses the factuality of his own tale when challenged to account for its extravagance, Crayon asserts here that the events are indeed "true history." What accounts for these changes?

An answer is suggested by the way in which Irving portrays Crayon's shock at discovering the changes that have overcome Tarry Town during his long absence. While the hollow once encouraged daydreaming and storytelling, the village has now transformed into the sort of burgeoning center of commerce that has little practical use for legends and tales. Gone is the Dutch architecture, replaced by "Grecian and Gothic styles"; the town has been organized into parceled lots with a fancy hotel as its centerpiece. Worse yet, the villagers are now wealthy merchants and the farmers have abandoned their fields to become "bank directors [who] drink claret and champagne." The "slumber of ages" has ended as the Edenic village falls into history. In the final sentence of the piece, Crayon recognizes the implications of these changes for his own writings about the region: "The antiquarian visitor to the Hollow, in the petulance of his disappointment, may pronounce all that I have recorded of that once favored region a fable" (29: 113). The tone could hardly be more distinct from the conclusion of the original tale. If "The Legend of Sleepy Hollow" suggests that stories enable a community's belief system, this later piece presages Benjamin's lament that modernization devalues the communicability of experiences that forge community ties. If the former claims that legends become true as their audience makes them meaningful, the latter anticipates a time when readers of Crayon's "antiquarian" writings will dismiss them as lies because they no longer possess the capacity to be rendered relevant.

2 Nathaniel Hawthorne: Extratextual Framing and Sermonic Rhetoric in "Wakefield"

"The Legend of Sleepy Hollow" is a story that claims to have no purpose beyond the pleasure of its own entertainment, but beneath the surface lies something more complicated. If the joke played on the intent old man in the concluding note dramatizes how the tale's truth is less important than its function, the ambiguity of the editorial framing rhetorically enacts that same point by inscribing into the text its own retelling. Hawthorne's "Wakefield" (1835) offers an intriguing contrast for several reasons. Most obviously, perhaps the narration is so prominent that it is difficult to speak of a storytelling frame per se; if separated from the addresses surrounding it, the plot of the London husband who abandons his wife for twenty years in order to monitor the effect of his absence hardly seems capable of standing alone. In this respect, "Wakefield" exaggerates a quality typical of Hawthorne's tales by eschewing the overt editorial framing that Irving employs in his two most famous stories. Instead, as G. R. Thompson argues, Hawthorne's addresses to the audience tend to foreground the narrative exchange to the point that "the existence of framing as a constituent of cognition" becomes a core dramatic theme.[26] While "Sleepy Hollow" defines itself as an oral story through a strategy of intertextual contrast, "Wakefield" provides an example of extratextual framing. Hawthorne's tale sets forth its interpretive expectations by directly addressing readers rather than dramatizing their participation through fictional models and antimodels of response. Yet its curious rhetorical power arises from something more than the immediacy that we feel when narrators speak to us. Rather, Hawthorne's storyteller defines his purpose by casting his tale's evaluative commentary into the style of antebellum sermonic rhetoric.

The fact that "Wakefield" claims to have a purpose also distinguishes it from "Sleepy Hollow." Hawthorne's narrator desires just the sort of moral fiction that the Knickerbocker postscript ridicules. The opening passage states the point: The story's utter credibility is the appeal of the germinal anecdote of the absent husband remembered from "some old magazine or newspaper." Wakefield's story is a "fact," "the strangest incident on record," a narrative "of the purest originality unexampled, and probably never to be repeated," so unique and original that "it has often recurred, always exciting wonder, but with a sense that [it] must be true." The story excites such wonder, in fact, that the storyteller tells it three times: first as a brief recollection, then as a half-paragraph outline, then as the full-length story. With each retelling, the narrator freely invents details, expressing little concern about violating the spirit of this "abstractly stated" kernel: "We are free to shape out our own idea [of Wakefield's character], and call it by his name." What licenses this creative freedom? "Whenever any subject so forcibly affects the mind, time is well spent thinking of it," he declares. "Thought has always its efficacy, and every striking incident its moral." Accordingly, "there will be a pervading spirit and a moral, even should we fail to find them, done up neatly, and condensed into the final sentence."[27] If Irving's oral storyteller implies that his tale has no pragmatic purpose, Hawthorne's narrator claims exactly the opposite. Storytelling, he seems to say, is a viable cultural practice as long as its point is a moral one.

Or does he? The bizarre assurance that a moral will be delivered "even should we fail to find [one]" implies an ulterior motive that makes the story anything but a "ramble." In fact, a great deal of the commentary generated by "Wakefield" insists that Hawthorne's narrative self-consciousness *must* be ironic and "disingenuous" if the story is to be regarded as anything more than a "stunt," or a "failure of development, a failure of creative energy." Even the tale's most famous admirer, Jorge Luis Borges, who rated it above *The Scarlet Letter*, qualified his enthusiasm by arguing that "the fact that Hawthorne pursued, or tolerated a moral purpose does not invalidate, cannot invalidate his work." Borges speaks for the bulk of modern audiences when he describes the concluding moral as "false," a concession to a didactic culture that "tried to make art a function of the conscience."[28] That effort is most jarring when, instead of dramatizing the matrimonial reunion, the narrator declares the scene superfluous and makes his point: "Amid the seeming confusion of our mysterious world, individuals are so nicely adjusted to a system, and systems to one another, and to a whole, that by stepping aside for a moment a man exposes himself to a fearful risk of losing his place forever. Like Wakefield, he may become, as it were, the outcast of the universe" (140). Because Wakefield *does not* lose his place forever, readers have struggled to reconcile the moral with the story. For those suspicious of didactic fiction, the conclusion transforms the tale into something harder and colder than the "meditation" originally proposed. At once abrupt and efficacious, it seems little more than a placebo, a pat maxim assuring us that metaphysical complexities can be distilled into simple grammar, that palatable answers never stale when refrigerated in the aphoristic present tense. If the beginning of the story tempts us with the opiate of imagination, these readers complain, the conclusion insists that we just say no.

But the moral is not the only aspect of the tale to trouble readers. The very tone by which the narrator addresses his collaborators is highly ambivalent: "If the reader choose, let him do his own meditation. Or if he prefer to ramble with me through the twenty years of Wakefield's vagary, I bid him welcome." While "we" constantly appears in narrative interjections like "we must hurry after him" or "we must leave him, for ten years or so," such sentences seem too directive, too imperative to encourage the pauses in reading by which "we" might do our share of the "rambling." At two key moments the storyteller even drops the pretense of collaboration to dramatize his private performance: "Poor Wakefield! Little knowest thou thine own insignificance in this great world! No mortal eye *but mine* has traced thee!" Later he halts the story to lament restrictions on his creativity: "Would that *I* had a folio to write, instead of an article of a dozen pages! Then *I* might exemplify how an influence beyond our control lays its strong hand on every deed which we do" (136; emphasis added). Such slips into the first person imply that "we" is little more than a rhetorical fiction, a convention that, however convivial or potentially engaging, serves as a controlling device. Given such curious maneuvers, Arnold Weinstein correctly describes "Wakefield" as "an experiment in narrational power."[29] But how to characterize that power?

Alexander Gelley offers one approach by examining how the story's syntax positions "us" vis-à-vis the drama. In a simple sentence like "amid the throng of a London street we distinguish a man," "amid" may modify either "we" or "man" so that "a situational determination of the reader in relation to the scene is both implied and blocked."[30] Syntax is a "form of access" by which we are placed in a spatial relationship with the events described. In the case of ambiguous modifiers—is that adverbial phrase misplaced or not?—our perspective upon the drama is uncertain and we are forced to make what Gelley calls a "specular investment," an imaginative projection of the scene within the limits the frame allows. The ambiguity that "amid the throng" creates is a minor example of the capacity for multiple interpretations, which is the central effect of Hawthorne's narrative framing. For readers who accept the storyteller's invitation to collaborate—the degree to which they imagine the narrative "we" as constituent of themselves—the framing places them in an immediate relation with the action. But for those doubting its sincerity, the effect can be alienating, distancing even, for it suggests rhetorical presumptuousness, a "speaking for" in which the narrator asserts mastery over readers' responses, rendering them a captive audience.

This spatial displacement is only one element of the tale's power, however. Equally important is a stylistic frame that stakes a claim for the importance of storytelling by drawing its rhetorical authority from sermonic discourse. The effect of Hawthorne's sermonic framing is suggested by an 1846 entry in Emerson's journal: "Hawthorn [*sic*] invites the reader too much into his study, opens the process before them. As if the confectioner should say to his customers Now let us make the cake."[31] It is unclear precisely to what text Emerson refers, though his mention of the author's study suggests the preface to *Mosses from an Old Manse*, in which Hawthorne invites readers to imagine themselves as guests at his home, reading his tales in manuscript form. Yet the rhetorical cookery criticized here could easily allude to "Wakefield," which employs the same form of address that Emerson satirizes: "In some old magazine or newspaper I recollect a story, told as truth, of a man—let us call him Wakefield—who absented himself for a long time from his wife" (130).

This "let us" device exemplifies what Lawrence Buell calls the "rhetoric of declamation" that antebellum authors absorbed from the era's oratorical culture. Whether associated with the pulpit or with politics, such rhetoric allowed writers to add a sense of interpersonal immediacy that infused the written word with the energy of oral performances. Evoking formal speech genres creates "contrasting plains of discourse," including odd tonal shifts, juxtapositions of formal and colloquial language, "collage[s] of the demotic and the highfalutin'."[32] Such contrast resonates in "Wakefield" in the "let us" phraseology, whose performative power echoes Old Testament rhetoric. It appears too in the odd interjections of King James archaisms: "Go quietly to thy bed, foolish man; and, on the morrow, if thou wilt be wise, get thee home to good Mrs. Wakefield. . . . Remove not thyself, even for a little week, from thy place in her chaste bosom" (133). Exclamatory utterances also ring with exaggeration: "Stay, Wakefield! Would you go to the sole home that is left you? Then step into your grave!" (139).

Attributing this baroque eloquence to the influence of oracular culture might make more sense had the tale been authored by Emerson, whose style bears the obvious influence of his training in the pulpit and the lyceum. But despite what would seem Hawthorne's lack of practical experience in such speech genres, critics have documented his familiarity with oratorical traditions and their influence on the "oral-aural cast" of his narrative styles.[33] Moreover, at least two of Hawthorne's most vocal contemporary supporters, Evert Duyckinck and Edwin P. Whipple, specifically equated the moral force of his tales with the sermon. Elevating his stories above the "dead truism[s]" proliferated by "common-place preachers," whose sermons failed to "reach the depth of thought and sentiment from which [Hawthorne's] seemingly airy sketches draw their life," both legitimated short fiction and gave readers a context within which to assimilate a story's point. Tales and sketches could be morally efficacious, affecting the reader's life as overtly as didactic discourse. Indeed, tales served that purpose better because they recognized the creative power of imagination.[34]

Because the storyteller describes "Wakefield" as an "article of a dozen pages," equating the frame with a speech genre might also seem to contradict the rhetorical situation established in the text. Yet the relevance of sermonic rhetoric to "Wakefield" becomes clearer if we read it in the context of *The Story Teller*, the unpublished story collection for which it was most likely written. To do so requires a speculative leap of faith because when the collection was dismantled and published in the *New-England Magazine* over the winter of 1834–35 Hawthorne did not retain his original prospectus, but left critics to reconstruct its contents through internal evidence. Despite the absence of proof that "Wakefield" was intended for the collection, the story's declamatory tone makes sense when read against the contrast between contemporary preaching styles depicted in *The Story Teller*'s presumed introductory sketches, "The Story Teller No. 1" and "The Story Teller No. 2." (An abridged version of these sketches appears in *Mosses* as "Passages from a Relinquished Work.") Before turning to the tale itself, it is necessary to summarize briefly the project to understand the role that its sermonic interjections serve.

Although an increasing number of critics now look to *The Story Teller* to illuminate Hawthorne's ideas about the function of storytelling,[35] few have acknowledged how cleverly he locates it within an important transitional moment in the history of American pulpit oratory. The narrator of "Passages" grows up under the patronage of his stepfather, Parson Thumpcushion, a dogmatic exegete who "pounds" his pulpit furniture as he "expounds" upon Scripture. His exhortative style leads the narrator to wonder whether the old man imagines himself holding "some Unitarian infidel at bay." For conservative Protestant sects like the parson's, Unitarians were "infidels" in part because their eloquence replaced moral instruction with moral impression. That is, Unitarians substituted the Word of God with words of Romantic feeling meant to inspire, as humanly as possible, divine sublimity. While the "stern old Pilgrim" raises his three sons through a rigorous program of moral instruction, his cold didacticism inspires a "bitter grudge" in the narrator, who resists committing himself to a profession the way his adoptive brothers have. (One is a minister, another a physician, and the third a shoe merchant.) Instead, the narrator proclaims an affinity with "wandering orators and poets," whose "exercise of narrative faculty" inspires a "flow of fancy" whose "indulgence [is] its own reward." Precisely because Thumpcushion "would rather have laid me in my father's tomb, than seen me either a novelist or an actor," the narrator decides to combine both professions by taking to the road as a "wandering story teller." "After all," he notes, in a sentence whose irony bespeaks Hawthorne's characteristic self-deprecation, "it was not half so foolish as if I had written romances, instead of reciting them" (10: 409).

Having abandoned the parsonage, the narrator soon meets an itinerant minister, Eliakim Abbott, a pious but exceedingly inept orator who functions as an ironic counterpart to Thumpcushion. Although his denomination is not specified, Eliakim satirizes just the sort of Unitarian whom the old man would enjoy throttling. As ministers of the patrician class, Thumpcushion and Abbott symbolize the gendered extremes of paternal and feminized authority that the narrator must negotiate in his storytelling. Although Eliakim is sincere in his evangelical mission, his poetic sensibility renders him a figure of derision, especially among the tavern-goers who crowd to hear the narrator. He is so sensitive, in fact, that the sound of his voice embarrasses him. While Eliakim's "address [to] sinners on the welfare of their immortal souls" draws a crowd of "about fifteen . . . mostly females," the narrator's performance solicits "bursts of merriment" from a high-spirited, overflow audience. The storyteller's success is as immense as the preacher's failure, but not for the reason that he at first assumes. If the sketch initially echoes Knickerbocker's postscript in celebrating imaginative stories over didactic literature, there is a quick change of temperament when the narrator realizes that his triumph is not necessarily the product of his narrative acumen. The audience's outbursts are inspired by "a stiff queue of horse-hair" that one of the theater's actors, a "young person of doubtful sex" named, provocatively enough, Little Pickle, has appended to his back, "where, unknown to me, it kept making the queerest gestures of its own, in correspondence with all mine."

The realization that the crowd's pleasure has little to do with his story leads to a moment of complex ambiguity. Writing his memoirs later in life as a "bitter moralizer," the narrator claims that the scene taught him "how much of fame is a humbug . . . how much bestowed on mistaken principles." The lesson may inspire his pledge to "write the book [*The Story Teller* itself] for the sake of its moral, which many a dreaming youth may profit by, though it is the experience of a wandering story teller" (10: 408). I say "may" here because the question of moral intent is again an example of the open-endedness that allows Hawthorne's tales to be read in at least two ways. Is the assertion of a pragmatic intent a sincere sign of the storyteller's desire to invest his adventures with some purpose? Or is it an ironic tweaking of the expectations of those stern, old Thumpcushions who define purpose in moral terms?

Reconstructing this frame suggests how indebted *The Story Teller* was to Irving's *Sketch Book*. While "Sleepy Hollow" is an oral story transcribed into writing, "Wakefield" is a tale written down at some point after its original performance. In both cases, acts of retelling are embedded in the narrative pretext, and the question of how stories change to meet the motives and expectations of each telling compounds the prevailing interpretive problems. While Irving superimposes writing upon orality, making it impossible to identify who tells the tale, Hawthorne juxtaposes these media with a metafictional twist. The framing in "Sleepy Hollow" celebrates the oral roots of the tale. Similarly, audience addresses in "Wakefield" imply that the "practised art" of storytelling is worthy of "the same prodigality as if [the narrator] were speaking for a great party, or for the nation at large, on the floor of the capitol" (10: 416). As an evaluative device, Hawthorne's rhetorical prodigality enhances the tale's sense of purpose by suggesting why it is important, why it is worth telling. Exploring how this style of address mediates our access to the plot helps us understand its potential effect on readers' responses.

David Leverenz proposes one answer to the question of effect when he describes how Hawthorne's interjections can induce "an acute desire for premature interpretation." The narrator tempts us to guess the overarching significance before we arrive at the final paragraph by assuring us in the opening passages that there is a point that can be "done up neatly" and "condensed." For Leverenz, self-conscious declarations of purpose allow Hawthorne's storytellers to satirize the "aggressive" and ultimately "self-revealing gaze" that they encourage in readers: "As detectives sniff and snoop through the underbrush of his tales, he lures them into the open, then humiliates them with their own intellectual prurience."[36]

The relationship between narrator and audience is more complex in "Wakefield," for its insistent imperatives ("watch him," "cast your eyes") necessitate participating in the story. These commands generate suspense by allowing us to explore why the tale is compelling—why Wakefield's adventure "appeals to the general sympathies of mankind." It seems safe to say that what engages us is *not* the plot's unraveling, for we know from the outset both the climax (Wakefield returns to his wife) and the resolution (he becomes "a loving spouse till death"). What makes the tale dramatic is not the sequence of events, but the relationship between those events and the interjections that surround, qualify, and modify them. As the storyteller admits in "Passages," plots are only "skeletons of tales" whose "filling up" is best left to "the inspiration of the moment." While he may keep in mind various "commencements and catastrophes" that will color his stories, narrating them is a spontaneous act: "I cannot remember ever to have told a tale, which did not vary considerably from my pre-conceived idea, and acquire a novelty of aspect as often as I repeated it" (10: 417). His stories never grow old or stale because he knows how to make them open-ended enough that diverse audiences can find them meaningful.

By relocating the drama from the plot to the process of evaluating its moral import, the storyteller's habit of "filling up" the tale encourages a style of reception that Louis O. Mink calls "configurational comprehension," a form of attentiveness that assumes a "synoptic vision," an "aerial overview." Interpretation is not an act of following a story, but of analyzing how, in Mink's words "one *has followed*" it. That is, in texts like "Wakefield" in which the outcome is known from the beginning, we are not obliged to anticipate the resolution but can focus instead upon the manifold ways in which it might have happened—and, by extension, to question why the storyteller chooses to tell it as he does. "Since we already know the story," Mink writes, "we can only play at following it. In the comprehension of the story as a whole, there are no discoveries and descriptions have no tense." As a result, significance is not found by expounding upon its meaning, as the Thumpcushions of the world do, but by cultivating its usefulness, its ability to be meaningful regardless of the contexts in which it might be read. Recognizing the generative power of a story requires reflecting upon how fictions "aim at producing and strengthening the act of understanding in which actions and events, although represented as occurring in the order of time, can be surveyed as it were in a single glance as bound together in an order of significance."[37] Such understanding is precisely the effect that the storyteller's sermonic interjections seek to achieve, for they de-emphasize the drama and challenge us to account for our interest in it, to explain why and how it engages us.

This imperative is most vividly demonstrated by the fact that the interjections contradict the plot. When Wakefield first flees to his hideaway and the narrator asserts that "it is perilous to make a chasm in human affections; not that they gape so long and wide—but so quickly close again," we must judge the validity of the narrator's assessment, reconciling it with what we know of character and motive. A close reader will question the storyteller's pronouncement, for we have already been told that Wakefield does indeed return home. At least in his case, those chasms *do not* quickly close. Elsewhere, the narrator casts a cold eye on the husband's habitual postponement of his return ("Not tomorrow—probably next week—pretty soon") by announcing that "the dead have nearly as much chance of revisiting their earthly homes as the self-banished Wakefield." Again, the assertion does not fit the story's ending. Similarly, as the husband imagines the unquestioning joy his wife will feel upon his return, the storyteller proffers this warning: "Alas, what a mistake! Would Time but await the close of our favorite follies, we should be young men, all of us, and till Doomsday." In each instance, the interjection is incongruous given the resolution that we know is imminent.

Such contradictions explain why critics have assumed that the storytelling is unreliable if not ironic. Yet when Robert L. Chibka complains that the tone of "moral panic" in these interjections is more "rhetorically effective than appropriate," he fails to question whether provoking an emotional response, and not subscribing to some ambiguous standard of appropriateness, might just be the purpose.[38] In voicing these proverbial statements, the narrator appeals to the way we think the tale *should have happened*, the likely outcome for a man less fortunate than Wakefield. "We know, each for himself, that none of us would perpetrate a folly," the narrator insists, and if so, it is for the reasons that the interjections state: We fear that the breach of human affection would close after our departure, that in abandoning family members to measure the depth of their love through their grief, we risk sore disappointment. Because the commentary voices the conventional morality that keeps most readers from "stepping aside," the story allows readers to test their belief in that morality. Much as Rip's twenty-year nap raises cackles of incredulity among his fellow villagers, what the narrator describes as Wakefield's "whim-wham" ideally forces readers to question any desire they might feel to slip out of the ties that bind them. Just as Rip's audience believes his story only after it is corroborated by Vanderdonk's authority, Wakefield's tale becomes credible only when measured against readers' individual commitment to those "nicely adjusted" systems of interdependence that the moral invokes.

The storyteller also invites audience participation by alluding to different ways he might have told the tale. At one point he wishes he could write Wakefield's story in a novel-sized folio instead of a brief article. This sudden self-dramatization of the narrator's limitations seems disingenuous. As Chibka asks, "Who"—other than the narrator himself—"has denied [him] his folio?" (227). Many a reader, furthermore, would likely appreciate a more explicit analysis of the influences determining Wakefield's actions. And yet a more specific rendering of motive would change how the narrator has chosen to present the story by making mystery into mere information, speculation into specification. To explicate would force the kernel of narrative to bloom unnaturally by forsaking what Benjamin again calls its "germinative power"—its ability to be meaningful in many different contexts. By emphasizing how he commits himself to telling the story, Hawthorne's narrator reminds us that his is only a version of it, only one attempt to explain the mystery. As Borges writes in exploring the appeal of the outline, "The interpretations of the riddle can be infinite" (223). To recognize and respect the generative power of the scenario, a good storyteller must acknowledge that a tale can never claim to solve the mystery, for to do so is to exhaust its power of perpetual relevance.

Unfortunately, modern prejudices against morals and maxims prevented Borges from recognizing how such evaluative devices also interpret the riddle, expanding rather than diminishing its ability to engage audiences. These prejudices arise from the mistaken assumption that an overtly stated moral purpose, even one as cagey as Hawthorne's, exhausts the plenitude of significance by imposing closure. But the storyteller explicitly warns against this idea by insisting on the proliferative nature of the moral's import. "Wakefield has given us much food for thought," the narrator declares in the final paragraph, "*a portion* of which shall lend its wisdom to a moral, and be shaped into a figure" (italics added). Unlike Ichabod Crane, who "swallows" tales whole, Hawthorne's storyteller partakes of only a helping of his narrative's potential significance, leaving the leftovers for subsequent readers to feast upon. The moral is not *the* meaning of the story, not *the* significance, but as Benjamin suggests, a symbol of its ability to be meaningful. To presume that the tale is ironic or sincere ignores the process by which one arrives at that conclusion. The conclusion fails to provide the practical advice or counsel that, according to Benjamin, constitutes the usefulness of a story. Yet that failure challenges readers to discover how the moral relates to the story by retracing their footsteps and reexploring the relationship between the sermonic interjections and the plot. The conclusion is an invitation to its beginning, a device that says to readers, "From this quirk of history we have made something significant, but we cannot presume to think we have told the entire story." As narrative theorists like Benjamin, Borges, and Mink suggest, the entirety of a tale can only be approached by asking how others have made sense of it—a process that is always an act of sharing.

In an essay on the development of the nineteenth-century American sermon, David Reynolds has explored how religious discourse increasingly used stories to make their lessons more entertaining. Rather than expound upon Scripture, ministers like Charles Grandison Finney encouraged colleagues to address congregations in "the language of common life" by adopting "illustrations . . . drawn from incidents real or supposed" so audiences could apply them directly to their life.[39] Writing in 1835, the same year that "Wakefield" first appeared in the *New-England Magazine*, Finney claimed that "a short story of some event real or imaginary" offered a far more powerful vehicle for dramatizing spiritual awareness than dry, doctrinal recitation. It is unlikely that "short story" here refers to the specific literary genre, since the term did not enter popular usage until fifteen years later. Still, the quote suggests the affective power attributed to oral storytelling traditions that Reynolds documents in the period. "Wakefield" offers a dichotomous example of a story that establishes its power by drawing from religious rhetoric. The "let us" phraseology, the maxim-like interjections, and the concluding moral can be interpreted as satirizing that rhetoric, but that fact does not violate the point that storytelling is the art by which we understand why a whim-wham like Wakefield's can "forcibly affect the mind."

3

Herman Melville: Intratextual Framing in "Bartleby, the Scrivener"

Critics have long recognized the influence of "Wakefield" upon Melville's "Bartleby, the Scrivener: A Story of Wall Street." Both tales belong to a genre, which also includes Poe's "The Man of the Crowd" and story collections like Willis's *Pencillings by the Way* and George G. Foster's *New York in Slices* (1849), that exploits the fear of urban alienation. Wakefield's and Bartleby's peculiar behavior is a response to an industrial culture that threatens the individual with anonymity. In each case, what generates suspense is the manner by which this theme of isolation shapes the telling of the story. Viewed from a distance that cannot quite be bridged, these *isolatos* appear as ciphers, in both senses of the word. As their withdrawal from the world of human interchange transforms them into nonentities, the mystery of their actions creates a riddle that readers must resolve, and their point is to challenge us to account for how we speak in the presence of their conspicuous silence.

But here the tales differ most greatly, for while the anecdote about Wakefield inspires heightened bursts of sermonic rhetoric, the style in which the story of the "pallidly neat, pitiably respectable, incurably forlorn" law-copyist is told seems to mimic the reticence of its titular hero. If Hawthorne's exclamations ring with oratorical exuberance, Melville's relative quietude implies an absence, a distancing of narrative presence, that for many critics symbolizes the condition of writing itself.

To recognize how the stylistic economy of "Bartleby" departs from the storytelling strategies that Melville had cultivated over the course of his career, one need only contrast its narrative voice to those of his two preceding novels. As any reader will quickly recognize, *Moby Dick* and *Pierre* synthesize a variety of speech genres, from sermons to sea chanteys to political stumping. According to Richard Brodhead, their baroqueness can be traced to Hawthorne, in whose tales Melville discovered justification for the expressive impulses that he had previously suppressed or discharged, fearing they were incompatible with the literary marketplace. Rather than pose the threat of mere "self-indulgence," rhapsodic digressions—what Brodhead calls Melville's "unleashing [the] urge to expression"—could demonstrate "a high obedience to a specially appointed vocation" in which literature assumed the lofty function of cultural prophecy.[40] Whether we speak of Ahab's loquacious Shakespearean soliloquies, Ishmael's rhapsodical flights, or Pierre Glendenning's evangelical declarations of artistic intent, Melville's style exploits a volubility that, by 1852, reviewers increasingly found grating.

The narrator of "Bartleby," by contrast, is a wholly antithetical creature, sentimental rather than philosophical, every bit as reserved in his expressiveness as the Melvillian prophets are grandiloquent. Indeed, an insistent irony emerges in the opening paragraphs as this "unambitious" lawyer distances himself from the forensic tradition of his profession by acknowledging that he "never addresses a jury, or in any way draws down public applause." He prefers instead to do "a snug business among rich men's bonds and mortgages and title-deeds" as a "conveyancer and title hunter, and drawer-up of recondite documents," as though he were silencing the art of advocacy in a sea of bureaucratic paper.[41] Bartleby, too, is a far more obvious symbol of writing than oratory. As a scrivener, he is condemned to the drudgery of copying the lawyer's documents, and during his rumored clerkship at the Dead Letter Office in Washington, he is said to have burned by the cartload mail that failed to reach its destination. Then as now, the Dead Letter Office is a powerful metaphor for the desires that go disappointed in communication. Yet because the word "letters," whether bringing to mind correspondence or alphabetic script, suggests exchanges dependent upon a material medium, the vast bulk of "Bartleby" commentary addresses this theme of failed communication as though it were strictly an issue of inscription. Even moments when the lawyer cannot understand why Bartleby says "I would prefer not to" are said to symbolize the alienation of writing.

So persistent is the tendency to equate the brevity of expression with writing that only one recent critic has ascribed to the lawyer's narration a "profoundly spoken quality" with a "poignant, special effect." In *The Silence of Bartleby* (1988), Dan McCall compiles a list of the narrator's self-corrective comments. Seemingly superfluous statements like "it is fit I make some mention," "I should have stated before," "here it must be said," and "to speak more properly" evoke the tentativeness and spontaneity of conversation, leading McCall to claim to "hear [the lawyer] speaking in every line."[42] One could point to other clues. The lawyer describes his story as a "meagre recital," a phrase suggesting an oral performance. News of Bartleby's employment at the Dead Letter Office comes "to [his] ear a few months after the scrivener's decease" in the form of a rumor (45). Like the fate of Ichabod Crane, which Tarry Town villagers learn through gossip, the scrivener's behavior can only be understood through a form of oral discourse deemed so insubstantial and inconsequential that the lawyer wonders whether he should even divulge it. Finally, lest we forget, Bartleby's "prefer not to" is itself a speech act that twists the tongues of those caught in its consequences.

The most conclusive proof that Melville invests an oral quality in his style is McCall's discovery of a probable source for the lawyer's much maligned closing meditation on the similarity of dead letters to dead men in Samuel Warren's *The Moral, Social, and Professional Duties of Attorneys and Solicitors* (1849). In drawing phrases from Warren's oration on the necessity of "effectual redress" in carrying out the law, Melville colors his narration with the antebellum rhetoric of declamation, just like Hawthorne in "Wakefield." And yet the oral strain here bears a different effect. The formal "let us" interjections and sudden breaks into King Jamesisms serve as extratextual frames leading us to *The Story Teller* and its contrast between storytelling and preaching to account for their purpose. But the spokenness of Melville's narration creates an intratextual frame, a "reading model" within the work that "comment[s] on aspects of its own genre through some little embedded episode, image or situation that serves as a part-for-whole mirror" (Reid 302).

Of course, critics often argue that the lawyer's exasperating struggle to understand Bartleby's actions mirrors the audience's effort to make sense of the story. And yet much commentary has proved surprisingly tone deaf to the complexities of the narration by claiming that the frame centers upon the relationship between the lawyer and Bartleby and not the roles of narrator and character that the lawyer simultaneously plays. In other words, his responses to Bartleby *in the story* do not influence reader response as much as his evaluation of them *in the narration*. As he recounts events, the narrator judges his actions, and his perspective shifts repeatedly from the time of the tale and to the time of its telling. Because we never witness his dealings with his scrivener without the intervening agency of his storytelling, any examination must consider the influence of retrospection upon his narrative performance.

This intratextual framing becomes most apparent whenever the "profoundly spoken quality" of his voice suddenly gives way to an oddly formal style replete with the judicial jargon and tortured syntax of legal documentation: "The conclusion of this whole business was, that it soon became a fixed fact of my chambers, that a pale young scrivener, by the name of Bartleby, had a desk there; that he copied for me at the usual rate of four cents a folio (one hundred words)" (25). Such passages are satirical inasmuch as they exaggerate the summational authority that writing assumes by its ability to organize, arrange, and order thoughts through complex syntactical structures. The subordinate clauses here seem designed to echo a legal contract. As though he were composing an abstract for a recondite document, the lawyer attempts to impose order upon his changing work environment by fixing the facts into a set form. The irony of these shifts into a more professional, authoritative voice arises from a recognition that, however compelled he might be to draw conclusions, the lawyer can never quite articulate the significance of "this whole business." For all the power of writing to set the discursiveness of thought in a linear, rational form, Bartleby eludes the logic of structure. But my cautionary use of the phrase "a recognition" suggests the central narrative ambiguity here, for while we may find ourselves sensitive to these stylistic shifts, nothing in the text formally tells us that the narrator intends to sound satirical. Is this irony staged by Melville at the lawyer's expense, or is he granting him the self-awareness sufficient to parody his thinking habits?

To broach the question of the narrator's reliability is to enter into an old critical conundrum, and yet the debate has proved decidedly one-sided, for most discussions of "Bartleby" treat him as a dupe, an object of Melville's disdain. It is true, as one critic claims, that "Melville forces us to judge the lawyer's every statement by reference to the mode of its being: by the lawyer's personal and class interests, age, gender, cultural matrix, and psychological economy."[43] Yet the fact that few critics acknowledge even *the possibility* that he might be judging himself by those same criteria is itself telling, for it suggests just how standardized, institutionalized even, this interpretation has become. To read the lawyer's narration ironically is now the "right" reading. Hershel Parker is emphatic about this point: while "the average reader of *Putnam's* probably sympathized . . . with the elderly narrator's perplexity," and while "most modern readers at first probably share" this response, "the best modern readers" resist that identification, recognizing instead that "all through the story [the lawyer] tells much more about himself than he realizes."[44]

The ironic reading does injustice to the intricacy of the narration, which helps us understand why a reader might sympathize with the lawyer for reasons far more compelling than mere ingenuousness. Instead of dismissing a sympathetic reading as naïve, we can examine how Melville's intratextual framing offers the possibility that the narrator possesses a deeper awareness of the situation than is normally credited to him. This framing can be traced in three textual patterns: (1) passages in which the lawyer either "revolves" evidence of Bartleby's behavior or "resolves" himself upon a particular course of action; (2) passages in which he comments as a narrator upon his actions; and, finally, (3) the concluding sequel, in which the purpose of the tale is revealed.

At a late point in the text, the lawyer describes how Bartleby's favorite word, "prefer," saturates the conversation in his office. Involuntarily, both he and his long-term scriveners, Turkey and Nippers, take to repeating it, employing it in contexts that the narrator deems "not exactly suitable." The lawyer admits, "I trembled to think that my contact with the scrivener had already and seriously affected me in a mental way. And what further and deeper aberration might it not yet produce? The apprehension had not been without efficacy in determining me to summary measures"

(31). By "summary" he means a quick deployment of commonsense propriety. But "summary measures" also characterizes a prominent narrative technique, for repeatedly the narrator halts his story to summarize the effects of a particular exchange with Bartleby. The "measures" by which he judges his responses to such scenes are of two distinct types: He may portray himself in the act of "revolving" or pondering a particular incident in his mind, or he may describe himself as "resolving" upon various schemes that subsequently fail to carry out their intent. Like the passage in which "the conclusion of this whole business" is recounted with legalese, these motifs assume a satiric tone by virtue of their exaggerated subordination and excessive reliance upon adverbs such as "then" and "thus," which lend written discourse the authority of sequentiality. The contrast between these passages and the conversational style creates an evaluative frame that asks readers to account for its function. What does it reveal about the lawyer, the narration demands, that he portrays his thinking in this "overwritten" form?

An early manifestation of *revolving* occurs after the scrivener has twice refrained from verifying his employer's documents, though he continues to copy them. Bartleby's "remarkable conduct" leads the lawyer to "regard his ways narrowly," a rather revealing adverb whose accuracy is confirmed when he ascribes this strange behavior to the "probable effects" of a malnourished diet: "He lives, then, on ginger-nuts [gingersnaps], thought I; never eats a dinner, properly speaking; he must be a vegetarian then; but no; he never eats even vegetables, he eats nothing but ginger-nuts." He ponders the effect of the spice itself: "Now what was ginger? A hot, spicy thing. Was Bartleby hot and spicy? Not at all. Ginger, then, had no effect upon Bartleby. Probably he preferred it should have none" (23). The humor here arises from the lawyer's struggle to reconcile the evidence that he "narrowly" observes within two specific forms of reasoning. The first quotation offers an example of deductive reasoning, while the second is a syllogism, similar to the parodic "ratiocination" offered by the shabby gentleman in the postscript of "The Legend of Sleepy Hollow." According to Walter Ong, both forms are expressive of a written consciousness since they structure expression according to a logic of "abstract" thinking rather than the "situational" or contextual "frames of reference" typical of oral cultures. Such forms are appealing because they promise that any phenomena, however bizarre, can be made amenable to reason simply by applying to them universal norms of common sense.[45] And yet in "Bartleby" such devices fail repeatedly to serve their purpose. For all the order and certainty that summational forms promise, the lawyer's *revolving* merely returns him to a state of speculation in which he can only wonder whether his employee "probably" preferred not to be agitated by ginger.

It is important to recognize the implications of the phrase *thought I,* which, like *revolving* and *resolving,* appears more than a half-dozen times. As an attributional device, *thought I* marks the narrator's analysis, or resolving, of the situation as he retells it. As this pattern of *revolving* emerges, the tension between expression and form becomes increasingly overt, a result, again, of the retrospective nature of the narrative stance. The struggle to deduce the source of Bartleby's despair at the time of the story manifests itself in structures that are at odds with the style employed at the time of the narration. Whenever the scrivener declares his preferences, the lawyer observes "all the quiet mysteries" surrounding him and then attempts to arrange the clues in a sequential form to resolve their mystery. However, as he describes the effects of his struggle, his judgments turn speculative rather than declarative, as though he were rejecting rational forms of thinking as artificial, empty containers. These contrasting styles create an undertow in the syntactical flow of meaning. If the sequential ordering suggests a desire for the centripetal pull toward certitude, the narrative style, by admitting its speculativeness, is centrifugal, radiating outwards to acknowledge an almost bewildering universe of possibility.

One passage in particular demonstrates how the interplay between story and narration generates this evaluative pattern. Rummaging Bartleby's desk for clues to his background, the lawyer discovers a savings bank book. To integrate this detail with the evidence he has already gathered, he recites a litany of the scrivener's peculiarities: "I remembered that he never spoke but to answer; that though at intervals he had considerable time to himself, yet I had never seen him reading—no, not even a newspaper; that for long periods of it he would stand looking out, at his pale window behind the screen, upon the dead brick wall." Once more, the past tense ("I remembered") marks this style as representing his thinking in the story, not the narration. The sequence of *thats* continues through nine subordinate clauses, noting Bartleby's fastidious temperance, his reticence, his immobility, culminating finally with this declaration: "And more than all that, I remembered a certain unconscious air of pallid—how shall I call it?—of pallid haughtiness, say, or rather an austere reserve about him" (28). Critics unsympathetic to the lawyer pass right over the narrative complexity here: if "more than all that" implies conclusive proof, the resulting aura of exactitude is punctured by the effort to find the appropriate language to characterize Bartleby, marked here by not one but three qualifiers ("how shall I call it?"; "say"; and "or rather"). In such instances, the narrator's tentativeness, his unwillingness to describe the scene without qualifying his presentation of it, creates a contrapuntal pattern to the syntax of certainty that dramatizes his reasoning habits as a character.

Analogous to such passages of *revolving* are those in which he describes how he *resolved* himself to courses of action that would reinstitute normalcy in the office. Like *summary, resolve* is a word rich in judicial connotation, and, indeed, his tone sounds like a formal decree, as though he were declaiming his intentions. These self-declarations are also cast in exaggerated syntax that emphasizes the ineffectiveness of his labored thought process.

Having discovered one Sunday morning that Bartleby has taken up residence at the office, the lawyer declares his intention to solve the mystery behind the man: "Finally, I resolved upon this;—I would put certain calm questions to him the next morning, touching his history, &c., and if he declined to answer them openly and unreservedly (and I supposed he would prefer not), then to give him a twenty dollar bill over and above whatever I might owe him, and tell him his services were no longer required; but that if any other way I could assist him, I would be happy to do so, especially if he desired a return to his native place" (29). Again, the lawyer attempts to predict Bartleby's responses by judging them according to logic; the preponderance of both sequential coordinates (*and, then*) and typographic cues (*&c.*) belies the writtenness of such thinking. And yet when Bartleby responds exactly as he predicts by declaring he would prefer not to discuss his personal history, the lawyer fails to dismiss him, thereby breaking his resolution. Instead, he pleads with Bartleby to operate under "the common us-ages of this office," only to have his injunction met with a dry rejoinder: "At present I would prefer not to be a little reasonable" (30). The exchange offers the earliest hint of why the lawyer is powerless to affect his employee; in trying to reason with Bartleby the lawyer attempts to place him in a system of common sense within which he refuses to be ensnared.

The most important of the lawyer's resolutions occurs when he describes how he draws from his "doctrine of assumptions" to persuade Bartleby to leave his office. That his reasoning borrows its authority from the logic of writing is explicit here: "There was no vulgar bullying, no bravado of any sort, no choleric hectoring, and striding to and fro across the apartment, jerking out vehement commands. . . . Nothing of the kind" (33). Instead of persuading Bartleby through an impassioned oratorical performance, he reasons with him by invoking common sense: "I *assumed* the ground that depart he must; and upon that assumption built all I had to say." This economical mode of argumentation, he adds, is preferred by the "dispassionate thinker." And yet precisely because Bartleby is a man of preferences rather than assumptions, the lawyer's resolutions were doomed to fail. That he, at the time that he tells the story, recognizes why his assumptions proved ineffectual is clear. "The more I thought over my procedure, the more I was charmed with it," he acknowledges—until he realizes that he had succumbed to the "fumes of vanity." However judicious this presumption of common sense, he now recognizes that the "assumption was simply my own, and none of Bartleby's." By acknowledging such failures, the storyteller models the self-reflection and awareness that the text demands of us as we attempt to articulate our own responses.

These resolving and revolving passages imply satire through the juxtaposition of form and expression. The exaggerated patterns of legalese suggest a cognitive scrambling for order, for some syntactical assurance that Bartleby's behavior can be comprehended. Because this patterning calls attention to itself through stylistic means, I characterize it as an internalized or embedded evaluative device. By dramatizing the lawyer's mind-set, the satiric style is an ideological marker of his belief system. A second prominent evaluative pattern is an external cue, for it characterizes the narrator's attitudes at the time that he tells his tale. These passages include a range of interpolated commentary, from imperatives addressed to readers ("Think of it") to the commonplaces by which he attempts to explain his actions ("Nothing so aggravates an earnest person as a passive resistance") to self-evaluations that reveal him judging his responses ("I might as well have essayed to strike fire with my knuckles against a bit of Windsor soap"). In ironic readings of "Bartleby," such interjections are considered sentimental digressions by which the lawyer avoids the "true" import of the tale—namely, his responsibility for Bartleby's death. (Ann Douglas goes so far as to dismiss his "sometimes meaningless garrulity" as an "onanistic indulgence.") Yet this evaluative framing serves the important function of involving the audience in the drama, for it models the process of self-analysis that we are asked to imitate as we read.

This function is best demonstrated by a passage that directly addresses readers, which occurs when the narrator describes the feelings that overwhelmed him upon discovering that Bartleby resided in his office: "Immediately then the thought came sweeping across me, What miserable friendlessness and loneliness are here revealed! His poverty is great; but his solitude, how horrible!" Except for a subsequent one-sentence command to the audience ("Think of it"), the present tense into which these exclamations are cast is fictional; despite their immediacy, they dramatize emotions experienced in the story, not at the time it is told: "Of a Sunday, Wall street is deserted as Petra; and every night of every day it is an emptiness. . . . And here Bartleby makes his home; sole spectator of a solitude which he has seen all populous—a sort of innocent and transformed Marius brooding among the ruins of Carthage!" The storyteller intervenes to judge the legitimacy of this image by distinguishing the "feeling of overpowering stinging melancholy" it inspired from a "not-unpleasing sadness" to which life had previously accustomed him. The recognition that he and Bartleby shared a "common bond of humanity," he confesses, created a profound awareness of gloom, which he dramatizes through another shift into the fictional present tense: "[I] thought to myself, Ah, happiness courts the light, so we deem the world is gay; but misery hides aloof, so we deem that misery there is none." Yet he then describes such responses as "sad fancyings—chimeras, doubtless, of a sick and silly brain" (28). Critics often quote the lawyer's claim to share a "fraternal melancholy" as evidence of his condescending pity while ignoring completely the imperative and the self-criticism. Such readings fail to recognize the purpose of this evaluative commentary. "Think of it" commands us to imagine the agony of Bartleby's isolation, and "sad fancyings" cautions against accepting our initial responses as adequate answers. If we do not account for the way the narration frames the action, we are apt to overlook the persistent judgments to which the lawyer subjects himself *and* the similarly high standard that he asks us to apply to our own reading.

The narrator stresses the need for such self-evaluation as he critiques the broader body of beliefs and assumptions that might shape audience responses—again, not in order to rationalize his behavior, but to encourage an engagement with the story that is at once emotional and self-reflective. At one point he explains why early feelings of sadness and pity gave way to the fear and repulsion that drove him to flee Bartleby's presence: "So true it is, and so terrible too, that up to a certain point the thought or sight of misery enlists our best affections; but, in certain special cases, beyond that point it does not. They err who would assert that invariably this is owing to the inherent selfishness of the human heart." In ironic readings of "Bartleby," such statements are disclaimers by which he justifies his actions. But for an audience who identifies with the narrator, his attempt to explain his feelings articulates a common body of response. He constructs here a network of identification that invites readers to imagine how they would react to similar emotions. Acknowledging that Bartleby exhausted his "sincerest pity," he asks us not to judge him but to question whether "repulsion" might arise from something far more ominous than "inherent selfishness"—namely, the failure of "effectual succor," our inability to minister to those indifferent to salvation. Just as he critiques his reactions to Bartleby, the narrator asks that we share that willingness to evaluate our responses to *him*.

In several passages, the tone of parodic self-criticism is so prominent that it is difficult to understand how critics can denounce him as naïve and unreflective. In one case, the lawyer's frustration is so great that he momentarily worries that he might be moved to violence, the same way John Colt killed Samuel Adams in a fit of passion in the 1840s. How did he prevent such an indiscretion? "Why, simply by recalling the divine injunction: 'A new commandment give I unto you, that ye love one another.' Yes, it was this that saved me." But it was not the "higher," humanistic principles of fraternal compassion that saved him; rather, he realized that he would be remembered as the first man to commit murder "for sweet charity's sake," just as Colt was remembered for his sudden burst of irrational anger. He then evaluates his response with an ironic bit of proverbial wisdom: "Mere self-interest, then, if no better motive can be enlisted, should, especially with high-tempered men, prompt all beings to charity and philanthropy." As if the sarcasm were not obvious enough, the loftiness of tone is deflated by a dismissive transition ("At any rate") in which he describes how such maxims soothed his "exasperated feelings" by allowing him to "benevolently constru[e] [Bartleby's] conduct." Self-serving benevolence is, of course, the charge that critics often level at the lawyer. Yet the fact that he ridicules it complicates claims that he learns little from this experience. Instead, his self-deprecation models the process of self-interrogation by which audiences are asked to challenge the complacency of their values.

No evaluative component has perplexed critics as much as Melville's concluding sequel, in which the lawyer relates the "vague report" of Bartleby's employment at the Dead Letter Office and then dramatizes the effect of its "certain suggestive interest" as he rhapsodizes on the tragedy of lost letters. Part of the critical enmity arises from aesthetic dissatisfaction. Because it is formally separated from the main narrative, the sequel is an addendum, an afterthought that ruptures what would otherwise be a dramatic continuity amenable to Aristotelian standards of development, climax, and denouement. Thus, one critic complains that the sequel is "a flaw because it takes the reader outside the confines of the story itself" by "add[ing] biographical information about Bartleby after enough has been said."[46] But the standards of enough said are distinctly modern in taste; this critic evaluates the story's form according to modernist aesthetics of brevity that would have Melville render the revelation of Bartleby's clerkship dramatically rather than discursively. Such judgments not only project contemporary prejudices against emotional affectivity onto an age in which it was more commonplace and acceptable, they miss entirely the purpose of the sequel. Like the storytelling scene in the postscript of "The

Legend of Sleepy Hollow" or the moral in "Wakefield," the conclusion articulates the story's situational self-reflexivity by suggesting why it is told as it is.

To understand this point, we should recognize that the narrator has told the tale at least once before. Shortly after Bartleby is removed to the Tombs, he seeks out the appropriate functionary at the Hall of Justice and testifies to Bartleby's essential good-naturedness by "narrat[ing] all [he] knew" (42). Did his testimony differ from the account presented to us? Perhaps not in the essential outline of events, but the evaluative commentary has undoubtedly changed, since between the time of the scrivener's death and his narration, at least two events occur that color and shape his retrospection. Hearing the rumor about Bartleby inspires emotions that he claims he can hardly express: "Dead letters! Does it not sound like dead men?" What generates these feelings is not only the gloomy image of Bartleby burning the letters, but the fact that he was "suddenly remov[ed] by a change in the administration." The narrator presumably identifies with this experience since, at some point subsequent to Bartleby's death, he has lost his Master of Chancery title due to a new state constitution that abolished the office. The cleverness of this connection arises from its muted presentation: While the narrator complains of losing his title in the opening paragraphs, the scrivener's termination is revealed only in the end, and at no point does Melville allow his storyteller to acknowledge explicitly what they share. Instead, these "sudden removals" subtly frame the narration, encouraging sympathetic readers to inquire how these events might make him reflect differently upon the experience of this "fraternal melancholy."

But as important as what the postscript tells us is the fact that it is a rumor. As McCall rightly suggests, the sequel challenges us to evaluate "the adequacy, not the veracity" of this "one little item of interest" that *might* explain Bartleby's inconsolable despair (133). Critics who complain that the conclusion too tidily rationalizes the scrivener's tragedy miss the point; the lawyer's inability to certify this information is the central clue to the well-wrought tentativeness of the storytelling. The rumor about Bartleby offers food for thought that may momentarily satisfy but cannot sate the hunger that narrative feeds. According to Jean-Nöel Kapferer a rumor, like a secret,

> increases the value of information and leads to an exacerbation of "desires to know more." As is classic in every market economy, a shortage leads to a black market . . . a circuit of unofficial, unguaranteed and unvalidated information, that is nevertheless immediately consumed and spread to the degree that the need to be informed has been frustrated.[47]

The lawyer never claims to solve the mystery; the rumor's effect is the best conclusion he can draw, and he shares it as a way of inspiring readers to contemplate its power over them. As a storytelling frame, the postscript is thus a device for passing along the story, and this act of sharing, if "Bartleby" can be said to possess a redemptive power, makes it so. Letters may speed toward death, the conclusion implies, but storytelling breathes a resuscitating life into tragedy.

Epilogue

Scenes of storytelling in these tales, whether overt or embedded, dramatize the making of multiple meanings through narrative exchange. As the short story begins to emerge in contradistinction to the tale, however, the function of narration is redefined from inspiring the affectivity of Romanticism toward a concentration on the formal properties of the aesthetic medium itself. An 1860 *Atlantic Monthly* article titled "The Carnival of the Romantic" by W. L. Symonds suggests nicely why short fiction would begin to embed narrative addresses:

> Between the vocal story and the story in literature there is an immense difference, like that between talking and writing, between life and art. The qualities in which the story-teller makes even frivolity weighty and dulness significant . . . the play of the eye, the lips, the countenance, the voice, the whole sympathetic expression of the person . . . are wanting to [fiction]; it has passed from the realm of life to that of art; it loses the charm which personal relation gives even the trifles.[48]

Because speech is dependent on "personal relation," the emotions that it produces are transitory, and its import evaporates once contact concludes. Writing, as a material medium, necessitates a significance that transcends the moment of exchange. To write for the truth thus requires an economy of expression that allows a reader to attend to art without being distracted by its presentation.

Although Symonds conflates all fiction with the novel, he expresses the common sentiment among nineteenth-century aestheticians that narrative caters to an unhealthy desire for stimulation.

"Story-telling," he continues, "is one of the graces of the art of life" but not the life of art, which cultivates the mature thought that allows appreciation for "form" rather than "flavor." Of course, Symonds's position that any fiction, once removed from the realm of "sympathetic expression," loses its charm is extreme but hardly uncommon. Realist storytellers countered this criticism by promoting "artistic impartiality" or narrative reticence that prompts thought over feeling. As William Dean Howells writes, "literary self-respect" is incompatible with "the old trade of make-believe" that was intent on stirring excitement. A style of narration "actuated by the motives and the passions in the measure we all know" benefits "grown persons" by reminding them of a simple truth: "Reality is romance." Significantly, Howells links this emotional economy with the brevity of American English: Once stories cease to "preach pride and revenge, folly and insanity, egotism and prejudice"—once, in other words, they cease to "put on fine literary airs"—they will "speak the dialect, the language, that most Americans know—the language of unaffected people every-where."[49]

The evocation of "unaffected" language to convey motives and passions that we all know dramatizes the conflict between stylistic economy and storytelling we will find in realist short stories. If we speak a common language, the imagined community that storytelling frames create between authors and audiences is redundant, for that relationship already exists, embedded within the style we share. Specifying the story's situational self-reflexivity becomes an artificial conceit. Yet a story featured in the *Atlantic Monthly* barely six months after the appearance of Symonds's "The Carnival of the Romantic" illustrates how ambiguously common language can affect interpretation when a speaker's identity is obscured. In Rebecca Harding Davis's "Life in the Iron Mills," the storyteller appeals to the reader's moral outrage while depicting the inhumanity of industrialization. The authority to make such appeals goes unspecified, however, for the voice might belong to a minister, a muckraking journalist, or a reformer. Indeed, one cannot even tell whether the voice belongs to a woman or a man. As befits print communication, the message eclipses the messenger.

"Life in the Iron Mills" is striking not merely for the reality that it represents but for the reality that it strives to effect. Two other postbellum stories, Sarah Orne Jewett's "A White Heron" and Charlotte

Perkins Gilman's "The Yellow Wallpaper," likewise dramatize how the verity that Howells assumes is common knowledge is a rhetorical construction fashioned through gestures of address. The three works are further linked by their awareness that these addresses often suffer gender stereotypes, for unaffected language in the realist era is increasingly described with metaphors of masculinity. To differing degrees Davis, Jewett, and Gilman confront the gender biases that distinguish reality from make-believe. Ultimately, they suggest that common sense is not an objective standard but a norm that we negotiate through stories.

Part 2

Making it Real: Direct Addresses, Gender, and the Realist Short Story

Prologue

When Rebecca Harding Davis died in 1910, eulogies recounted how her most famous short story, "Life in the Iron Mills," challenged cultural assumptions about women's writing. As the *New York Times* reported, many of her original readers "thought the author must be a man" because "the stern but artistic realism of the picture she put alive upon paper, suggested a man, and a man of power not unlike Zola's."[1] Although the analogy is anachronistic—Zola was unknown in America when "Life" was published in the *Atlantic Monthly* in April 1861—the suggestion that Davis wrote like a man is by no means unique. Elizabeth Stuart Phelps, whose novel *The Silent Partner* (1871) owes an obvious debt to the story, likewise argued that while her "intensity" was "essentially feminine . . . her grip was like that of a masculine hand." The effect for Phelps was at once liberating and inspiring; reading the tale prompted a "distinct crisis . . . at the point where the intellect and the moral nature meet," thus dramatizing the affective potential of an activist strategy of narration that was "never possible after reading to ignore. One could never again say that one did not understand."[2]

Phelps's language here is revealing: *grip* captures the rhetorical power of Davis's exposé of working conditions in Wheeling, Virginia (now West Virginia), the steel town on the Ohio River where she spent most of her life. With documentary details welded into long, iron-hard descriptive passages, the style is at times startlingly sparse and visual, with conjunctive images like "the pig-pens, the ash-heaps covered with potato skins, the bloated, pimpled women at the doors" (48) as clear and focused as a photograph. *Intensity*, meanwhile, conveys the emphatic tone of Davis's direct addresses, which are typical of the era's didactic fiction: "Stop a moment. I am going to be honest. This is what I want you to do. I want you to hide your disgust, take no heed to your clean clothes, and come right down here with me,—here, into the thickest of the fog and mud and foul effluvia. I want you to hear this story" (13). But the terminology should also raise eyebrows, for what makes *grip* particularly masculine and *intensity* "essentially" feminine?

The question provides a springboard for the concerns addressed in this part of the book: (1) the function of directly addressing the reader in realist short stories and (2) the role of these addresses in the development of a women's realism that confronts and appropriates stereotypes of female expressiveness to retain a degree of affectivity in the storytelling exchange deemed inessential by mainstream male realists. In the tales analyzed in the previous part of the book, the act of narration was foregrounded often to the point that the storytelling dominated the stories. In this section, however, we will discover a greater tension between stylistic economy and storytelling as narrators abruptly halt otherwise dramatic action to comment upon it, defining for us the significance of the events rendered. The purpose of direct addresses is not dissimilar from that of the more expansive and discursive framing strategies employed by Irving, Hawthorne, and Melville: Both techniques are tools by which a text's situational self-reflexivity reveals to readers the interpretive expectations it is willing to accommodate. But because invocations to the audience during the realist period are defined as an artistic flaw, the conflict between our two connotations of *economy*—between the aesthetic function of presentational immediacy and the cultural function of storytelling—will be more pronounced. Until recently, extant criticism has tended to come down squarely on the side of stylistic economy by dismissing narrative interjections as disruptive, alienating, and a sure sign that the intent is didactic rather than artistic. Yet direct addresses can be shown to serve at least two specific cultural functions: (1) they allow storytellers to acknowledge a range of potential reader response, and, in so doing, (2) they provide devices by which narrators can qualify or hedge their styles of representation and thus extend to readers a greater degree of interpretive freedom. The result is what we might call collaborative realism, a mode of narration in which verisimilitude is not an extratextual standard universally subscribed to by readers but a textual reality that must be negotiated in the process of its articulation.

As a starting point for understanding the tensions between realism, gender, and direct addresses, we should recall Robyn Warhol's argument that, during the Victorian era, narrative interjections were identified increasingly as a "woman's strategy, to be applied at moments when [the audience's] emotional receptivity should be most sensitive, and to be avoided by practitioners of self-referential 'high art.'"[3] By "practitioners" she means William Dean Howells and Henry James, the two realists most often associated with the doctrine of objectivity. Early twentieth-century critics, including Percy Lubbock and Fred Lewis Pattee, often equate objectivity with narrative presence to suggest that realist writing precludes complete quietude on the part of a storyteller. Yet, as any reader will recognize, Howells and James openly stage their stories. Even in James's complex late style, which typically employs an undramatized narrative voice, one discovers obvious storytelling cues in the form of self-corrective comments, as in this randomly chosen sentence from "The Jolly Corner": "When I say [Spencer Brydon] 'jumped' at it I feel the consonance of this term with the fact that—at the end indeed of I know not how long—he did move again, he crossed straight to the door."[4] Warhol pinpoints the key difference between stances when she speaks of "emotional receptivity." While Davis's addresses are emphatic, pathetic in their appeal, the self-reflexivity evinced by Howells and James is rigorously analytical. While nineteenth-century reviewers collapse the distinction by referring generically to an author's "digressions," the stylistic economy of realism can be said to elide the affective timbre of the address, not necessarily the convention itself, which is why Howells and James are sometimes criticized for "expatiating" excessively.[5]

Howells's *Criticism and Fiction* explains why emotional interjections were deemed inappropriate to realist art. In the book's central chapters, he excerpts an essay by Spanish author Armando Palacio Valdés that attributes the "decadence of contemporary literature" to the rage for "effectism . . . the itch of awaking at all cost in the reader vivid and violent emotions, which shall credit to the invention and originality of the writer." Although Howells severely qualifies Valdés's complaints, he nevertheless absorbs the disdainful rhetoric used to characterize affectivity by denouncing as "primitive" the "high-strung," the "blood-curdled," the "goose-fleshed," and the "hair-breathed"—in short, any fiction that appeals to readers who, because they are "tired of thinking," want the "relaxation in feeling—feeling crudely, grossly, merely" (247).

This aversion to feeling is important because it illuminates a central point of divergence between the tale and the short story. Though the Civil War has long been regarded as the single greatest cause for the emergence of more realistic short fiction, editors and critics as early as the 1850s began calling for an artistic alternative to the stories published in *Godey's Lady's Book*, the *New York Ledger*, and other popular periodicals. As a prime vehicle for ethical exhortation, the tale had been corrupted by "stereotyped incident," "hackneyed plots," and, most severely, by "unnatural language" that appealed to "uncultivated instincts." Those phrases, coincidentally, appear in an essay by Alice B. Neal Haven (best known as the author of *The Gossips of Rivertown*, an influential short-story collection) that originally appeared in *Godey's*, the very publication accused of pandering to the "uncultivated."[6] While standards of "naturalness" are notoriously subjective, mid-nineteenth-century assessments of the tale generally share the assumption that moral edification crippled artistic expression, creating the need for an entirely new form of short fiction that would value verisimilitude above all else.[7] The critical vocabulary promoting the realist short story often draped its attacks on "unnatural language" in feminine garb. Indeed, envisioning his realist advocacy as a war, Howells boasted memorably that he was "banging the babes of romance about." Yet as editor of the *Atlantic Monthly* after 1869, he accepted stories by Rose Terry Cooke, Harriet Beecher Stowe, and Harriet Prescott Spofford, all of whom directly addressed their audience. At one point, he even claimed that the stories of Sarah Orne Jewett and Mary Wilkins Freeman were "faithfuller and more realistic than those of the men."[8]

Howells' appreciation for these writers highlights the obvious fact that realism was not sex exclusive. While many of their male contemporaries shamelessly manipulated the pathetic force of didacticism, several women realists satirized exhortative styles as perpetuating insuperable sexual stereotypes. Rose Terry Cooke, for example, parodies the moral pragmatism of direct addresses in

"Miss Muffett and the Spider" (1860). Writing "in the author-itative plural," the editorial "we" recasts the Mother Goose nursery rhyme as a didactic allegory on proper female behavior. The satire is every bit as acid as Twain's parody of sentimental poetry in *Huckleberry Finn*, replete with exclamatory declarations of intent: "I am going to write a story, instead of a treatise solemn and staid, a story illustrative of a distich of Mother Goose—not, oh! not after the faithless fashion of 'him who told the wondrous tale' of Mother Mary—a prophecy that indicates to the philosophic mind the reign of that sensational periodical, *The Daily Ledger.*"[9] The analogy between typological narratives (a common variety of the popular tale) and nursery rhymes reveals just how tenuous the religious authority that informed didactic storytelling was in the eyes of many realists.

As Cooke's story suggests, narrative styles did not necessarily reflect sexual difference. Instead, realism assumed a masculine tenor as its aesthetics were articulated. In the *Atlantic* in the 1860s and 1870s, it is repeatedly defined as a form of stylistic economy in which "telling a thing is enough and explaining it too much." By the mid-1880s, Turgenev embodies the ideal because he is "a realist in the sense of hiding himself." According to James, the objectivity resulting from authorial silence grants audiences the latitude to explore "the relation between the cultivated fancy and the visible, palpable facts of the world." By cultivated, James means a storytelling style that prompts aesthetic rather than emotional responses. The *Atlantic*'s reviewers developed a set list of terms to describe the proper tone and approach that would inspire this aesthetic effect. Realism's *accurate observation* and *graphic* or *sober fidelity* defused the *excess of fancy* and *ornamental excesses* of sensational narrative styles by allowing audiences to focus on the drama rather than the storyteller's presence. Its *authenticity* and *poetical insight* would correct the *exaggerated absurdities* and *rash indignities* of popular fiction. Above all, realism would offer an *analysis of passion* rather than *sordid delineations* of it. Significantly, some types of realism violated the same taboo as sentimental fiction by too strenuously manipulating emotions. What critics called "photographic" realism, the harbinger of naturalism, was repeatedly dismissed for not aspiring to *artistic literalness*. James ridiculed Davis's style, for example, on at least two occasions in the late 1860s for its "injudicious straining after realistic effects which leave nature and reality at an infinite distance behind and beside them."[10] In other words, Davis violated standards of authorial silence by overdramatizing her subject and creating a harsh, deterministic picture of the world. The judgment points to an intriguing paradox of the era: When stories by women writers lacked "cultivated fancy" or "poetical insight," they were not rejected for being too sentimental but for being too realistic. The *Atlantic*'s editor, James T. Fields, asked Davis to revise her second submission to the magazine, "The Story of To-day" (published in book form as *Margret Howth*) because it "assembled the gloom." Horace Scudder, who assumed the editorship of the *Atlantic* in the early 1880s, returned "The Yellow Wallpaper" to Charlotte Perkins Gilman with a rejection notice famous for its own terseness: "I could not forgive myself if I made others as miserable as I have made myself!" The disdain for emotional styles is best embodied in a comment from an anonymous *Atlantic* reviewer in 1871: audiences' "chords of feeling" were being "rasped and twanged like fiddle-strings by the hysterical performances of some of our authoresses."[11]

A word choice like *hysterical* is telling: as a diagnostic judgment, it alludes to the emergence of a critical vocabulary grounded in the presumed objectivity of professionalism rather than the religious institutions from which didactic fiction drew its moral authority. As cultural historians note, the impetus toward professionalization in the post-Civil War decades created a class of experts charged with upholding norms of reality, whether in science, medicine, law, or journalism. Writers may never have enjoyed the prestige or lifestyle accorded physicians and lawyers, but many laid claim to the "cultural authority both to possess and to dispense access to the real."[12] If Romanticists like Irving, Hawthorne, and Melville expressed their ambivalence by cultivating the persona of a marginalized observer, many male realists aspired to the status of arbitrators. At its most pragmatic, as Howells would claim, such privilege meant that a storyteller need not "[account] in any way for his knowledge of the facts," thus drastically redefining the short story's structure of narrative address.[13] In the tale, a storyteller's social status often bears a demonstrable influence on style as the narrative frame contextualizes the transmission of the story by offering audiences ideal or ironic models of reception. Yet in realism, that identity is often extraneous because the audience is subordinated a priori to the narrative perspective. Any deviation from an economical norm of expression risks being labeled "supernatural," "fanciful," or, more extremely, "hysterical." Because masculine values predominantly define this model of reality, pejorative terms like *hysterical* are associated with supposedly feminine attributes; indeed, in the later years of the century, the act of storytelling itself is equated with effeminate behavior. As Frank Norris claims, a man simply writes more realistically than a woman because he "is not troubled with emotions and has no overmastering desire to communicate his sensations to anybody." A woman writer, because she "is impressionable, emotional, communicative," cannot cultivate the necessary aesthetic distance to write objectively.[14] Facing such prejudices, storytellers interested in evoking a tangible sense of narrative exchange were forced to appeal to the reader through ever more embedded codes of interaction.

With different degrees of openness, Rebecca Harding Davis, Sarah Orne Jewett, and Charlotte Perkins Gilman confront gender stereotypes of storytelling prevalent in the realist era. In doing so, their work illustrates the interpersonal function of the direct address. Far from being a lapse of aesthetic taste, this convention allows storytellers to acknowledge the potential diversity of audience response and solicit multiple interpretations of their tales. As Karl Kroeber explains, storytellers emphasize the open-endedness of their stories by appealing to as many different readers as possible. They define their audience as "having diverse occupations, prejudices, and life experiences, so that their 'community' depends on the acceptance of their acknowledged differences." Rather than proliferate a singular vision of reality, such narrators "*connect* differentiated groups and individuals" as they mediate between multifarious perspectives. In so doing, they define "the reading of [their stories as] a different imagining process from one of reading most modern [texts] 'addressed' to readers undefined, anonymous, and conceived as responding in purely aesthetic terms."[15] In other words, direct addresses reveal how a storyteller *negotiates* rather than *assumes* the right to tell a story.

The three stories analyzed here illustrate how this connecting function of storytelling was increasingly subordinated to plot over the course of the realist era. In "Life in the Iron Mills," Davis's often disconcerting shifts in tone and style—what one critic has described as her "bizarre complex of tones and appeals—now the voice of the Christian reformer . . . now the muckraking journalist"[16]—can be read as a concerted effort to shape the widest possible variety of reader responses. The manner by which she strives to assimilate different types of readers into an audience is wholly unique, for although gender differences are an obvious theme of the story, she refrains from specifying either the sex of her narrator or her fictional readers. Many contemporary critics, of course, assume that the storyteller is a woman by overidentifying the narrative voice with the author, just as Davis's original audience, according to the *New York Times*, believed that the author must have been a man.[17] Davis not only published the story anonymously, but in the text itself she elides references to her storyteller's sex, which is why I use the term *she/he* throughout my reading. De-emphasizing the narrator's sex allows Davis to move freely among styles of address without accounting for the authority of the narrative voice. Nor do narrative interjections invoke the conventional sex roles of the era by addressing the audience as "dear lady" or "dear gentleman reader." Instead, "Life in the Iron Mills" genders its readership rhetorically, not dramatically, by establishing different degrees of intimacy suggestive of the segregated spheres of influence. That is, the narrative voice fluctuates between an aggressive, almost hortative public style and a more intimate, private one. Because the networks of identification created by these addresses are constructs not of social identity (the diverse occupations and life experiences that Kroeber specifies) but of social modes of expression, the text becomes the site where an audience's diverse assumptions of authority—who has the right to address whom—are activated. Davis's style thus serves a paradoxical function as gendered appeals become devices by which gender assumptions are questioned and undermined.

Jewett likewise deals with the influence of sexual difference on narrative style, though her audience addresses are far more oblique than Davis's. While "Life in the Iron Mills" juxtaposes at least two distinct interpretive postures by mingling styles of address, "A White Heron" refrains from establishing any clear narrative stance, placing the audience instead in an ambiguous triangular relationship with the characters and the storyteller. Reticence should not be confused with silence, however, for the narrator is an active agent in Jewett's story. Embedded evaluative devices, including questions, modal hedges, and descriptive detail, function as techniques of "suggestion"—an important word for Jewett—that orient attention toward incongruous details in the story's realist fabric. These hints of unarticulated meaning become occasions for a hesitation or pause that invites a reader's active participation in the resolution of the text's mysteries. "The Yellow Wallpaper," meanwhile, offers the most complex insight into the influence of gender on realism. Gilman fashions an increasingly unrealistic style that implicitly critiques the assumptions of reason that underpin realistic forms of representation by emphasizing a woman's struggle to resolve her "habit of storymaking" with her husband's restrictive, rational perspective.

Despite their different functions, addresses in these texts dramatize the ambiguous space of exchange in storytelling. While negotiating the terms of representation, the injunctions defer or hedge their own authority, necessitating audience response if sense is to be made of narrative statements of fact, thus engaging the audience in a collaborative vision of truth. If realist critics argue that excessive feeling violates the aesthetic norms of verisimilitude, these writers intimate the exact opposite: for them, nothing confirms the reality of representation better than an audience's emotional response.

4

Rebecca Harding Davis: "Life in the Iron Mills" and the Cross-Gendered Text

Patricia Yaeger has called attention to the various sociolects in "Life in the Iron Mills" that dramatize class differences. Representing the pocket, the heart, and the head of the world, three middle-class men stroll the mill debating the deplorable condition of the workers' lives, speaking in "several rhetorical modes to dissemble economic distances that would otherwise be unbearable."[18] Kirby, the son of the owner, exemplifies the language of laissez faire: "*Ce n'est pas mon affaire*. . . . The Lord will take care of his own; or else [the laborers] can work out their own salvation." Dr. May offers Scriptural aphorisms in a philanthropic spirit. He believes that "much good was to be done . . . by a friendly word or two," but his maxims are compromised by his social status, for he "talk[s] down to the capacity of his hearer." Mitchell, a "thoroughbred gentleman," is the most problematic, precisely because he most resembles the middle-class audience of the *Atlantic Monthly*. Educated, artistic, contemptuous of "one-idead men," his "taste, culture, [and] refinement" allow him to view morality as a philosophical rather than social issue. He alone recognizes what Hugh Wolfe tries to express in the statue shaped from scraps of korl, but he refuses to articulate the connection that he feels. When pressed by a "chafed" May to offer the sculptor a pittance of hope or encouragement, he says, "I am not one of them. . . . Reform is born of need, not pity" (38–39). According to Yaeger, Davis uses the debate between the three men, which runs roughly a third of the story, to dramatize the subterfuge of middle-class language. She "points to the ease with which well-to-do men and women create figures of speech, and contrasts this glibness with the laborious speech and the wage labor of the iron workers."

To avoid succumbing to this "glibness," Davis's storyteller must qualify the narration. Yaeger argues that she/he "breaks her [*sic*] own metaphors" and other "rhetorical flourishes," ending with an image of the korl woman, Wolfe's statue, which symbolizes "the terrible silence within speech, [of] the blasphemous exclusion [from language] of those who need it most." Yet Yaeger's own language implies that Davis's "flourishes" have yet to be broken completely. The story, she claims, "ends drenched in sentiment, but . . ." (273). As with the *New York Times*'s description of the story ("stern but artistic realism"), a strategic conjunction is called upon to excuse Davis's style. Other critics have spared such subtlety. Robert F. Marler bluntly describes "Life in the Iron Mills" as "overwritten," while a recent biographer of her son, Richard Harding Davis, laments that "the scrape of reality sandpapered off" only "some of her sentimentality." Sharon M. Harris, in the most extensive study of the author's career to date, argues that the direct addresses are ironic. Rhetorical "exaggeration" should dissuade, not encourage, a sentimental identification with the laborers.[19] The instinct to justify the story's emotional injunctions illustrates just how deeply contemporary tastes are saturated by the realist prejudice against affectivity. What has gone unexplored is the persuasive power that such a style might sway on an *Atlantic Monthly* readership, which, since the founding of the magazine in 1857, had been exposed to numerous "political arguments" couched in evocative emotional appeals. Although rhetorical modes may *dissemble* economic differences, they nevertheless allow the storyteller to *assemble* the widest possible audience within a class-circumscribed readership. By mingling communicative strategies culturally coded as masculine and feminine—a strategy that Warhol calls "cross-gendering"—Davis prevents the story from being categorized as solely addressing one sex or the other.

To put it another way, negotiating the real in "Life in the Iron Mills" requires telling two stories in two distinct styles. On the one hand, the tale is about Hugh Wolfe, an iron puddler and artist who is wrongly accused of stealing Mitchell's wallet and who later commits suicide in prison. His is a stereotypically masculine narrative of an individual's struggle against adverse social circumstances to realize "a consciousness of power . . . free to work, to live, to love! Free! His right!" (47). The narrative interjections that characterize his tragedy are aggressive and reprimanding, rebuking the fictional addressee (who becomes a character much like Mitchell) for ignoring the conditions of the workers. According to Warhol, this "distancing" strategy may alienate the actual reading audience when the fictional "you" is described in detail. By "[providing] so much information about this 'you' that" he or she assumes the dimension of a character, the narrator "necessarily places a distance between the actual [audience] and the inscribed 'you' in the text" (29).

Another story deserves telling, however, which centers on Deborah, a hunchback whose unrequited love for his cousin Wolfe dehumanizes her. She looks to him "as a spaniel [looks to] its master" (23); elsewhere, she is described as a witch, one of the "fierce devils [that] whisper in [Wolfe's] ear" (45) tempting him, like a deformed Eve, to snatch the delusive apple of a better life. (She steals the wallet that lands him in prison.) Wolfe's struggle is a social narrative in which the "vigor of a man" degenerates into "a meek woman's face" (24). Because Deborah's tale concerns romantic love, some critics complain that it ignores the economic status of women.[20] Yet inasmuch as Deborah embodies emotions traditionally associated with femininity, sympathy in particular, she serves an important function, for she acts as the nexus for what Warhol labels an "engaging" narrative strategy that encourages the audience to assume the role of the fictional reader. As Warhol suggests, "Using narrative interventions that are almost always spoken in earnest, [an engaging] narrator addresses a 'you' that is evidently intended to evoke recognition and identification in the person who holds the book and reads, even if the 'you' in the text resembles that person only slightly" (29). Again, because Davis does not ascribe a sex to her fictional readers, these strategies are gendered according to tone or, more appropriately, according to what George L. Dillon calls rhetorical "footings," the relative degree of engagement that various linguistic features evoke between a speaker and addressee.[21] The distancing strategy projects the superiority, formality, and confrontational aura of "masculinized" writing, while the engaging mode conveys the equality, informality, and obliqueness of "feminized" styles.

The opening frame suggests how intricately these strategies are interwoven. On the one hand, the tale begins with an aggressive challenge ("A cloudy day: do you know what that is in a town of iron-works?") that begs the reader's response: "What do you make of a case like that, amateur psychologist?" (11–12). Characterized later as an "Egoist, or Pantheist, or Arminian, busy in making straight paths for your feet on the hills" (14), the fictional reader is at worst indifferent or at best unsympathetic to the characters. Yet the narrator admits uncertainty about how to tell the story that undercuts the superiority of this initial stance. Three times in the opening frame she/he characterizes the narration as "idle," critiquing her/his own tendency to romanticize the laborers. By admitting uncertainty about the performance and opening storytelling techniques to evaluation, the narrator is vulnerable to the same criticisms as the addressee.

As the storyteller invites us to descend into the pits, she/he reveals the purpose of the story: "I want to make it a real thing to you" (13–14). But making the story real depends on the audience's ability to "see it clearly," an imperative that is increasingly voiced in sermonic rhetoric that appeals to a Christian vision of authority through Biblical allusions. The power of observation is linked to spiritual perception: "whatever muddy depth of soul-history lies beneath [the surface] you can read according to the eyes God has given you" (23). Subsequent addresses are even more emphatic: "Be just when I tell you about this night, see him as he is. Be just,—not like man's law, which seizes on one isolated fact, but like God's judging angel, whose clear, sad eye saw all the countless cankering days of this man's life, all the countless nights, when, sick with starving, his soul fainted on him, before it judged him and this night, the saddest of all" (25–26). *Just, judging, judgment*, these cognates form the vocabulary of the distancing strategy. The particular rhetorical practice invoked here is the jeremiad, a "mode of public exhortation," according to Sacvan Bercovitch, "designed to join social criticism to spiritual renewal, public to private identity, the shifting 'signs of the times' to certain traditional metaphors, themes, and symbols."[22] By 1861, the American jeremiad had long evolved from a Puritan sermon into a mode of middle-class social prophecy. While at best pseudo-theological as it was absorbed into secular discourse, it nonetheless offered a profoundly emotional style of address for abolitionists, evangelists, and politicians. Bercovitch describes its persuasive force as "a movement from promise to experience—from the ideal of community to the shortcomings of community life—and thence forward, with prophetic assurance, toward a resolution that incorporates (as it transforms) both the promise and the condemnation." The jeremiad is a "ritual of consensus" because it negotiates a vision of reality according to an ideal grounded in (presumably) shared values. Its strategic maneuver is "affirmation through lamentation" (203). As part of a distancing strategy, it convinces the audience that the storyteller preaches to the choir. It is the fictional reader, not us, who has failed the moral standard. The more this textual "you" is characterized as transgressing these shared values, the less the actual audience is compelled to identify with it. Though the narrator assumes a superior footing, the distance between the fictional addressee and the audience exonerates the latter from her/his wrath by speaking *for* rather than *to* us.

At certain points, the storyteller distances the audience from the fictional reader by projecting the attitudes of "you" into the prejudices evinced by Mitchell or May. After Wolfe's trial for stealing the wallet, for example, the doctor reads the report to his wife: "Scoundrel! Serves him right! After all our kindness that night! Picking Mitchell's pocket at the very time." Mrs. May promptly denounces the "ingratitude of that kind of people." May judges Wolfe the way that the narrator warns the fictional reader not to by exhorting him to "be just." The narrator goes on to lament the sentence, dramatizing the injustice of such judgments: "Nineteen years! How easy that was to read! What a simple word for Judge Day to utter!" (51). "Judge Day," who presides over Wolfe's trial, echoes both judgment day and May, equating the doctor's offended philanthropy with blasphemous egotism. Because he fails to examine the "crime" in the larger social context, failing to "see [Wolfe] as he is," May is not a deep reader.

But it is Mitchell who, by sparking the iron puddler's temptation, offers the most consistent model for "you." After the three men leave the mill as the furnaces temporarily shut down for Sunday morning, Wolfe remains on the cinder road outside the works, struggling to understand why he cannot rise above his grimy existence. The narrator expresses the pain of his situation: "Do you remember rare moments when a sudden light flashed over yourself, your world, God? when you stood on a mountain-peak, seeing your life as it might have been, as it is?" (40). Rhetorical questions like these are ambiguous devices. They simultaneously enact superiority while appealing to a sense of solidarity: Superiority because the narrator is not interested in the question's answer, but only in asserting that Wolfe's confusion is an emotional experience as profound in a laborer as in an educated, reflective audience. But rhetorical questions also enact solidarity by appealing to the cultural value placed in that moment of revelation, the Pisgah vision of instant awareness central to the middle-class *Bildungsroman*, the narrative of development. Its power lies in the positing of typological experience. (As Bercovitch notes, Pisgah is a central symbol of the jeremiad tradition.) Wolfe's vision raises a new consciousness of his "squalid daily life" as the coarseness, the ashes, "tonight . . . [become] reality."

Not surprisingly, his vision is of Mitchell, "all-knowing, all-seeing, crowned by nature, reigning,—the keen glance of his eye falling like a sceptre on the other men." Wolfe, too, shares those qualities: "Through the years he had day by day made this hope a real thing to himself,—a clear, projected figure of himself, as he might become" (40–41). His vision is nothing if not the American dream of self-making. Linking Wolfe with Mitchell through a revelation, the storyteller casts his struggle not as a threat to the middle class but as a longing for assimilation within it. Describing Wolfe's ambition as "a real thing" recalls earlier promises to "make [the story] real." What is posited here is not a documentary reality, not a transcription, but the subtle negotiation of a social reality that has failed its promise. "Look at me!" Wolfe cries to Deb. "Is it my fault I am no better?" His frustrated individualism is indicative of the lament. As Bercovitch notes, mid-century jeremiads typify individualism as "an exemplum of American enterprise" rather than "something unique [like] . . . a Byronic of Nietzschean assertion of superiority." The individual is "a model of progress and control that typifies the society as a whole" (156). As an artist trapped in an inhuman environment, Wolfe marks the failure of that social progress.

Critics often characterize Wolfe's temptation as a fall into bourgeois values: In deciding to keep the stolen money, he abandons his class in a desperate attempt to escape the social riddle of his reality. According to the jeremiad model, however, he fails the *ideal* vision of middle-class values. His reality no longer aims toward its providential promise but remains static and self-content, grounded in pragmatic justifications. While bearing witness to this typological narrative (which might be called the last temptation of Wolfe), the audience simultaneously observes the reading of the story itself while being warned against repeating Wolfe's error.

Both dramas revolve around the inexorable gulf between divine and human justice. Wolfe recognizes that keeping the wallet does not violate God's law; as Deborah tells him, it is Wolfe's right. The recognition arrives "veiled by no sophistry," but the line is ironic because the storyteller shows the sophistry of Wolfe's own thought creating a private reality. He is blinded by an image of himself "as he might be, strong, helpful, kindly. . . . What wonder if it blinded him to delirium,—the madness that underlies all revolution, all progress, and all fall?" The question leads to the most complex direct address in the story:

> You laugh at the shallow temptation? You see the error in its argument so clearly,—that to him a true life was one of full development rather than self-restraint? that he was deaf to the higher tone in a cry of voluntary suffering for truth's sake than in the fullest flow of spontaneous harmony? I do not plead his cause. I only want to show you the mote in my brother's eye: then you can see clearly to take it out. (46)

The terms of this lament (full development vs. self-restraint, higher tones vs. spontaneous harmony) are exceedingly vague, but they posit a subtle contrast between individual and social progress. The narrator's own tone suggests that such a contrast is too easy, too "shallow," implying that the audience must look deeper to resist forming a judgment of Wolfe's temptation. The last line paraphrases Matthew 7:4–5, again staging reception as spiritual perception: "Judge not, that ye be not judged." Distance here is an ethical imperative. To "see clearly" the reader must see Wolfe's tragedy as a symbol of a larger social failure in which progress is defined as "fancied rights" and "dreams of improved existences."

Significantly, after the scene in which May offers his judgment, the distancing strategy disappears as the addresses instead qualify and hedge the narrator's own perspective. This rhetorical "softening" occurs at an important thematic juncture at which Wolfe, imprisoned, recognizes his alienation both from Mitchell and, more important, from his fellow workers and Deborah: "A longing seized him to be spoken to once more" (59). Sensitive to this sudden need for contact, the narrator's language softens: "He thought it was to be for the last time. For the same reason, it was, I suppose, that he strained his eyes to catch a glimpse of each passer-by, wondering who they were, what kind of homes they were going to, if they had children" (58). As Wolfe struggles to make connections, the narrator relaxes the assurance with which she/he claims to know Wolfe's motivations ("I suppose" as opposed to "I know"), opening a space for the audience to enact its own identifications. By not characterizing the fictional reader's response, she/he makes narration an act of empathy, subtly negotiating a joint perspective on the action.

As Jane Tompkins notes, numerous women writers, including Harriet Beecher Stowe, Maria Cummins, and Susan Warner, incorporated the jeremiad into their style. The "sentimental power" of the address was grounded not in the social authority of Puritan ministers, obviously, but in the emerging "new matriarchy" of the antebellum era in which women embodied "the most traditional values—religion, motherhood, home, and family."[23] Davis's use of the jeremiad does not fall into this tradition because she does not re-frame its providential sweep into a thematic framework specifically identified with women's culture. Wolfe's temptation takes shape as a stereotypically masculine narrative in which the individual must escape society in order to realize his innate self-worth; this story then becomes the subject of the narrator's persuasive injunctions. Deborah's story, meanwhile, is a romantic drama that pivots upon a variation of the marriage plot central to the sentimental tradition. But while many tales of the era portray marriage as a reward for virtue, Davis inverts its resolution, turning motifs of romance into touchstones for the audience's receptivity. Expectations for a love story offer an opportunity to persuade the audience that the desire for love (and, more broadly, the feeling of connection that community affords) are universal emotions. However less dramatic than Wolfe's conflict, Deborah's drama serves as the sympathetic center of the narration, allowing the storyteller to engage the fictional reader through more intimate, personal appeals.

The function of sympathy in "Life in the Iron Mills" further departs from the sentimental tradition by asking us to identify with a wholly untraditional image of the feminine. In many sentimental tales, sympathy is an appeal grounded in the assumption that an essential or true womanhood transcends regional, racial, and socioeconomic differences. While Davis's storyteller does appeal to the dissolution of class boundaries, the structure of sympathy instituted through the engaging narrative strategy encourages the audience to project itself—without pity—beyond privileged experience into the life of a woman deformed both by the work place and enculturated notions of femininity. Crafting a fictional reader willing to see beyond Deborah's "thwarted woman's form" (21), the narrator redefines the transactive nature of sympathy to broaden the opportunities for connection.

The difference between the distancing and engaging strategies is manifest most obviously in the tone of those interjections that establish how Deborah's character should be read. Whereas the fictional "you" must be commanded to "see [Wolfe's motivations] clearly," the distinguishing features of the cousin are immediately visible: "When she walked, one could see that she was deformed, almost a hunchback"; "She was hungry,—one could see that easily enough" (17). The "one could see" phrase conveys an equality of perspective: The storyteller and reader already share the same way of looking at the world. Although *one* traditionally evokes formal writing, the impersonality of the pronoun can invite more readers to identify with the address, precisely because it no longer requires them to assume the specific, scripted role of an amateur psychologist or Egoist.

Equality is further conveyed through the use of rhetorical hedges, adverbs of uncertainty like *perhaps* and phrases like "it might be" that stage the act of representation as self-conscious speculation. At one point, the storyteller suggests that if Deborah were an artist, "perhaps . . . the picturesque oddity" of the mill would feed her imagination and make her nightly walk to deliver Wolfe's dinner a less painful enterprise. The line introduces a contrast between the woman and Wolfe: While she only sees the mills as a hellish environment he displays an artistic imagination that, as we have seen, inspires him to identify with men like Mitchell. But *perhaps* also introduces the rhetorical motif of narrative inquiry by which the narrator refrains from claiming to know Deborah's motivations. Unlike Wolfe, whose despair is heightened by the exclamatory tone of the distancing strategy, Deborah is less a psychological agent than a matrix of unpredictable, potential actions. Though the cause of her grief becomes increasingly obvious—Wolfe prefers the more traditional "girl," Little Janey, over his cousin—her responses are not easily projected.

Early in the story, for example, the narrator suggests why Deborah, unlike other women at the cotton mill where she works, abstains from alcohol: "Perhaps the weak, flaccid wretch had some stimulant in her pale life to keep her up,—some love or hope, it might be, or urgent need. When that stimulant was gone, she would take to whiskey" (17).[24] By rehearsing this outcome, which the conclusion proves wrong, the narrator reiterates prevailing middle-class assumptions about laborers—namely, that most if not all eventually succumbed to dipsomania. What obscures the irony of the storyteller's asserting these prejudices is the close identification struck with the fictional reader. Here there are no commands to judge as God would judge. Instead, narrator and audience are presumed to share these opinions. Yet because *perhaps* renders such attitudes only *potential* endings, their authority is undermined. Having appealed to beliefs that readers might hold, the storyteller can introduce new probabilities of motive and more subtly orient the audience to alternative story lines without directly chastising it.

Another obvious rhetorical hedge is introduced as Deborah naps upon a pile of ashes in the mill. Looking like a "limp, dirty rag," she is "not an unfitting figure to crown the scene of hopeless discomfort and veiled crime." Indeed, she is even a more fitting figure "*if one looked deeper* into the heart of things" (21; emphasis added). Again, there is no command to look deeper; *if* renders the act of speculation conditional. Obliqueness more gently encourages the audience to assume the role of someone whose simple curiosity is the catalyst of sympathy. The narrator quickly repeats the formula in the form of a rhetorical question: "Deeper yet if one could look, was there nothing worth reading in this wet, faded thing, half-covered with ashes? no story of a soul filled with groping passionate love, heroic unselfishness, fierce jealousy?" (21). Here the "if" clause mutes the aura of superiority that makes the rhetorical question an ambiguous device for establishing solidarity. One may recognize an imminent answer; we may sense that the storyteller is on the verge of telling us that there is something worth reading in Deborah's story, yet the address is non-confrontational. We are not required to ask why we might overlook the value of Deborah's story.

Instead, Wolfe's attitude toward his hunchback cousin dramatizes the need for readers to speculate, to make connections between themselves and the character. He treats her with condescending pity: Just as Mitchell observes Wolfe with the curiosity that a rare mosaic inspires, the iron puddler treats his cousin with the same kindness reserved for the rats in the cellar. In both cases, sympathy is impossible because the object of identification has been dehumanized. The storyteller, by contrast, strives always to humanize Deborah by noting points of connection that an audience may share. Critics who complain that the romance plot elides class status overlook the manner in which the speculative act invites the audience to draw its own conclusions. Wolfe's pity "*might* be that very knowledge" (emphasis added) that brings to her face its haunting look of "apathy and vacancy." This possible explanation is then made more concrete by appealing to the audience's experience: "One sees that dead, vacant look steal sometimes over the rarest, finest of women's faces . . . and then one can guess at the secret of intolerable solitude that lies beneath the delicate laces and brilliant smile" (22). The rhetorical hedge ("might") becomes an opportunity for the storyteller to invite the reader to hypothesize ("one can guess") about the motives of the character. Deborah's environment may deform her more "fiercely" and "perpetually" than middle-class women, but the source of that deformity, solitude, threatens us all.

The oblique footing is not consistently maintained, however. Just as the storyteller employs a more engaging strategy after Wolfe's imprisonment, so, too, certain injunctions in Deborah's tale distance the audience. As she lies on the ash heap, for example, the hunchback imagines Little Janey "clinging" to Wolfe. "You laugh at it?" the storyteller abruptly asks. "Are pain and jealousy less savage realities down here in this place I am taking you to than in your own house or your own heart,—your heart, which they clutch at sometimes?" (23). The scripting of a different reader role here is obvious; the shift from "one" to "you," the more confrontational tone of the rhetorical questions—the fictional reader is now obstinate, doubtful that a woman like Deborah could be conscious of an emotion as complex as jealousy. The dramatic break into a more exclamatory mode of address seems to impede the sympathy in which the audience has been encouraged to partake by forcing connections. Yet such appeals stress the importance of emotional honesty shared by Deborah and the storyteller and eventually extended to the reader. As Warhol suggests, earnestness is an essential quality for writers attempting to engage their audience, for by legitimating emotions as honest and valid, they justify the pathetic force of storytelling and can thus convey the "truth" of "sensation and genuine experience" despite the "deceitful" context of fiction (108). As long as the storyteller's emotions are "real," the audience can allow itself to be moved. For Davis, Deborah's earnestness is the source of her internal beauty. When she tries to convince Wolfe to keep the wallet, the storyteller describes her as speaking "in deadly earnest," her "frantic eagerness" engendering "a power akin to beauty." Wolfe, however, fails to recognize the beauty of emotional honesty: "He thought the woman mad, tried to check her, but she went on, fierce in her eager haste." Before he can stop her, the narrator intrudes to contextualize Deborah's emotions: "Mad? Yes! Are many of us mad in this way?" (43). Unlike the confrontational rhetorical questions of the distancing strategy, this question solicits an intuitive "yes" that links Deborah, the narrator, and the reader through a recognizable emotional response. By not negatively characterizing the fictional reader's response, the storyteller allows us to see beyond the pejorative connotations of madness to recognize the impulse behind Deborah's actions.

This strategy of engaging the audience through earnest speculation helps resolve some of the ambivalence contemporary readers may feel toward the story's conclusion. Several critics find Deborah's conversion to Quakerism impalpable, seeing in the implicit Christian resolution a highly suspect ending to a story so powerfully grim. Such complaints not only overlook the power that, as Tompkins has demonstrated, such sentimental conclusions possessed at the time (139); they likewise miss the dramatic motifs of identification and the complementary tentativeness of the narrator's style. After Wolfe dies, Deborah intently watches the Quaker woman who comes to prepare the body for burial. With her "homely body," the Friend is an obvious physical counterpart of the hunchback. Indeed, the connection between the two women is rhetorically cemented through the repetition of key words. Just as Deborah was in "deadly earnest" when convincing Wolfe to keep the wallet, the Quaker possesses a "clear and earnest" face. Just as the hunchback "keenly" observes the woman, the Friend "keenly" observes Deborah staring at the hills where Wolfe will be buried. Not surprisingly, the Friends themselves are described as "earnest" (63). While the connections are subtly established, they convey a more mutual sense of community than the egoism that Wolfe abstracts from Mitchell. Indeed, joining the Quakers after serving her prison term, Deborah discovers what she has long awaited: she is "much loved by these silent, restful people." Freedom from the marriage plot grants her the acceptance that she craved from Wolfe.

Even though Deborah's story is resolved, the conclusion is open-ended. The storyteller speculates about the aftereffects of her loss of Wolfe: "There may be in her heart some love denied her here,—that she shall find him whom she lost, and that then she will not be all-unworthy. Who blames her? . . . What blame to the meek Quaker, if she took her lost hope to make the hills of heaven more fair?" (64). The rhetorical hedges ("there may be," "if") and interrogatives establish a style of representation concerned less with mimetic accuracy than intersubjectivity. Whereas Wolfe's death is described in a pseudo-sensationalistic style ("Nothing that moved, save the black nauseous stream of blood dripping slowly from the pallet to the floor!"), Deborah's emotions remain inconclusive and ambiguous, rendered in a manner that asks us to ponder their significance more deeply. Making a story real requires a significant emotional investment on our part; oblique appeals create a silent space for readers' responses to answer or resolve, however tentatively, the issues raised through inquiry.

Rather than distance the audience from "natural" norms of truth, Davis's textual interventions help effect reality by inviting subtle collaborative acts. The acknowledgment of the potential diversity of audience reaction relies on appeals grounded in gender assumptions, and the complex intermingling of footings ultimately highlights the superficiality of descriptions like "masculine grip" and "feminine intensity." The effect of this blending can be read in Phelps's claim that the story eroded the artificial barrier between the intellect and the emotions, a barrier obviously gendered in the nineteenth century. Nina Baym has argued that women writers of Davis's generation were forced to identify themselves as women, either "by tricks of style—diffuseness, gracefulness, delicacy; by choices of subject matter—the domestic, the social, the private; or by tone—pure, lofty, moral, didactic."[25] "Life in the Iron Mills," however, reveals how some authors worked for expressive freedom from these confines—a freedom enjoyed by storytellers and readers alike.

5 Sarah Orne Jewett: "A White Heron" and the Power of Suggestion

Although, like "Life in the Iron Mills," "A White Heron" does not ascribe a sex to its narrative voice, none of Sarah Orne Jewett's contemporary readers ever accused her of writing like a man. The reason is due partly to the literary genre with which she was identified. By the time she submitted the first of her many contributions to the *Atlantic* ("Mr. Bruce" in 1869), the realistic effects available to storytellers had diversified to include *couleur locale* or regional imagery distinct from the urban panorama of the Boston-New York literary axis. While New England local color now refers predominantly to women writers, the term was less gendered in the nineteenth century, applied first to George Eliot's novel *Romola*, then to the stories of Bret Harte, Edward Everett Hale, Harriet Beecher Stowe (post-*Uncle Tom*), Rose Terry Cooke, and Mary Wilkins Freeman, among others.[26] But if the phrase did not connote a wholesale women's tradition as it does now, critics nonetheless perceived and promulgated connections between the rich detail of these descriptive styles, the relative plotlessness of the short story as compared to the novel, and women's supposed creative strengths, effectively creating a set of gendered assumptions by which the work of writers like Jewett was judged.

Horace Scudder's review of her 1890 story collection *Strangers and Wayfarers* demonstrates how such assumptions shaped the responses of realist critics. Scudder argues that two conditions make the short story a viable literary form: When the subject matter is "virgin soil," a storyteller can assume that the novelty of the topic will create a certain curiosity on the part of readers. But even if that soil is "worn out," as in the case of New England subjects, writers have an advantage, because audience familiarity licenses further miniaturization of the dramatic scope: "He—or more likely she—may with entire confidence assume this general knowledge [of regional peculiarities], and proceed at once to expend art upon the nice details, to individualize, to discriminate, to disclose distinctions which the casual observer may overlook."[27] The self-corrective pronoun shift from he to she here seems more intentional than spontaneous; though perhaps meant to convey a (debatable) statistical fact—more women write short stories about New England than men—the description ties the assumed expressive habits of women to the limitations of the genre. To "expend art upon the nice details" is to write within the constraints of form, for as a character study, the short story can never be more than a *tableaux vivant* of detail. Without the novel's expansiveness, which allows characters to develop through dramatic events, the resulting pictures can only be static and suggestive. Short fiction, in a sense, can accommodate only the pretext of a tale. "We accept the characters made to hand," Scudder claims, "and ask only that the occasion of the story be adequate."[28]

Such comments betray his diminished expectations of the genre. When, in another review, he confesses that he "scarcely" expects "that Miss Jewett will ever attain the constructive power which holds in the grasp a variety of complex activities and controls their energy, directing it to some exclusive end" (his definition of a novel), his praise for her ability as a short-story writer "to conceive a genuine situation, to illustrate it through varied characters, to illuminate it with humor and dewy pathos" seems at best mild enthusiasm.[29] Scudder's comments suggest the degree to which gendered assumptions were ingrained in realist aesthetics, an equation that has long posed a tricky question for literary historians. Does the aesthetic program of realism, as Ann Douglas and (far more tentatively) Michael Davitt Bell suggest, restrict women writers to "impoverished" portraits of domestic routines by assuming that they are inherently inadequate to fulfill its standards? Or, as Josephine Donovan, Elizabeth Ammons, Anne Romines, and a host of others argue, do these non-linear, descriptive styles constitute a woman-oriented realism that resists and subverts the mode's masculine biases?[30]

The two positions are not mutually exclusive: That the short story could represent for critics like Scudder a feminized form appropriate for expressions of "dewy pathos" need not mean that a woman writer comfortable in its spatial intimacy could not gratify those gendered expectations while revising them from within. In "Life in the Iron Mills" Davis invokes and subverts audience assumptions about masculine and feminine communicative styles by eliding the sex of her narrator, and tricking readers into assuming that they are addressed by either a man or woman; by contrast, Jewett willingly inhabits those assumptions by marking her style as feminine in "A White Heron," even while declining to specify her storyteller's sex.

But there is a second reason why Jewett's style was less likely than Davis's to be judged as masculine writing: The devices that could be regarded as expressive (*i.e.* feminine) disruptions of the fabric of realism had expanded to include a variety of more embedded forms of address. If prejudices against emotional interjections could lead an enthusiastic reader of Davis's story like Phelps to ascribe them to an "intensity" and earnestness that was "essentially" feminine, Jewett's style would seem by contrast subdued. Only in her earliest stories, some of which were written before she turned twenty, does she dramatize the responses of a fictional "you." In her first collection of stories, *Deephaven* (1877), she employs the first-person retrospective stance that Melville adopted in "Bartleby," a device then known as the "assumed narrator." Jewett would cultivate and refine her use of this technique throughout her career, culminating with her masterpiece, *The Country of Pointed Firs* (1896). But while the assumed narrator was touted as a prime device for hiding the author's narrative presence, she was repeatedly criticized for intruding into her stories. Reviewing her 1879 collection, *Old Friends and New*, Scudder suggested that she avoid "the form of study which permits her to be present during most of the action" so she "might gradually strengthen . . . [an] ability to conceive of a story which had its own beginning, middle, and end and was not taken as a desultory chapter of personal experience."[31] In his review of *Strangers and Wayfarers*, he again complains of Jewett's excess presence and recommends narrative silence, which "leaves the reader to his own conclusions. . . . [as writers] rarely impose their reflections upon his attention" (847). He then offers a succinct definition of realist affectivity: "True artistic creation wakens the creative reception, and for the time being makes the reader also an artist" (850). Again, Jewett's style for Scudder prevents this artistic creation because her overt presence seems to impose a response on the reader.

Jewett's most anthologized story, "A White Heron," offers a complex example of how her style invites a reader's creative reception. With its undramatized yet imminently active narrative presence, the text sits midway on a scale of embedded addressivity between "Life in the Iron Mills," with its overt invocations to fictional readers, and "The Yellow Wallpaper," whose structure of address is hidden within the pretext of private diary writing. Although Jewett's storyteller indulges in a number of exclamations, interrogatives, and idiosyncratic descriptive detail, the only "you" addressed is Sylvia, the nine-year-old protagonist, not the reader. While the story has not challenged critics to justify these intrusions to the degree that "Life" has, much debate remains regarding their purpose and effect.

Elizabeth Ammons, for example, argues that the "ultrafeminine" final paragraph, whose "flowery, personal invocations and hovering apostrophes" command the "woodlands and summertime" to share their secrets with Sylvia, formally "rips the fiction." Just as the child confounds the hunter's plot to capture the bird, the "flossy feminine" style of the closing passage interrupts the "traditional male-defined narrative structure" of the coming-of-age story, in which a "sexy young man saves a sexually awakening heroine . . . [thus] assert[ing] the triumph of heterosexuality over matrisexuality."[32] Because its heightened style calls attention to the constructedness of the plot, the structure of address denaturalizes the realism of the textual world, distancing the ideal female reader from its immediacy in order to remind her that its story line seeks to integrate women in a world of masculine values.

By contrast, Terry Heller argues that far from distancing the reader, Jewett's intrusions create a "rhetoric of communion" that unites "the narrator and reader in concert with a sort of consciousness in nature." Noting that Ammons' argument focuses exclusively on the apostrophe of the closing paragraph to the detriment of several less explicit devices, including tense shifts, exclamatory interjections, and the addresses to Sylvia, Heller suggests that the narrative voice encourages a sympathetic identification with the character by "claim[ing] to speak for the reader, voicing what should be the reader's thought." At one point Sylvia jars the perch of a sleeping bird in her eagerness to discover the white heron's nest. The narrator exclaims "Alas, if the great wave of human interest which flooded for the first time this dull little life should sweep away the satisfaction of an existence heart to heart with nature and the dumb life of the forest!" (15). For Heller, the interjection models the audience's ideal response: "It is as if the narrator and the reader looked each other in the eye and understood our agreement as we watch Sylvia ignorantly moving toward an undesirable fate."[33]

But to argue that the story inspires creative reception by distancing *or* engaging readers oversimplifies the interpretive work that the relative embeddedness of Jewett's narrative addresses demands. In "Life in the Iron Mills," the storyteller's interjections inform us how we should contextualize the fiction in order "to make it a real thing." But because "A White Heron" does not formally inscribe the responses of a fictional reader into the story, the networks of identification extended to actual audiences are more ambiguous. As a result, determining both how these intrusive devices should influence our reading and how they should be reconciled with the surrounding realistic elements is more problematic. Indeed, I would suggest that the authority a reader invests in the storyteller depends upon his or her very awareness of *being addressed*, for one can read "A White Heron" without necessarily recognizing that it is a "told" story in the way that "Life" insists that it is.

Louis A. Renza illustrates the range of interpretive uncertainty that the story accommodates by not establishing a clear footing with its audience. His deconstructive treatment is by far the most controversial reading of "A White Heron," undoubtedly because he explores the possibility that Jewett's "narrational modus operandi" is only putatively "feminine" and that beneath the gendered style lies a preoedipal identification with an absentee father figure that determines her strategies. In two novels written in the same period as Sylvia's story, *A Marsh Island* and *A Country Doctor*, patriarchal figures such as Israel Owen and Dr. Leslie protect "untamed" female protagonists from the prescriptive social stereotypes that other characters seek to apply to them, thus "exempt[ing them] from patriarchal institutions or conventions which these fathers only *appear* to represent by virtue of the social and/or sexual identity." What if, Renza asks, Jewett internalizes this "father/daughter relation" in "A White Heron"? The narrator, after all, "allows Sylvia time to absorb the 'gifts and graces' and 'secrets' of nature by herself or before she will have to enter 'the great world' of heterosexuality-defined relationships prefigured by her experience with the hunter," just as those father figures enable Doris Owen and Nan Prince to elude that world.[34]

For our purposes, we might explore what would happen were a reader to assume a similar filial role in relation to the storyteller's authority. That is, if the narrative interjections articulate the ideal audience response, as Heller argues, might the "rhetoric of communion" not silence our creative reception because these interjections tell us how to react? And by presuming to speak for both the character and the audience, might the storyteller not serve a rhetorical function analogous to the dramatic function served by the hunter, who overwhelms Sylvia into an "awed silence" in which "there was no such thing as speaking first"? If we enact a sympathetic identification with Sylvia, might the storyteller's exhortative tone focus our creative attention much as assertive addresses focus the child's attention: "Now look down again, Sylvia, where the green marsh is set among the shining birches and dark hemlocks; there where you saw the white heron once you will see him again; look! look!" (18). And if one is tempted to defer to this exclamatory tone, might the storyteller effectively ask readers to relinquish their "secrets," their personal responses, just as the hunter "gallantly" tells Sylvia to "speak up"? Must the audience, too, "be persuaded to tell"? If the narrator "asserts communion," as Heller claims in what seems an oxymoronic choice of phrasing, might an audience feel that the "sound of [its] own unquestioned voice" should terrify it, just as Sylvia's terrifies her?

But similar questions arise if readers find the narration so intrusive, so paternalistic that they feel distanced from the textual reality. As Renza notes, the narrator's addresses to the child "literally displace the reader's proximity to the girl's thoughts or actions" (106). Other emphatic interjections ("No, she must keep silence!") serve the same purpose. The lack of a scene in which Sylvia decides not to tell the hunter where to find the heron (for she is determined when she climbs down from the pine tree to reveal the secret) also creates what Renza calls a "withheld space" by which the storyteller refrains from speaking the "secret" of "A White Heron" itself. Like Sylvia, the narrator "cannot tell the heron's secret," for to do so would be to "give its life away" (21). But does this withholding not place readers in the same role as the hunter? Does our presumed desire to know both the heron's secret and the reason that Sylvia cannot reveal it create for the narrator a pressure to tell? Are readers not also "well worth making happy while [they wait] to hear the story she can tell"? (20).

Such questions dramatize the consequences of Jewett's semi-embedded narrative agency: Without some explicitly articulated footing by which we can judge how a narrator addresses us, we enter the story with an unscripted role in its unraveling. But rather than portray Jewett's intrusive devices as fostering anxiety or alienation, I want to suggest that they inspire a more positive sort of creative reception. That Jewett imagined storytelling as a collaborative art is clear from an oft-quoted letter in which she attributes her aesthetic sensibility to her father. "A story," she writes, "should be managed so that it should *suggest* interesting things to the *reader* instead of the author's doing all the thinking for him, and setting it before him in black and white. The best compliment is for the reader to say "Why didn't he put in 'this' or 'that.'"[35] Elsewhere, she complains that in Jane Austen's work "all the reasoning is done for you and all the thinking. . . . It seems to me like hearing somebody talk on and on and on while you have no part in the conversation, and merely listen" (qtd. in Fields 135). (Intriguingly, *Atlantic Monthly* reviewers in the same period often cite Austen as an exemplar of authorial reticence.) As with many other realists, conversation provided Jewett a central metaphor for dramatizing the storytelling exchange. But if, for example, Howells likened reading to "sit[ting] at fine ease, and talk[ing] over . . . such matters of literary interest as may come up from time to time" without audiences being "allowed to interrupt,"[36] Jewett imagines narrative reticence as rescuing us from silence. Late in life, Jewett defined her style as "imaginative realism," in which a "reticence or bravery of speech" relies on the "power of suggestion" to allow the audience to express the "unwritable things that the story holds in its heart" (qtd. in Fields 119). Such phrases recall Scudder's comments on artistic creation and suggest that Jewett, too, believes that creative reception is vital to the narrative exchange. But whereas Scudder argues that creativity demands emotional silence from the author, Jewett's reticence implies a more prominent interaction in which supposedly intrusive devices serve as turn-taking gestures, cues that invest, through emphasis, suggestive power in certain details. Dramatizing the storytelling exchange as a conversation allows us to read reticence as a textual pause that provides readers an opportunity to contribute to the story's significance.[37]

One way to understand the rhetorical distinction between reticence and silence is to explore its thematic function in "A White Heron." Like Deborah in "Life in the Iron Mills," Sylvia is the sympathetic nexus of the narration; she even comes to Mrs. Tilley's lonely farm from "a crowded manufacturing town" not unlike Davis's Wheeling. And just as Deborah is for a time deformed by Wolfe's emotional opacity, Davis's narrator likewise implies that a woman's emotions can render her subservient to men. Both Davis and Jewett employ what Annis Pratt calls the metaphor of "canine servitude," because while Deborah looks to Wolfe "as a spaniel to its master," Sylvia feels affection for the hunter as "a dog loves."[38] Yet Sylvia, more than Deborah, perpetuates a world of communicative harmony. She listens "with comfort and companionship to the drowsy twitter of a half-awakened bird" and hears the thrushes "with a heart that beat[s] fast with pleasure" (14–15). Sylvia's communion with nature arises from her fear of people. Fortunately Mrs. Tilley's farm is a world where the stray cats purr louder than humans dare talk and upon her arrival, she whispers her joy at not having to interact with others. The natural world, the story implies, operates according to implicit codes of mutuality. When those codes are ignored or upset, as when Sylvia inadvertently prevents a toad from returning to its home under the doorstep (11), that natural order breaks down. Not surprisingly, the heron also symbolizes an orderly reticence, for what sends the elusive bird from his perch on the ancient pine is a "company of shouting catbirds," whose "fluttering" and "lawlessness" destroy his contemplative peace.

Like the shouting catbirds, the hunter threatens the integrity of this realm because he violates these codes. Though he speaks in a "cheerful and persuasive tone," always kind and gallant, he frightens Sylvia into an "awed silence" with his "determined and somewhat aggressive" whistle. Invited to supper, he listens to Mrs. Tilley as she tells him about her four dead children and her vagabond son Dan who is "no hand to write letters." When she mentions Sylvia's knowledge of the woods, however, he loses all pretense of empathy: "The guest did not notice this hint of family sorrows in his eager interest in something else" (9). He even interrupts the old woman, twisting the conversation to discover whether Sylvia can help him track the elusive bird. His agenda becomes more apparent the following morning as they search for the heron. The little girl intuitively walks behind the hunter, refraining from initiating dialogue: "The sound of her own unquestioned voice would have terrified her,—it was hard enough to answer yes or no when there was need of that" (13). Sylvia's silence here is far different from her reticence among the thrushes. It is no longer a listening strategy, for the power that the hunter embodies has quieted her.

The child's hesitation to speak in his presence even "when there was need" suggests that in the dominating medium of masculine language, a woman cannot help but be hushed, like the very birds the hunter shoots down. The metaphor of "going gunning" in this sense symbolizes the phallic power that silences women. Emily Dickinson's "My life had stood—a loaded gun," a poem that employs much the same imagery as Jewett's story, offers a valuable contrast here. In both cases, the loaded gun represents the power of masculine language to control and limit the expression of female experience. By identifying her life through this symbol, Dickinson's speaker admits not only the appropriation of her speech ("The Owner passed—identified / And carried me away"), but how her voice now fires upon other women figures ("And now We hunt the Doe"). The poem suggests that, for a woman's expression to carry any authority, she must speak with a man's aggressiveness so that "None stir the second time / On whom I lay a Yellow Eye." But while "gunning" language may be empowering, it deprives the speaker of experiencing the mutuality of communication. She gains "the power to kill" only by sacrificing "the power to die."[39]

By contrast, Sylvia's ambivalence toward "gunning" prevents that appropriation of voice. Regardless of whether her silence is instinctual or a self-conscious choice, it frees her from his masculine communication style. When the hunter abandons the farm, his disappointment leaves the girl with a "sharp pang," which lasts only momentarily before she becomes again a compassionate listener: "She forgot even her sorrow at the sharp report of his gun and the piteous sight of thrushes and sparrows dropping silent to the ground, their songs hushed and their pretty feathers stained with blood" (21). As a pun, "sharp report" evocatively fuses the noise of the fired rifle (a noisiness similar to the industrial cacophony that Sylvia escapes) with the "piercing" mythos of male language. But "report" also alludes to the realist style of *reportage*, the storytelling strategy whose definition of creative reception demands an objective, unemotional authorial silence. If the storyteller is to avoid hushing readers by not placing them in a position of "merely listening" in which they have "no part in the conversation," the narrative intrusions must foreground details and images whose relevance to the textual fabric must be determined through individual responses.

Jewett's use of interrogatives exemplifies the interpretive questions raised by her intrusive strategies. When the hunter asks if he might spend the night at Sylvia's house to "go gunning" in the morning, the narrator poses two seemingly straightforward questions that dramatize the depth of the little girl's fear: "Sylvia was more alarmed than before. Would not her grandmother consider her much to blame? But who could have foreseen such an accident as this? It did not appear to be her fault, and she hung her head as if the stem of it were broken" (6). These interrogatives are not rhetorical questions like those used in "Life in the Iron Mills." They are, rather, examples of free indirect discourse, an attributional form in which a storyteller voices a character's unspoken thoughts or emotions. Although it creates the illusion of unmediated access to an internal psychological landscape, free indirect discourse can have two effects: It may inspire readers to identify with characters because the dramatic immediacy implies that the storyteller presents their emotions sympathetically, or it can inspire a distancing when we suspect that they are presented ironically. What makes Jewett's use of this style intriguing is her unwillingness to clue the reader to one option or the other. However active, the storyteller does not present him/herself as an authority like Davis's narrator in "Life." As the story reveals, Mrs. Tilley not only refrains from blaming the child but embraces the hunter, who awakens her "long slumbering hospitality." She invites him into the house and begins "gossip[ing] frankly" about the intimate tragedies in her life. In fact, Mrs. Tilley only rebukes Sylvia when the she *fails* to help the hunter. For whatever reason, the child misjudges her grandmother's response, and the interrogatives serve as a cue to the tension that the hunter inspires.

In other passages, the device invites readers to question the reliability of Sylvia's and the narrator's perspectives. Having climbed the pine tree, Sylvia catches a panoramic sight of the world beyond Mrs. Tilley's farmhouse, seeing for the first time the church steeples, the villages, and the sails of ships at sea. This visual rapture lasts only a moment before she questions its worth: "Where was the white heron's nest in the sea of green branches, and was this wonderful sight and pageant of the world the only reward for having climbed to such a giddy height?" (18). Voicing the child's thoughts allows the storyteller to dramatize Sylvia's loss of empathy. By assuming that this pageantry is an insufficient reward for climbing the tree (as *only* suggests), Sylvia places an unnatural value upon it.

As if to redouble this clue toward the young man's influence, the storyteller redirects Sylvia's attention by telling her to look "where [she] saw the white heron once," cautioning her not to send "an arrow of light and consciousness from [her] two eager eyes" lest the bird detect her presence. To be privy to the heron's secret, Sylvia must return to the state of congenial sympathy with nature, and, to do that, she must recognize that her gaze is a potential weapon, not unlike the hunter's gun, to earn her reward. And yet when the heron leaves its perch, annoyed by the catbirds, the storyteller describes him as moving "like an arrow" (19). Here the arrow alludes to the solemn bird's natural poise and speed, the very qualities that will be exterminated if the hunter manages to shoot and stuff it. In a standard reading of "A White Heron," the arrow links the girl and the bird as correlative symbols, yet its disparate use, once to imply Sylvia's dangerous attraction to the hunter's values, once to imply the natural world threatened by them, makes that equation problematic. Instead, the narrator is warning us not to expect a "reward" from the story similar to what Sylvia expects; we are reminded that this textual reality is a construct whose significance must be determined through our active involvement.

Modals also contribute to the reticence of Jewett's style. They appear more frequently after the hunter introduces himself, enhancing the contrast between the aggressive, "gunning" masculine style and the more supportive, interactive female style of conversation, which, alongside the hunter's language, appears unassertive. As in "Life in the Iron Mills," the modals "hedge" the realistic style, eroding its mimetic authority by emphasizing its tentativeness. And yet there is an important difference here: While Davis's narrator uses them to engage the reader by conveying an equality of perspective, Jewett's storyteller again raises questions about who is telling the story. Sylvia's struggle to climb the pine tree is rich in the suggestiveness that modals convey:

> The tree seemed to lengthen itself out as she went up, and to reach farther and farther upward. It was like a great main-mast to the voyaging earth; it must truly have been amazed that morning through all its ponderous frame as it felt this determined spark of human spirit creeping and climbing from higher branch to branch. Who knows how steadily the least twigs held themselves to advantage this light, weak creature on her way! The old pine must have loved this new dependent. More than all the hawks, and bats, and moths, and even the sweet-voiced thrushes, was the brave, beating heart of the solitary gray-eyed child. And the tree stood still and held away the winds that June morning while the dawn grew bright in the east. (16–17)

For many critics, the pathetic fallacy dramatizes Sylvia's sympathetic identification with nature; as Heller suggests, "contributing freely to her vitality, unconscious of danger, all living things abet Sylvia in what could turn out to be her greatest error. Implicit in such gifts from nature is an assurance that unity of spirit . . . is the more powerful force in Sylvia's life" (188). But why would the tree love the child *more than* the hawks and thrushes, especially when the "determined spark of human spirit" that it supposedly feels is inspired by her desire to please the hunter? The modals here ("must truly," "must have") are clues that this assertion of "unity" is a speculative act whose uncertainty confers to readers interpretive latitude. At such moments, the storyteller stitches a wealth of perspectival ambiguity into the fabric of verisimilitude, leaving it to us to resolve the questions this style internalizes in the text.

One final aspect of Jewett's technique allows for prospective textual pauses: the use of descriptive modifiers, including a rich variety of adjectives, adverbs, and even her playfully deceptive use of the definite and indefinite article. Again, such modifiers are traditionally associated with the supposed floweriness of feminine speech.[40] Their luxuriance raises questions of ambiguous effect. On the one hand, they might limit the space for audience response by overdetermining the narrative picture. Nineteenth-century realist criticism rebuked writers for breaking standards of economy to indulge in literary or rhetorical figures. Scudder complains, for example, that Jewett's style in *Old Friends and New* leaves characters "cling[ing] to her skirts [as] she leads them about with her." Yet many of these descriptive devices actually raise interpretive issues by again calling attention to the storyteller's subjectivity. Mistress Mooly is described as a "hornéd torment"; birds say goodnight with "sleepy twitters"; "nodding" rushes grow in the swamp. The adjectives employed to humanize nature dramatize the curious idiosyncrasy of the narrative perspective and create the textural peculiarity of this world.

Additional cues appear in the adverbs that modify nearly every piece of direct quotation. Jewett's characters do not merely "speak"—they speak "kindly," "graciously," "frankly," "doubtfully," "eagerly," or "desperately." These descriptive tags mark the storyteller's evaluation of various speech acts, which impinge upon the mimetic purity of the dialogue by revealing how each quotation passes through that perspective as it is "reproduced" in the act of telling. As a result, the audience must reconcile the narrator's interpretation with its own sense of the developing character dynamics. When, for example, the hunter tells Sylvia and her grandmother that he means to "get [the region's rare birds] on [his] own ground," Mrs. Tilley asks "doubtfully" whether he cages them up (9–10). Of course, the birds are not caged, but stuffed and put on display. The adverb implies that Mrs. Tilley knows the answer to her own question; to some degree, she must be aware that the hunter's presence threatens her farmland values. This hint recalls Sylvia's worry, noted earlier, that the grandmother would blame her for bringing this dangerous intruder into their world. Yet Mrs. Tilley's actions hardly seem to be influenced by this realization, for she would rather please the hunter than her granddaughter. The old woman either forgets what the young man represents or is simply willing, in exchange for ten dollars, to compromise her principles. Either way, with one adverb, the storyteller hints at a hidden depth of tension in an otherwise stagnant or flat character.

No element better symbolizes Jewett's suggestiveness than the portrayal of the white heron itself. Indeed, the incongruous details that invite the audience to articulate the textual ambiguities begin and end with the difference between *a* white heron, as the title insists, and *the* heron, as it is referred to throughout the story. More than one reader has committed the same error as Mary Wilkins Freeman, who, thanking Jewett for praising her novel *A Humble Romance,* claimed that she "never wrote a story equal to [Jewett's] 'The White Heron.'" Perhaps because he quotes Freeman's letter, F.O. Matthiessen also misreads the title in his 1929 study of Jewett's career.[41] The confusion arises because the bird is discussed in decidedly singular terms, as *that* heron, as *it*. The hunter initiates the ambiguity: "I caught a glimpse of a white heron three miles from here on Saturday, and I have followed it in this direction. They have never been found in this district at all. The little white heron, it is" (10). Not indigenous to the district, the bird is a refugee, a lonely exile much like Sylvia, pursued by a predator as it struggles to find sanctuary. Its mythic elusiveness leads Sylvia to think of it as *the* heron, too, as she remembers "that strange white bird" of the swamp.

Yet when Sylvia finally sees that "white spot of him like a single floating feather," the text offers one understated detail: "The heron has perched on a pine bough not far beyond [Sylvia], and cries back to his mate on the nest, and plumes his feathers for a new day!" (18–19). There is no further reference to the mate. Neither Sylvia nor the storyteller comments on its presence, so there is no way of determining whether this second bird is also a white heron. (White herons, or snowy egrets as they are more commonly called, occasionally crossbreed with the blue heron species.) Marvelously understated, the detail is a narrative luxury seemingly inconsequential to the point. It creates what Roland Barthes calls *l'effet du réel*; as a "referential illusion," it contributes little to the plot but instead enhances the texture of the scene, making it seem more real.[42] The implications are more complicated, however, for it implies that the secret Sylvia discovers is not the heron's nest but its family. She may refuse to reveal the bird's hiding place out of respect for its beauty, but equally likely, she is not willing to destroy its domestic harmony. The mate is a cue that the herons, as obvious figures for the text itself, symbolize its multiple meanings. The difference between "The White Heron" and "A White Heron" is the difference between one story and countless stories, the difference between a Howellsian monologue and a more interactive dialogue. The secret that the narrator cannot speak, inasmuch as they can be spoken, is the indeterminacy of the text. The question "Who can tell?" thus becomes an invitation, a gesture of sharing that encourages the reader to answer, simply and confidently, *I can*.

The devices discussed here are the more obvious signs of narrative presence; readers may find themselves responding to more embedded markers of address depending on their sensitivity to the storyteller's mediating role. Regardless of what particular cues engage our attention, examining how Jewett's style rescues us from "having no part in the conversation" allows us to rethink the thematic and aesthetic significance of the story's key word, "silence," which is the focus of great critical debate. In a feminist reading, Sylvia's silence is power, for, as Ammons writes, her sudden unwillingness to speak functions as a "contrasting rhetoric" to the narrator's exhortations in the final paragraph (16). By occupying polar stereotypes of feminine expressiveness—the publicly mute woman and the voluble, excited talker—both the child and the narrator inspire readers to redefine these roles as we ascribe to them an emotional depth that transcends stereotypes. For a historicist like Bell, however, silence is "rather strange and chilling as an emblem of literary or artistic vocation, suggesting that to withdraw . . . might be to renounce expression altogether." For him, it is difficult "to distinguish Sylvia's victory over the noisy urban intruder, as she stuns herself into protective dumbness, from defeat" (192). But in terms of narrative strategy, silence is not a renunciation of rhetorical power but a conscientious unwillingness to deploy it. More akin to reticence, narrative silence formalizes space for our creative reception. The beauty of Jewett's style rests ultimately in the way that her semi-embedded addresses enable the inevitable exchange of the storytelling process. By asking us to explore the narrator's subjectivity and the unarticulated motives of its characters, "A White Heron" invites a conversation in which our response is the agency that makes it real.

6 Charlotte Perkins Gilman: "The Yellow Wallpaper," Storytelling, and "Getting Real"

Unlike Jewett, Charlotte Perkins Gilman cared little about suggestiveness. She wrote to preach: "If it is literature," she said, "that is an accident."[43] In the case of "The Yellow Wallpaper," the didactic impulse is understandable given its well-known autobiographical genesis. In 1887, Gilman (then Charlotte Stetson) borrowed a hundred dollars and entered a Philadelphia sanitarium operated by Dr. Silas Weir Mitchell, a neurologist practicing an immensely popular curative for physical exhaustion. Gilman sent the doctor a list of her symptoms, which included depression, anxiety, and occasional uncontrollable outbursts. Having already treated two of her cousins, he promptly dismissed the letter as "self-conceit." (Coincidentally, Mitchell treated Davis for a similar bout of exhaustion in the mid-1860s.) According to Gilman, the treatment was designed to return the patient to "as domestic a life as possible." She was confined to bed, isolated from everyone except the doctor and his staff, hand fed, massaged, and, in all likelihood, given thrice daily enemas. After a short time, she returned home. "Have but two hours' intellectual life a day," the doctor prescribed for continued recuperation. "And never touch pen, brush or pencil as long as you live."[44]

But Gilman did touch pen, finding in work a routine far more therapeutic than the enforced passivity of the rest cure. After divorcing her husband and moving to California, she fictionalized her experience in the powerful story of a woman who, incarcerated by her physician-spouse in the nursery of their rented home, grows obsessed with the wallpaper pattern surrounding her. Yet if Gilman intended to preach, the resulting story is hardly didactic. Cast in the form of an unabridged diary, the text lacks a storytelling frame that would dramatize its effect on an ideal reader and thus render its curative powers explicit.[45] Instead, the diary is a "found" text addressed not to readers but to an undramatized, ambiguous "you" who is alternately a fellow conspirator and captor. As if to heighten this theme of frustrated communication, the woman speaks of writing on "dead paper," a phrase reminiscent of the "dead letters" that Bartleby purportedly carted to the flames. The contrast is important. If "Bartleby" marks Melville's adoption of a retrospective style whose evaluative commentary frames our access to the plot, "The Yellow Wallpaper" foreshadows the modernist form of brevity by depriving us completely of authorial contact. In the absence of an overt, foregrounded communicative structure, one discovers a drastically revised storytelling contract in which the text's situational self-reflexivity is difficult to decipher. Because it defers so much interpretive authority to the audience, Gilman's method would seem to violate her professed point.

The reception history of "The Yellow Wallpaper" illustrates the consequences of this strategy, for the story was not widely read as social criticism before its Feminist Press edition in 1973. As Gilman notes in her autobiography, audiences congratulated her for conveying mental deterioration with such verisimilitude, while detractors wondered whether she insulted those struggling "against an *heredity* of mental derangement" (120; emphasis added). In other words, the woman's breakdown was interpreted as a consequence of her personal pathology. Gilman even remembers one reader who, so certain that the story was pure autobiography, deposited an unsolicited diagnosis on her front porch—which she promptly instructed her second husband to burn without reading (314). While perceptive critics recognized that the husband's rest cure exacerbated his wife's anxiety, the story's indictment of marriage so upset readers that its sexual politics were for the most part undiscussed.[46] Gilman publicly declared her purpose in a now-famous 1913 article published in *Forerunner*, a progressive newspaper that she wrote and financed. The story "was not intended to drive people crazy, but to save people from being driven crazy," she announced before boasting that "it worked."[47] She repeated her didactic claims several times before her death in 1935, even limiting her ideal readership to a specific audience: "One girl reads this, and takes fire! Her life is changed. She becomes a power—a mover of others—I write for her."[48] But while Gilman was recognized as an authority on household management, publishing several works on domestic science and women's economics, "The Yellow Wallpaper" was largely ignored. Howells included it in a 1920 short-story anthology, one of only a half-dozen reprintings over the next half-century. If Gilman hoped to prompt debate about the medical establishment's treatment of women, it seems fair to ask why she employed an ambiguous style of narrative address that failed to foreground her point.

Exploring this question, Wai Chee Dimock has argued that the story presupposes a specific type of addressee, one "whose sanity and rationality are the very credentials by which she [the reader] can diagnose the ailments of the characters. . . . someone . . . always granted a clear knowledge, both of the 'reality' of the wife's madness and of the 'reality' of the marital situation." Perhaps a more explicit storytelling frame would make this ideal reader too visible in the text, allowing the audience to mimic rather than presume this "clear knowledge." As Dimock goes on to suggest, the sanity and rationality upon which Gilman's ideal reader is predicated is "created in the image of professionalism at its most idealized, endowed with the sacred attributes of specialized knowledge and interpretive competence," attributes that in the 1890s were denied to the "girls" that Gilman hoped would "take fire" and become "mover[s] of others" by reading her work. To rectify this discrepancy, the story's narrative method seeks to enact a "transformative agency" that will imbue in the latter those "sacred attributes" denied to the former. To achieve this imperative, the "literary form . . . compromises a network of knowledge between author and [audience], a network maintained largely at the expense of the characters in the story."[49] "The Yellow Wallpaper" makes its point then not only by dramatically rendering the constraining of the woman's interpretive authority but by challenging readers to overcome similar constraints imposed upon them.

Unfortunately, Dimock does not specify where this "network of knowledge" is established. What clues might help an audience get the point? An obvious starting place is the woman's own evaluative commentary, whose relative veracity we judge much as we do the narrator's interjections and asides in "Bartleby." Throughout her diary entries, we happen upon repeated stylistic cues meant to dramatize her condition; these cues function as embedded evaluative devices that we measure against our personal standards of what is real and normal. Consider an early statement like "John laughs at me, of course, but one expects that in marriage." Resonating with defeat and resignation, the confession is a stoic recognition that in her marriage the only reward for self-expression is ridicule. Yet some readers will distance themselves from the implications of this *of course*, despite their empathy for the protagonist, for those who *do not* expect marital ridicule will question whether this assertion represents the values the story endorses. (Sadly, some readers *do* expect to be laughed at and may not sense an ironic inflection.) Audiences familiar with the autobiographical background of "The Yellow Wallpaper" will find it especially difficult to believe that this sentence speaks Gilman's attitudes toward domestic relations.

To put it another way, Gilman employs evaluative gestures ironically. As the story develops, the diarist's commentary becomes for us "double-voiced" utterances by which we distinguish the implied author from her character. These ironic touchstones are most evident in Gilman's use of rhetorical devices traditionally intended to endorse the idea that standards of verisimilitude are uniform because they are self-evident and obvious. As the story ultimately reveals, devices like *of course* are persuasive tactics, for they pressure us to "get real" by conforming to the presumed commonality of common sense. By exaggerating her narrator's use of these evaluative cues, Gilman draws attention to the verbal tools that enable the social construction of reality. To expedite its express purpose of making the story a real thing, "Life in the Iron Mills" weaves together various rhetorical footings, from imperatives ("see it clearly") to more subtle participatory invitations ("if one could see"). "The Yellow Wallpaper" may draw from a less diverse pool of devices than "Life," yet it uses them to make a similar point about the function of storytelling. Both texts reject the notion that narration is an aberrant art because it produces fictions that distract from reality. Rather, storytelling is the process by which the real is collaboratively constructed. Gilman's story goes a step further by dramatizing what happens when the narrative faculty is repressed. As her husband insists she must abandon her "habit of story-making" to regain her health, the woman finds her method of making sense continually dismissed as a "slight hysterical tendency." As a result of this pressure, the narrator gradually adopts her husband's rhetoric of realism, but instead of recuperating, she retreats deeper into an alienated fantasy world. While the story dramatizes our need to make feelings and phenomena meaningful through the medium of narration, it also underscores the need for a communal, supportive audience sensitive to this function.

By and large, the critical consensus regards "The Yellow Wallpaper" as an allegory of gendered reading in which John exerts his authority as both husband and doctor to impose upon his wife the interpretive protocols of his profession. According to Annette Kolodny, "John not only appropriates the interpretive processes of reading—diagnosing his wife's illness and thereby selecting what may be understood of her 'meaning'; reading to her, rather than allowing her to read for herself—but, as well, he determines what may get written and hence communicated." Rebelling against her confinement, the woman "progressively gives up the attempt to *record* her reality" and "instead begins to *read* it—as symbolically adumbrated in her compulsion to discover a consistent and coherent pattern amid 'the sprawling outlines' of the wallpaper's 'pointless pattern.'"[50] But rather than just *read* the pattern, the narrator tries to solve the mystery of her obsession by telling a story. As she admits, she has long overcome fear by crafting fanciful tales:

> I used to lie awake as a child and get more entertainment and terror out of blank walls and plain furniture than most children could find in a toy-store. I remember what a kindly wink the knobs of our big, old bureau used to have, and there was one chair that always seemed like a strong friend. I used to feel that if any of the other things looked too fierce I could always hop into that chair and be safe. (15)

Narrative is a coping strategy vital to her mental health: By imagining knobs as kindly eyes and chair arms as a comforting embrace, she humanizes frightening phenomena, naturalizing them so she may feel secure in her world.

Similar imagery appears in a contemporaneous essay by Frank Norris, who describes storytelling as an instinct learned in childhood: "The child . . . dramatizes every object of his surroundings. . . . the easy chair is a comfortable old gentleman holding out his arms, the sofa a pirate brig or a Baldwin locomotive, and the child creates of his surroundings an entire and complex work of fiction of which he is at one and the same time hero, author and public."[51] As Norris complains, maturity often kills off this "little story-teller" by teaching us to cringe with embarrassment at remembering such fantasies; only artists retain their narrative instinct, which distinguishes them from mere "novelists of intellect" who lack imaginative prowess. (Even more important, he argues that the "gift" of narration is compatible with short-story telling, not "the art of composing novels," which is an "accomplishment," rather than an "endowment.") Norris's essay offers an important cultural backdrop against which the relationship between John's indifference toward "talk of things not to be felt and seen and put down in figures" (24) and his infantilization of his wife stands out more clearly. For Norris, storytelling is a child*like* impulse, but for John it is child*ish*. By coercing her to check her "imaginative power" and forcing her to get real he demands that she see the world from a far more terrifying perspective that passively accepts its reality instead of making it real.

Throughout the story, several patterns, both symbolic and rhetorical, dramatize the pressure the wife feels from John to curb her narrative impulses. The windows in the nursery where she is confined offer an obvious example. In one entry, she describes the "mysterious" arbors, "riotous" flowers, and "gnarly" trees visible from her room. Such modifiers highlight the "romantic felicity" of her perspective, dramatizing her certainty that an aura of Gothic mystery surrounds this "haunted house" that the couple rents during her convalescence. From an adjacent window, she can see a shaded lane and bay. This second window frames John's way of seeing, for instead of imagining the scene with her romantic flourishes, she simply describes it as "lovely." In fact, whenever she projects her viewpoint onto his by pretending that strangers trespass from the arbor to the lane, he warns her "not to give way to fancy in the least." Because "a nervous weakness like [hers] is sure to lead to all manner of excited fancies," John says "[she] ought to use [her] will and good sense to check the tendency" (28–29). The windows are metaphors of her dilemma. If she does check her narrative tendency by looking only through John's perspective, seeing the sights as he insists she must, she finds herself robbed of her meaning-making faculty. If she insists on the sanctity of her own window to the world and continues to indulge in storytelling, she is doomed to be condemned as excessively fanciful, childish, and sick.

Of course, the story's central symbol is the wallpaper. In several descriptions of its "sprawling flamboyant patterns," the diarist tries to make sense of the pattern according to John's interpretive habits. "Dull enough to confuse the eye in following, pronounced enough to constantly irritate and provoke study," its "lame uncertain curves" resist rationalization (26). The wallpaper simply will not make sense. "There is a lack of sequence, a defiance of law, that is a constant irritant to a normal mind," she complains. She will achieve normality if she can only determine its "principle of design." "I will follow that pointless pattern to some sort of conclusion," she promises, even if it flouts the "laws of radiation, or alternation, or repetition, or symmetry, or anything else that I ever heard of." But the struggle is emotionally taxing, for she exhausts herself "in trying to distinguish the order of its going in that direction" (31).

The pattern only begins to make sense when the diarist abandons John's realist perspective and allows herself to explain the design through an act of narrative invention. Just as her childhood furniture inspired nocturnal fears until she humanized it as eyes and hugs, the wallpaper's "undulating" disorderliness becomes less terrifying when it takes shape as "a woman stooping down and creeping about." Obviously, the wife projects her own pathetic situation into the pattern, but far from deviant, that act of storytelling is a perfectly rational way of understanding such phenomena. These necessary fictions allow us to assume control over events that might otherwise overwhelm us; through a story, we make them comprehensible. At first, the wife wants nothing more than to escape the gaze of the woman, but as she next imagines prison bars forming across the figure, she finds herself engaged by the plot unfolding before her eyes. "Life is very much more exciting now than it used to be," she reports, "you see I have something more to expect, to look forward to, to watch." The story's development captures her attention because she is trying to determine its point: "I don't want to leave, not until I have found it out," she admits, fearful that were John to know about her interest, he would remove her from the room (35).

Ultimately, she does get the point of this story she unknowingly crafts: The imaginary woman is attempting to escape her imprisonment. But if narration is a medium for making sense of the world, why does this therapeutic form of storytelling not help the wife recover and make her own escape? Why does "The Yellow Wallpaper" end with the startling image of her creeping along the floor, crawling over the body of John, who faints from shock upon seeing the spectacle?

A clue to the answer rests in the evaluative commentary that establishes the wife's relationship with her imagined audience. In "Rip Van Winkle," Rip's equally fantastic tale of dozing through two decades is accepted as truthful in his village as soon as Peter Vanderdonk, the keeper of local lore and myth, testifies to its merit. But the wife lacks such support, and without a community willing to recognize that we comprehend reality through stories, she begins to address a fictional "you" whose responses she can only presume. At times, this fictional reader is a confidant: "I think that the woman gets out in the daytime. And I'll tell you why—privately—I've seen her!" (38). As "privately" implies, she presumes an audience interested in hearing the story, one who, unlike John, will not casually dismiss it as a symptom of her condition. But in her final entries, this "you" becomes an agent of her husband who tries to control her story-making: "I am securely fastened now by my well-hidden rope," she declares in the last passage. "You don't get *me* out in the road there!" (41). This redefinition of the fictional reader's role is accompanied by the increasing adoption of John's persuasive tactics. Just as John pressures her by adopting certain rhetorical strategies meant to persuade her that she has stepped outside the bounds of reality, she deploys these same devices against *her* imagined audience. Our ability to recognize the increasing prominence of this evaluative pattern is imperative to understanding why storytelling fails to enable her recuperation. Deprived of a sense of narrative as an exchange between storyteller and audience, she exerts the same authority to which she is subjected and thus fails to negotiate with her addressee a communal sense of the real.

One such evaluative pattern centers around the use of *of course*, which appears in "The Yellow Wallpaper" more than a half-dozen times. As a mark of insistence, the phrase conveys a sense of irrefutable certainty as a speaker validates a statement by invoking what are supposedly communal standards of obviousness. If we disagree with this non-negotiable norm, *of course* implies, we stand outside the circle of common sense. Yet the very need to resort to such insistence can undermine this intended effect, for, as linguist M. A. K. Halliday perceptively notes, "We only say we are certain when we are not."[52] Because it conveys both vehemence and tentativeness, *of course* implies hidden motives and anxieties that undermine the persuasiveness of its appeal.

An obvious example of the (un)certainty that *of course* projects occurs when the wife questions John's diagnosis. Frightened by the wallpaper pattern, she wants to abandon the house, but he flatly refuses: "I cannot possibly leave town just now. Of course, if you were in any danger, I could and would, but you really are better, dear, whether you can see it or not. I am a doctor, dear, and I know." John enacts here what sociolinguists call a self-repair, an utterance that attempts to qualify or revise the implications of a previous statement. If the first sentence suggests that his professional obligations are his primary concern, John must immediately correct this impression by assuring his wife that were her condition "really" serious, he would sacrifice them to hasten her recovery. Unfortunately, the narrator does not recognize these nuances, for *of course*'s illusion of certitude binds her to his judgment, cowing her into agreement: "So of course I said no more on that score," she admits at the scene's conclusion (33–34).

At first, her use of *of course* signals her own lack of rhetorical power: "John does not know how much I really suffer," she writes in an early entry. "He knows there is no *reason* to suffer, and that satisfies him. Of course, it is only nervousness. It does weigh on me so not to do my duty in any way!" (28). Her use of the qualifier is a self-repair like John's, but it is an ironic one, for instead of enforcing her take on her condition with the rhetorical armor of insistence, she gives in to his authority. She initially challenges John's conviction that she invents her ailing, and her *of course* seems to validate that very attitude by agreeing that it is "only" excess fancy. In a sense, her initial use of the phrase parallels her use of *perhaps*, which dramatizes the tentativeness of her self-expression: "John is a physician, and *perhaps* . . . *perhaps* that is one reason I do not get well faster" (24). Using a marker of emphasis to convey the woman's uncertainty, Gilman provides a tool for decoding her point. As the wife defers to John's diagnosis, events in the story insist that she is "really" suffering more than "nervous depression." The resulting dissonance between the narrator's self-assessment and the plot suggests irony, which allows us to infer the narrative purpose of the otherwise absentee implied author.

As the wife is intrigued by the imaginary woman, a different type of ironic use of *of course* becomes apparent. Instead of marking her acquiescence, this irony revolves around her absorption of John's insistent style of persuasion. Rather than convey tentativeness, it registers her increasing vehemence. "I never thought of it before, but it is lucky that John kept me here after all," she writes upon first deciphering the woman in the wallpaper. "Of course, I never mention it to [him] any more—I am too wise,—but I keep watch of it all the same" (32). There is not the slightest hint of a self-repair here, for *of course* signals her certainty of the pointlessness of telling John about the woman's appearance. Smart enough to know he would think she was crazy, she acknowledges that she must keep this story to herself. The irony is that instead of sharing this insight with her fictional reader, she presumes him or her already privy to it. To her, John's disbelief is as obvious as her detrimental fancy is to him. Instead of staging her evaluative commentary with more collaborative, invitational cues, she employs the same emphatic habit as her husband and thus reinscribes his rhetorical power in her narrative style.

This reinscription crescendos in the wife's final diary entry, in which she not only fantasizes about the woman's escape from the wallpaper but becomes an active agent in her liberation by stripping the paper from the wall. The shapes in the pattern seem to laugh at her: "All those strangled heads and bulbous eyes and waddling fungus growths just shriek with derision!" Angered by this response, the wife threatens to jump out of the window, which she thinks would "be an admirable exercise." Immediately, however, she changes her mind: "I wouldn't do it. Of course not. I know well enough that a step like that is improper and might be misconstrued" (35). She implies that a logic of propriety influences her actions, and proper behavior, as *of course* suggests, is a standard shared by the reader. What makes suicide an illogical option is her certainty that John would misinterpret her motives; he would read her death within the plot of hysteria that he has been projecting upon her and not within the story line of imprisonment that she acts out. For her actions not to be "misconstrued," she must convince both her husband and her reader that her reality is perfectly rational, and doing so requires a style of communication stripped of emotional tentativeness. John's "objective" persuasive cues afford her the agency previously denied her, but it is a power she wields against her reader. The tone of "I know well enough" is as defensive as it is emphatic because, in her isolation, the wife has come to imagine addressees as adversaries. Storytelling is not a collaborative practice for negotiating common sense but a tactic of power used to vindicate one version of reality over another.

A similar evaluative pattern centers upon the coordinating conjunction *and*. Like *of course*, Gilman initially exposes its role in John's rhetoric of insistence: "My brother is also a physician, and also of high standing, and he says the same thing," she reports. These clauses and phrases form a sequence of accrued information intended to convince her to trust the accuracy of John's diagnosis. The narrator's brother has an immediate personal connection to the patient, *and* he is a doctor, *and* also well respected in the community, *and* if his diagnosis matches John's, she has little power to question her treatment. This is the basic function of *and*: It organizes idea units into a sequence to create the illusion of progressive logic. Gilman then exposes the source of this pattern of concatenation's persuasiveness by parodying the form: "So I take phosphates or phosphites—whichever it is, and tonics, and journeys, and air, and exercise, and am absolutely forbidden to 'work' until I am well again" (25). Here the conjunctions convey an appalling randomness; the repetition infuses the utterance with an air of exasperation that dramatizes the wife's lack of participation in her treatment. The rapid-fire linkage of phosphites *and* tonics *and* air *and* exercise reveals that her husband's judgment owes its authority to a syntactical form, not to any inherent reason or good sense.

Gilman does not employ this parodic pattern consistently, however. In the early diary entries, she more often plays off the conjunction's interactional function, which typically signals one's intent to continue talking by not offering the listener a conversational pause or hesitation within which the latter might respond.

Initially, this desire to keep speaking may not appear a strategy to silence the audience but simply an effort to provide additional clarifying information: "Of course I don't [cry] when John is here, or anybody else, but when I am alone. And I am alone a good deal just now" (31). In this case, *and* is a self-repair that, by showing how deliberatively she analyzes her condition, dramatizes her effort to craft "a real earnest reasonable talk" that will convince John she is rational and sensible. As the wife becomes involved with the wallpaper, however, conjoined sentences do not seem to revise or enlarge her meaning but merely to link ideas together: "Sometimes I think there are a great many women behind, and sometimes only one, and she crawls around fast, and her crawling shakes it over. Then in the very bright spots she keeps still, and in the very shady spots she just takes hold of the bars and shakes them hard. And she is all the time trying to climb through" (38). More than just a rambling speech style, these random connections dramatize her frenzied need to record her impressions before John catches her writing them down. If these conjunctions reveal her fear of being forced to abandon her storytelling, they also manifest the strategy by which she precludes any potential interruption. In a sense, *and* allows her to plaster over the space between sentences and silence the natural pauses in rhythm before they can silence her.

Karen Ford has noted an evaluative pattern centering around the use of *but,* "the conjunction of contradiction," which by her count appears in "The Yellow Wallpaper" some fifty-six times to symbolize the "unheard of contradictions" in the wife's struggle to tell her story. At several early points, she tentatively describes her feelings only to defer to John's opinion: "I get unreasonably angry with John sometimes. I'm sure I never used to be so sensitive. I think it is due to this nervous condition. But John says if I feel so, I shall neglect proper self-control; so I take pains to control myself—before him, at least, and that makes me very tired" (25). Unable to converse with her husband without him interrupting to insist upon the primacy of his diagnosis, she internalizes this corrective impulse and begins to censor herself: "Every time the narrator speaks," according to Ford, "she is interrupted and contradicted until she begins to interrupt and contradict herself."[53]

While several passages like the one cited above dramatize the wife's abrupt concession to John, others mark her burgeoning effort to harness the conjunction's power of contradiction to insist upon the sanctity of her own feelings:

> I don't know why I should write this.
>
> I don't want to.
>
> I don't feel able.
>
> And I know John would think it absurd. But I *must* say what I feel and think in some way—it is such a relief.
>
> But the effort is getting to be greater than the relief. (31–32)

The first four sentences convey her uncertainty about the salutary effects of writing in her diary; rather than make her feel better, it seems only to exhaust her and make her a convenient target for John's condemnations. The first *but*, however, shows her impulsive commitment to her self-expression, her intuitive awareness that she *has* to record her impressions. While this assertiveness is immediately eroded by the second conjunction, which again shows her conceding to John, the sentence nevertheless establishes a less conciliatory use of *but* by which the wife appropriates the rhetorical power used against her.

This assertive pattern is again most obvious in the final diary entries, where *but* is not a marker of concession but a sort of cognitive pivot by which she insists on the realism of the story playing out in the wallpaper. When Jennie, the housekeeper employed by John to watch over her, notices the strips of paper peeled from the wall, the diarist for the first time admits her obsession with the pattern. Convinced that John and Jennie know about the trapped woman but have chosen to ignore her story, the wife utilizes *but*'s power to interrupt in order to exclude them from witnessing or participating in its outcome:

> Jennie looked at me in amazement, but I told her merrily that I did it out of pure spite at the vicious thing.
>
> She laughed and said she wouldn't mind doing it herself, but I must not get tired.
>
> How she betrayed herself that time!
>
> But I am here, and no person touches this paper but me—not *alive*! (39–40)

In the final sentence, "but I" marks her place in the plot, her performative relationship with the text she literally tears apart. Similarly, "but me" emphasizes her exclusive authorship of that story, her unwillingness now to share it with any audience. Having been isolated and alienated by John's rhetoric of insistence, she uses its power to craft a reality she alone will enjoy.

This evaluative cue also foregrounds another type of narrative irony that, in these final passages, erodes the status of the diary as an unmediated text. As both Paula Treichler and Richard Feldstein have noted, a perceptive reader must account for the paradox of the diary's very existence, for the narrator appears to have stopped writing, yet the narration continues.[54] Significantly, *but* becomes the most visible cue for underscoring this abandonment of writing, for it emphasizes the simultaneity of narration and action: "Outside you have to creep on the ground, and everything is green instead of yellow. But here I can creep smoothly on the floor, and my shoulder just fits in that long smooch around the wall, so I cannot lose my way" (33).

What Treichler describes as this "unfolding in an impossible form" marks the rejection of a narrative constraint that subsequently becomes a keystone of modernist storytelling strategies—namely, the logic dictating that story and narration should be separated by some degree of time. In realist writing, subordinating the narrative act to the plot requires some internal justification for the story; thus, the observer-narrator recounts a past event, and storytelling is neatly transformed into remembering, which removes the desultory aura of make-believe and invests it with credibility. Yet, as Feldstein argues, attempts to logically explain the production of the final diary passages are frustrated by the text. We may conclude that the woman writes down the scene just after John faints, or she may recall it much later, just as Gilman composed the story after emerging from her treatment. What makes such explanations uncomfortably speculative is the sense that the narration no longer seems written at all; as Feldstein suggests, the "transcription [is] inexplicably interrupted and succeeded by a spoken account" that is marked by a shift in word choice. The woman describes herself as "telling" instead of writing, and "no matter how we choose to read this contradiction . . . it will remain unassimilable to an interpretation of the text" (315).

The shift from retrospective writing to the immediacy of speech has another effect so obvious that its importance can easily be overlooked. The switches in and out of present tense in the final entry ("Why there's John at the door!") foreground the act of storytelling, the very agency suppressed throughout "The Yellow Wallpaper." The woman's creeping is her way of telling the story she is forbidden to write down. Equally important, the concurrence of a written pretext with a verbal style of narration reveals the concealed presence of the implied author as a constructive agent in the unfolding of events. The material presence of the diary allows us to read the woman's thoughts as wholly self-contained, as a found text delivered without editorial mediation. The ephemeral nature of the spoken word, by contrast, implies that the story must be retold for it to remain alive. Thus, even if the story lacks a narrative frame, it nonetheless reveals itself as a text in transmission. It remains unclear whether Gilman herself was aware of the change in her style—nothing in the manuscript suggests a conscious revision away from diary writing[55]—yet the gesture inscribes in the narrative act an odd doubling of the story itself. Just as the wife tears down the wallpaper (her storytelling medium) so, too, the implied author strips away her original fictional conceit. While the wife does this because she is isolated from a supportive community that understands the function of storytelling, Gilman's abandonment of the diary ensures readers' active involvement by forcing them to account for this unexplained shift in the story's structure of address.

Epilogue

The switch from diary writing to perceptual impressionism in "The Yellow Wallpaper" aptly describes the shift from realism to modernism. The "you" addressed by the wife may be a figment of imagination, but it amplifies the situation of all storytellers who are aware that narrative presupposes an audience. Like Davis and Jewett, Gilman manipulates this second-person pronoun to dramatize the role of readers in exchanging stories. If Davis and Gilman conceive of storytelling as a political enterprise meant to effect a particular social change, Jewett is less of an activist, but the metaphor of conversation by which she defines narration is equally at odds with the objective imperative of realist aesthetics. For all three writers, representing the real involves more than transcribing the world into words. Reality requires consensus.

But Gilman presages modernism in another important way. When she revealed the autobiographical origins of the story in "Why I Wrote 'The Yellow Wallpaper'" in 1913, publicity had become an accepted form of news, creating celebrities out of public figures whose personality merited detailed analysis. That same year, Gertrude Stein was the subject of a "profile" in a magazine called *Arts and Decoration*, published to commemorate the Armory Show, the controversial exhibition that first exposed modernism to American audiences. (Despite her stylistic affinities with modernism, Gilman dismissed the show as a blatant display of egoism.) The article draws an extended analogy between Stein and artists like Picasso and Matisse whose work she collected: "She has taken the English language and, according to many people has misused it, or has used it roughly, uncouthly and brutally, or madly, stupidly and hideously, but by her method she is finding the hidden and inner nature of nature."[56] The threat posed by Stein's method is greatly exaggerated here, for at the time she was far better known as an art collector than an artist. Her short-story cycle *Three Lives* (1909), whose publication she had financed, generated lukewarm reviews, with one critic speaking of it as "an extraordinary piece of realism," perhaps the only time in her career she would be accused of such a thing. The "many people" who claimed that she abused the language refers mainly to her brother Leo, with whom she shared the increasingly famous atelier at 27, rue de Fleurus in Paris until the previous year. Written by her good friend Mabel Dodge, the article was conceived specifically to publicize Stein, and it worked. A *New York Times* reporter, Carl Van Vechten (who would become a crucial supporter), quickly dispatched an article on her, and within the year, both the *Chicago Tribune* and the publishing house Putnam's satirized her style—this at a time when her work was not only unknown but virtually unavailable. Stein spoke of publicity as "*la glorie*," assuming that it would attract commercial publishers and a mass audience. Instead, more than twenty years would pass before her readership approached the disproportionate amount of press that she received.

For reasons to be explored, Stein's shorter prose pieces are not often associated with the short story, but public perceptions about her style illustrate an important paradox surrounding modernist storytelling. On the one hand, modernist strategies strive to deconstruct a reader's sense of address by complicating the reception of voice. A single word may contain multiple perspectives that preclude the luxury of a uniform narrative perspective with which one might identify. Yet the devices that constitute these meanings may assume extratextual associations that allow one to distill from those many voices the sound of an implied author. What facilitates such an interpretive strategy is a burgeoning cultural fascination with personality. As interviews and profiles popularize authorial personae in the twentieth century, style becomes a manifesto of singular consciousness, a trademark form of expression whose peculiarities assume ideological significance outside of their textual usage. The authorial ethos of a Gertrude Stein, an Ernest Hemingway, a Djuna Barnes, or a Richard Wright thus offers an abstract substitute for the addressivity that modernist strategies elide.

Part 3

Cultivating Voices: Attributional Devices and Authorial Styles in Modernist Short Stories

Prologue

As Horace Scudder's criticism of Jewett's style suggests, a short story was judged aesthetically "true" by late nineteenth-century reviewers if it prompted "creative reception." That is, if authorial reticence allowed readers to focus on the content without the undue distraction of narration. Realist storytellers were not averse to affecting their audiences; rather, the short story distinguished itself from the tale in the target of its appeal. If, as its detractors complained, periodical fiction of the 1850s aimed to excite audience emotions, realist stories were intellectual pursuits concerned with cultivating aesthetic rather than moral temperaments, which were considered too emotional in character. Many critics believed that narrative interjections dictated reader response, and their unwillingness to read direct addresses as invitations to diverse readers highlights the realist habit of assuming narrative authority through an objective, communal style.

This third section of my study explores a different sort of creative reception, one that critics decidedly would not endorse because it circumvents the intensity of response that modernism as a literary style is said to demand. The double meaning of my title, "Cultivating Voices," drawn from Stein's "Miss Furr and Miss Skeene," reveals the textual space in which the conflict between brevity and storytelling expresses itself. The phrase alludes to the range of attributional devices by which the voices of various characters are inscribed into modernist stories. Whether dramatized through the use of indirect speech, direct dialogue, or free indirect discourse, these expressive habits assume more prominence in the narration, embedding the communicative structure so that readers must work to recuperate a sense of addressivity. Yet these same stylistic devices also serve an extratextual function. As tools by which a writer can convey "the very element of individuality . . . through which the individual consciousness [seeks] to distinguish itself, to affirm its incomparable originality" in the literary marketplace, they help construct public perceptions of an author's own idiosyncratic voice that readers can then call upon to shape their sense of significance.[1] The double meaning of voice creates the opportunity for an interesting interpretive phenomenon. If attributional devices complicate reception by decentering the modernist storyteller's voice, we can explore how audiences might compensate for the resulting demands by invoking the extratextual connotations of style. Before examining this issue, however, it is necessary to ask both why the modernist short story further embedded the genre's conative function and why authorial styles might provide a device for recuperating it.

The critical dissatisfaction with the tale expressed by mid-nineteenth century criticism has an interesting analogue in the transition between realism and modernism. Just as earlier reviewers disdained the "hysterical" interventions of narrators, many twentieth-century critics denounced writers for pandering to audience emotions. As Herbert Ellsworth Cory complained in *The Dial*, the "highly wrought technique" of the short story reduced it to the "patent medicine of modern art" by making "the disorders of the age more deep-seated while it brings factitious recreation." These disorders are not unlike the cultural pitfalls that, in the eyes of realist critics, the tale of the 1850s serviced—namely, the common reader's hunger for stimulation. "We do not want the short story," Cory assures his audience,

> We *think* we want it. In our healthier moments we condemn our modern speed mania. In our healthier moments we desire the literature of cool reflection. The very technique of the short story is pathological, and titillates our nerves in our pathological moments. The short story is the blood kinsmen of the quick-lunch, the vaudeville, and the joy-ride. It is the supreme art-form of those who believe in the philosophy of quick results.

He concludes by predicting (wrongly, of course) that any controversy over the short story's literariness will soon become a moot point, for as the genre "degenerates" on the newsstands where it absorbs the sensational styles of journalism and advertising, its "senility . . . augurs the sounds of voices more sonorous, the early appearance of a larger art."[2]

Cory's complaint conflates two meanings of brevity, for "larger" refers not only to physical size but to endurance. By assimilating the speed of modernity, the short story exhausts its relevance, becoming just another commodity routinely purchased, consumed, and discarded. If "pathological" echoes realist complaints against the degenerate affectivity of the tale, it also alludes to the interpretive conventions instituted by the mass-market magazines that rose to popularity in the last quarter of the nineteenth century. As Christopher Wilson has shown, periodicals like *The Saturday Evening Post*, *The World's Work*, and *Ladies' Home Journal* adopted "simple, direct, persuasive" styles crafted to "cut through the reader's barriers of resistance and 'impose' an idea." Instead of the genteel, conversational tone struck by the previous generation of editors like Howells and Scudder, reading was redefined into an aggressive act of "buttonholing" the addressee. The relative reticence that would awaken creative reception had given way to crass consumer appeals. Editors of mass-culture periodicals like Frank Munsey actually thought of themselves as quite discriminating about what constituted good fiction: short stories were "not dialect sketches, not washed out studies of effete human nature, not weak tales of sickly sentimentality, not 'pretty' writing." Rather, they were conveying "a force . . . that means something—in short a story. Good writing is as common as clam shells, while good stories are as rare as statesmanship."[3] Despite such claims, many critics and reviewers found the force of these "gripping" styles their own brand of "pretty writing," so easily mass produced that they were shucked like the average clam shell.

By far, the most common complaint lodged against the short story between 1900 and 1930 was that it had eroded form into formula. Cory's argument may have been inspired by a 1915 *Atlantic Monthly* essay by Henry Seidel Canby, who likewise labels the genre a "patent medicine . . . constructed by [a] formula," which he divides into four parts: a flashy beginning consisting either of dialogue or action, a plot that will "move, move, move furiously, each action and every speech pointing directly toward the unknown climax," the climax itself, and, finally, a "last suspiration . . . sometimes a smart epigram, according to the style of the story, or the 'line' expected from the author." The formula "is a very good one," Canby admits, but only for readers desiring "merely effective storytelling" in which "the means of telling the story fit the ends of story-telling as neatly as hook fits eye."[4] Such criticism was leveled at the literary short story, not just popular, mass-market fictions. Canby stresses that, regardless of the place of publication, "the majority of the stories come from the same mill, even though the hands that shape them may differ in refinement and taste." The efficacy of reading was more than a matter of market conditions; the compatibility between the means and ends of short-story telling was a quirk of history in which the brevity of form accommodated the most desultory effects of the prevailing cultural pace.

Even two critics with a personal investment in the genre would express severe doubts about whether short fiction could survive the planned obsolescence of consumer culture. In the same year that *The Development of the American Short Story* (1923) appeared, Fred Lewis Pattee described the new contagion of brevity as "rush[ing]" the reader "from episode to episode as the motorist of today rushes through the landscape, or as the eye of the 'movie fan' races from 'reel' to 'reel.' No more is there repose, no more is there life seen steadily and whole. The art of the short story . . . is the art of securing instant returns with no thought beyond."[5] According to Pattee, the pleasure afforded by the short story is an "unearned" reward; his metaphor of "instant returns" hardly seems accidental in an era when stock speculation challenged moral conceits of hard work and humility.

For Edward J. O'Brien, the lack of reflection afforded by the speed of modernity augured something more dangerous than literary commodification; brevity had become a narcotic that induced audiences into passive, mechanistic habits of thinking. Because it proliferated "types" that could be consumed with minimal effort, the modern short story was as dangerous as the technological innovations that increasingly regulated the rhythm of life. If the vague equation between the short story and fascism that runs through O'Brien's *The Dance of the Machines* (1929) strikes one as paranoid, his criticism is all the more intriguing because, as editor of the *Best Short Stories* series from 1915 until his death in 1941, he arguably promoted the genre more than any other critic in the first half of the century. (Pattee, in fact, dismisses O'Brien's series for "deal[ing] almost wholly with current newspaper material, the most of it drawn from the sordid and sensational areas of life," a charge that is patently untrue.) Not only did he defend the short story against the animadversions heaped upon it by the likes of *The Dial*, but he actively promoted emerging modernists, breaking his own rules for compiling his anthology in 1923, for example, by including Hemingway's "My Old Man," though the story had never before appeared in print. (The author's appreciation somewhat dimmed when he discovered his story was credited to "Ernest Hemenway.") Yet O'Brien places blame for the efficiency of reading that brevity promotes not upon the genre itself (as Canby and Cory do), but upon the cultural rhetoric of the era. Both commercial and literary writers had succumbed to the "patter" of advertising, for even those "talented artists who honestly believe that they are doing their best and frequently are doing so" find themselves resorting to rhetorical gimmickry just to cut through the glut of modern communication.[6]

The persistence of such criticism in the 1920s and 1930s begs a question: If, as Cory, Canby, Pattee, and O'Brien all complain, the short story suffers a susceptibility to technique that makes its reading too efficacious to be considered art, how does the genre come to be regarded by succeeding generations of critics as the quintessential medium of modernist expression? How, for example, can Austin Wright argue that the short story realizes the aesthetic aims of the mode better than other genres? How can Suzanne Ferguson claim that it "manifests its formal allegiances" to impressionism "even more obviously than does the novel"? Or how can Dominic Head assert that "the short story encapsulates the essence of literary modernism"?[7] Precisely because these later critics identify within it *another type of brevity* that confounds the easy alliance of means and ends, or that efficiency of storytelling of which Canby complains. By destroying the continuity of presentation, the techniques of modernism are said to impede those socially conditioned interpretive strategies that O'Brien claims mechanize reader responses. Instead, we find ourselves immersed in styles of representation that do away with internalized textual authority. According to Wright, the absence of a conventional narrator figure demands more creative reception because "the degree of dependence placed upon the reader's inferences is the most elementary measure of an author's intervention or non-intervention into his story." So elided is the addressivity of the modernist story that *narrator* is no longer an appropriate term; he offers *dramatist* as a substitute: "The narrator draws inferences from unspecified signs, leaving it to the reader to imagine what the signs must have been; the dramatist presents the signs and leaves it to the audience to draw the inferences" (326).

Perhaps the definitive attributional device for prompting audience inference in modernism is free indirect discourse, which, as we briefly suggested in our discussion of "A White Heron," promises direct access to a character's unspoken emotions. It should be stressed, however, that the technique offers the *illusion* of non-intervention or immediacy. The narrative act remains implicit, embedded in the dramatic context, since the speech or thoughts of a character are represented—or, better yet, re-presented—in a manner that inscribes the presence of a storyteller. Narratologists point to the "backshifting" of tense and the conversion of personal pronouns from first to third person as evidence of this presence. In a simple sentence like "She thought she was beautiful," the character's "original" quotation has been transformed—"I" becoming "she," "am" becoming "was." Karl Kroeber suggests how the dialogism of the device affects reception: if the "teller function" of traditional narratives encourages us to identify with a storyteller's perspective, free indirect discourse "intensifies, complicates and subtilizes that identifying tendency. The result . . . is a demand for continuous complex intensity of response . . . [that] arises from readers' conscious engagement in a linguistic performance. One cannot respond to the basic sylleptic bind—do these words represent the character's or the narrator's perception?"[8]

Yet narratologists like Kroeber too often generalize about this effect without asking how audiences might circumvent its "complex intensity of response." What goes unexamined is how extratextual values ascribed to the particular manner by which a writer minimizes his or her presence might become part of the expressive intonation perceived in the reading act. In other words, in the absence of an overt narrator, audiences may turn to the implied author, that behind-the-scenes shape shifter manipulating its sympathies, whose presence they perceive in the form of trademark stylistic devices and techniques. Michel Foucault has described this interpretive prerogative as the "author function," by which readers delimit meaning in deference to the values embodied by a writer's public identity. Because it allows them to reinstitute the textual authority formally elided, style in this sense can serve as a "principle of thrift in the proliferation of meaning."[9]

Significantly, many critics of the short story in the 1920s link just such an interpretive thriftiness to the baleful brevity of cultural rhetoric. As O'Brien complains, the magazine trade traps writers into perpetuating a product identified by their peculiar habits of expression:

> If the American short storywriter [sic] achieves a satisfactory mechanical product which the magazine of large circulation finds acceptable to its advertisers, he is not allowed to practise literary birth control. . . . The most popular writers of short stories in the most popular American periodicals have a definitely recognized pattern from which they do not widely depart. It is known as their 'style.'

A writer's need to advertise this style is symptomatic of our obsession with "veneer," the "deft, slick patter" that gives "flavor" to the product. Recall as well Canby's complaint that the short-story formula dictates an ending, a "last suspiration," that delivers "the 'line' expected from the author." For both critics, style is a brand name that inspires consumer loyalty by promising the homogeneity of expression and content.

The stories analyzed in the following chapters illustrate the interplay between character voices and trademark authorial styles by examining the interpretive work created by a range of attributional devices. In "Miss Furr and Miss Skeene," Stein employs "diegetic" or indirect speech acts, in which character voices are summarized within the authorial style, to invite reader collaboration. In "Hills Like White Elephants," Hemingway, by contrast, stages long interchanges of dialogue that efface his presence. But while he strives to omit all clues of a narrating consciousness, one particular mannerism typical of his style, repetition, becomes the most obvious expression of his agency.

Stories by Barnes and Wright typically incorporate more diverse attributional devices, creating double-voiced narratives whose meanings require some intertextual association with the authorial ethos. "Run Girls, Run" is a dense, allusive story that juxtaposes Elizabethan and modern idioms as it revises stereotypes of femininity perpetuated by Western mythology. The parody arises from an inherent contrast between formal oral discourses drawn from Barnes's theatrical background (the soliloquy and epic formulae) and typographic devices (parentheses, orthography). In "Almos' a Man," Wright juxtaposes free indirect discourse with a more mimetic form of perceptual representation, interior monologue, creating a pattern of perspectival shifts marked by movements in and out of African-American dialect. This pattern dramatizes his desire to liberate his authorial style from the pejorative stereotypes of minority expression that might affect readers' reception of his character's thoughts. In these four stories, audience addresses may be only whispers on the printed page, their volume increasing the more an individual reader associates stylistic gestures with ideological significance. In this sense, despite the modernist prejudice against storytelling, these stories invite a diversity of reader response not unlike the difference more formally inscribed into realist stories through textual interventions.

7

Gertrude Stein: Indirect Speech in "Miss Furr and Miss Skeene"

Stein declares in *Geography and Plays* (1922) that "I do not like stories," an assertion with which, if her exclusion from the canon of the modernist short story is any indication, genre critics have concurred.[10] Though *Three Lives* (1909), her first published book, is a story cycle modeled on Flaubert's *Trois Contes*, little in her subsequent *oeuvre* complements traditional notions of storytelling. Indeed, reading "Miss Furr and Miss Skeene" specifically as a short story requires some preliminary justification. Obviously, the bulk of Stein's work is non-mimetic, foregrounding stylistic effects like rhythm and repetition over theme and content to dramatize her belief that art need not tether its relevance to a particular time and place. Rather than depict a chain of localized events, many of her texts, both structurally and rhetorically, revolve around the moment of composition, and their creative genesis is maintained in a continuous present tense that aims to shelter them from history. For Stein, it is imperative that words resist "outside" social contexts that might limit their meaning, which is why she routinely borrows from the structuralist vocabulary of grammar to describe the effects of her writing. The sentence, not the utterance or speech act, is the fundamental unit of language because it exists "contained within [itself] and anything really contained within itself has no beginning or middle or ending."[11] Her writing thus challenges the very idea of storytelling as communication, often to the point where concepts like plot, characterization, and point of view sound like a dead language when applied to her fiction. As if to heighten this threat to narrative norms, she locates much of her work within traditional genres, most famously, the "autobiography" of her companion, Alice B. Toklas. Subtitles identify other pieces as plays, novels, and opera librettos. *Blood on the Dining-Room Floor* (1933), which has inspired an increasing amount of commentary in recent years, even celebrates the conventions of the mass-market whodunit while subverting them. The only story that she does not set out to rewrite, it seems, is the short story.

Stein herself is partly to blame for this perception. Though she contributed numerous brief prose works to little magazines like *Broom*, the *Little Review*, and *The Reviewer*—many of them posthumously collected by Robert Bartlett Haas in *Reflection on the Atomic Bomb*—she never speaks of a short form in her lectures and criticism, conflating, instead, narrative with the novel. Nor have critics identified within these pieces the standard structural criteria of the canonical modernist story (the epiphany, for example). Stein goes unmentioned in Wright's *The American Short Story in the 1920s*, and though "Melanctha" and "The Gentle Lena" (both from *Three Lives*) now make rare appearances in more progressive story anthologies, her briefer prose is more characteristically read as poetry. James R. Mellow and Wendy Steiner both compare "Miss Furr and Miss Skeene," for example, to the style of lyric portraiture gathered in *Matisse Picasso and Gertrude Stein* (1933) and *Portraits and Prayers* (1934).[12] Nor does anything in the story's original context in *Geography and Plays* suggest that it should be regarded as more of a narrative than the collages of doggerel, closet drama, and meditative prose that compose the rest of the collection.

Yet *Vanity Fair*, reprinting the piece in July 1923, subtitled it "The Tale of Two Young Ladies Who Were Gay Together and How One Left the Other Behind" and added an introduction that specifically labels it a short story. Probably written by Edmund Wilson, the magazine's managing editor, the note is important for how it attempts to frame Stein's prose for the reader. Among the many stories that *Vanity Fair* published during Wilson's tenure (1920 to late 1923), only "Miss Furr and Miss Skeene" necessitated prefatory remarks; equally experimental texts by other writers are identified with a particular genre only in the table of contents. *Vanity Fair* may have been one of the few publications with an enviable circulation to offer Stein wide exposure before 1933, yet its editors were apparently uncertain about how a mass readership might receive her writing. Nearly apologizing for her inventiveness, the introduction assures the audience that the story is comprehensible: "In one of Miss Stein's simpler manners, [it] should convince those readers who have hitherto been baffled by her later and more telegraphic style that she is really a writer of remarkable abilities."

Rather than "telegraphic," Stein's manner might be described as "telescopic." Sing-song rhythms condense and distance the drama, often obscuring the fact that there is a plot. After leaving her parents' home to cultivate her voice, Helen Furr meets Georgine Skeene, with whom she becomes "regularly gay." Hints of tension develop between the women, for Miss Furr does not like to travel as much as Miss Skeene, and when they visit the "quite pleasant home" that Helen has left, she refuses to stay. Men also pose a vague threat: "There were men there then who were dark and heavy and they sat with them . . . and they went with them," though where and what happens is inconclusive. By the final paragraph, the women drift apart: "Helen Furr was living somewhere else then and telling some about being gay and she was gay then and she was living quite regularly then." Ostensibly, when Stein wrote the piece in 1908, some fourteen years before it was published, she based the characters on a lesbian couple, Ethel Mars and Maud Hunt Squire, who frequented her Paris atelier at 27, rue de Fleurus. The story may also capture private uncertainties about romantic entanglements. Still recovering at the time of its composition from an early, unsuccessful relationship with May Bookstaver, which provided the basis for her first novel, the posthumously published *Q.E.D.*, Stein had met Alice B. Toklas only a year earlier, and the women would not "marry" for two more.[13] Whatever autobiographical tones resonate here, "Miss Furr and Miss Skeene" is not the happy story that its playful style suggests. As Marjorie Perloff argues, the change that Helen Furr undergoes must be inferred through the "permutation of a highly selected group of ordinary words" that creates "the skeleton narrative of any number of possible stories" from which an audience ultimately fashions its interpretation.[14] Interpretive freedom is most obvious in Stein's use of the word *gay*. Though contemporary audiences, accustomed to its slang association with homosexuality, may identify a Sapphic subtext more quickly than a 1920s readership, for whom the word primarily meant "happy" or "festive," no internal evidence confirms or denies the couple's lesbianism. Nothing within the story limits the word "gay" to a single, substantive meaning. How the reader interprets the relationship between Miss Furr and Miss Skeene effectively determines the outcome of the story.[15]

An equally important word, *telling*, alludes to a less obvious paradox between style and subject. To cultivate her voice, Helen Furr must tell others about being gay. The first major reference to speaking appears roughly halfway through the story when the women visit Mr. and Mrs. Furr, presumably Helen's parents. Miss Furr "said she would not stay, she said she did not find it gay, she said she would not stay where she did not find it gay, she said she found it gay where she did stay and she did stay there where very many were cultivating something" (19). When her companion leaves and Miss Furr realizes that "she was not at all feeling any need of having Georgine Skeene," her voice is superfluous: "She could use it and she did use it but then there was not any way of working at cultivating a completely pleasant voice when it has become a quite completely well enough cultivated one, and there was not much use in using it when one was not wanting it to be helping to make one a gay one. Helen Furr was not needing using her voice to be a gay one" (21). Only when she begins to learn from "very many [who were] telling about using other ways in being gay" does she begin cultivating it once more. By "telling," Miss Furr is then "teaching" others how to develop their voices, "telling about little ways one could be learning to use in being gay . . . telling them quite often, telling them again and again" (22). As Richard Bridgman suggests, the word *cultivation* evokes artistic development so that, by the end of the story, Helen Furr's "telling" seemingly becomes a form of public performance. Bridgman may overdetermine the word by describing Miss Furr and Miss Skeene as singers, yet, as with numerous works by women modernists, the story grounds the struggle for self-expression in the creation of an alternative, coded language comprehensible only to a small audience.[16] Without an appreciative community of "gay" listeners, the tale implies, there is "not much use in using" Helen Furr's voice.

The paradox is that while Miss Furr cultivates her voice, Stein never allows it to be heard, thus excluding readers from being the ideal audience that can recognize or benefit from Helen's developing talent. Indirect speech acts distance the voices of these characters by narrating speech acts with only the vaguest hint of their content or tone. When Miss Furr refuses to remain at her parents' home, for example, repetition conveys her dissatisfaction. A rhetorical effect, not what she says or how she says it, intensifies the emotion of the scene. Similarly, while Miss Furr tells others how to be gay, the storyteller offers no clue about how her newfound confidence affects her voice. While the story line implies a change in tone or tenor, the evidence never surfaces through the authorial style, leading to an obvious if frustrating question: Why does Stein refrain from slipping into the voice of her character?

The simplest explanation is that she is working in an anti-representational mode. While other modernists fragmented character through interior monologue and free indirect discourse, Stein foreshadows postmodernists by reducing the emotional complexity of her fictional people to linguistic abstractions so that, ultimately, the understated pun on "fur" and "skin" implies more about the sensuality of the characters than the story itself is willing to admit. Indirect speech also complements her desire to free narrative from time. By avoiding dramatic scenes she can ignore the contextual conditions of a speech act, those "social, historical, meteorological, physiological" influences that shape meaning.[17] Without reference to a specific historical moment, her abstract words maintain their omnitemporal aura.

Such explanations, however, do not adequately illustrate the effect that abstraction might have on readers. A less obvious justification for speech summary centers on Stein's attitude toward writing and orality and the reception activity that each inspires. Direct speech evokes oral conversation in which participants alternately speak and listen; Stein tries to prevent this model of interaction, composed of two distinct activities, from serving as an interpretive analogy to writing and reading. Instead, her style ideally provokes a response that, not unlike "The Yellow Wallpaper," must "compose" the story's significance. But if Gilman seems to rely on a reader's ability to recognize authorial inflections within her diarist's utterances, Stein's narrative authority is even more transparent, for she fashions a metaphorical conversation not between her and the audience but between her words and the audience. As Harriet Scott Chessman remarks, "Stein suggests that the act of creating becomes an act intricately bound up with the act of receiving; the two acts, mysteriously, often appear to occur simultaneously and can no longer be easily distinguished."[18]

Intriguingly, Stein's style is founded on a stringent distinction between speech and writing. "Of course I don't talk as I write!" she replied to a question asked by more than one suspicious reader. In an important series of lectures delivered at the University of Chicago in 1935, she explained that "you do not cannot must not shall not write as you talk" because "when you talk . . . what you say has no importance mostly to any audience because any audience has no feeling that they are an audience not while everybody is just talking" (*Narration* 54). Conversation is such an ordinary, commonplace exchange of words that we grow complacent and accept conventional meanings. The key to reception is recognition on the part of writer as well as audience. To illustrate its importance, Stein describes how she translated the poems of a young French poet. Translation is significant here because it is literally a rewriting in which reading and composition are incorporated into the same act. The work of this young poet, however, possessed a "certain smoothness" that alienated her from the creative process. "Hitherto I had always been writing, with a concentration of recognition of the thing that was to be existing as my writing as it was being written," she says. But in these poems, the recognition had already been achieved: "there it was it was already recognition a thing I could recognize because it had been recognized before I began my writing." As a result, she could only be "carrying out" an idea that already existed: "And then suddenly I realized . . . that the words come out differently if there is no recognition as the words are forming because recognition had already taken place" (52). Playing the part of a reader, Stein dramatizes why writing must incorporate the process of its own becoming. Without self-reflexivity, the differing roles of writer and reader solidify into insuperable identities, and art, for the latter, becomes a vicarious experience rather than a creative revelation. Only when we discover a writer in the process of naming words can recognition survive the original scene of composition and endure as a repeatable event.

According to Stein, recognition rarely takes place in oral conversation because speakers fail to exert the self-reflexivity that makes them, at the same time, listeners:

> When you write this is of course recognition there is the recognition that you recognize what you write as you write, while as you talk there is of course some recognition but really is there any real recognition of what you talk as you talk. I myself think not, and therefore naturally not you do not write as you talk. . . . There really is no real reason why you should since after all you are not your audience as you talk nobody really is not really as anybody talks that is just talks. (54)

Recognition in conversation is theoretically possible, however. Listening (and, by extension, reading) becomes a simple act of reception because "everybody gets tired . . . everybody always has to be listening to something, that is the way it is always anybody has to be listening to something that is what makes life lived . . . you are always listening to some one to something and you are always telling something to some one or to any one." It takes "genius" and energy to tell and listen at the same time. Much of *Narration,* in fact, is concerned with how various modern media (newspapers and history books especially) bifurcate this process by making listening "too easy."

Reading "Miss Furr and Miss Skeene" in the context of Stein's theories of reception suggests that she submerges speech events because these fictional exchanges would allow the audience simply to eavesdrop. A dramatized pattern of "just talking" implies that meaning can be located in the call and response of the characters, not in the audience's own dialogue with the text.

An interesting paradox in Stein's deconstruction of writer/reader roles further illuminates the effects of her telescoping style. Written as a lecture, *Narration* was originally heard rather than read (though the published version appeared almost immediately in 1935), a fact addressed in her discussion of recognition. She suggests that while the oral performer is "physical[ly] exciting," his presence "destroys the physical something that a writer is while writing" because "while he is writing that physical something by existing does not connect him with anything but concentrates him on recognition." In the act of writing, identity formation is a perpetual mutation of self, cast as discovery or surprise, so that, in a sense, self-consciousness precipitates self-creation. But oral performance physically ties the voice to the body, to an identity no longer in transit but stabilized within a figure or form. In this sense, direct speech might actually pose a threat to the cultivation of Helen Furr's voice. Were her words offered in dialogue, the audience might associate voice with body, activity with substance. Words might become flesh too easily if offered in quotation by referring to a thing rather than a process. De-emphasizing talk through the attributional device of indirect speech thus allows Stein to develop a voice without reference to a "corpo-reality" that would arrest its formation.

Indirect speech is a fundamental device for inspiring simultaneous listening and speaking in the reception act because, according to V. N. Volosinov, it presupposes "an analysis simultaneous and inseparable from transmission."[19] When summarizing someone else's speech, we transform it by emphasizing a particular feature; implicit in this act of emphasis is some form of analysis by which we single out and judge as important the aspect subsequently highlighted. Direct quotation is a passive or mechanical reproduction of a speech act, but the analysis inherent in indirect speech alters the original utterance. Inscribed within the reception act then is a necessary rearticulation of content that collapses the distinction between passive listening and speaking; this collapse makes the process, I assert, analogous to the "recognition" that for Stein, is essential.

Various styles of indirect speech resonate with different types of analysis. Summary may emphasize the theme or referent of the original message. It is a type of analysis that "receives an utterance purely on the thematic level and simply does not 'hear' or take in whatever there is in that utterance that is without thematic significance." The dichotomous type focuses upon the "texture" of the transformed speech by "incorporat[ing] into indirect discourse words and locutions that characterize the subjective and stylistic physiognomy of the message viewed as expression" (130–31). In fictional discourse, of course, previous utterances are hypothetical. But while Stein merely pretends to summarize what Helen Furr says, it is debatable whether audiences make this distinction and interpret indirect speech in fiction differently from actual conversations. For those who do not, we might say that the emphasized aspect of the message (either the referent or the texture) helps clue the audience to whatever expressive traits the storyteller feels are important about the character. In more mimetic texts, determining what type of analysis the narrator performs necessitates only listening, for we can grow attuned to features of a character's voice even while only passively participating. But a telescoped narrative, because the traits of fictional speech acts are described rather than performed, prompts us to hear and speak at once, for in attempting to recover an irrecoverable original utterance, we must invent the answer to our own question. Reception and creation thus become interchangeable activities.

At first glance, Volosinov's analytic paradigms might seem wholly inapplicable to Stein's indirect speech. Talk is so transformed that its original content and texture are equally obscure: "Very many were telling about using other ways in being gay." What is important here, however, is how Stein literally depersonalizes speech by transforming words into textures. "Very many" refers to a constituency identified only by its large membership; like a Greek chorus, this plurality is represented as speaking with one voice in one instance. Even though the summary acknowledges various "ways" to be gay, it fails to discuss any of those differences. For Volosinov, the "maximal compactness" achieved when numerous reported utterances are "received as one whole block of social behavior" indicates a content analysis where "only the 'what' of speech is taken in and the 'how' is left outside reception" (119). Yet Stein substitutes her *how* for the *what* of this chorus as the rhyme ("ways"/"gay") foregrounds the sonic texture of her style rather than any feature of the character speech. Similarly, the phrase "she told many then the way of being gay" compresses Helen's speech to the point that her original meaning and manner are irretrievable. The only referent to *gay* is the texture that it assumes in the narrative context.

Indirect speech also distances tensions between Miss Furr and Miss Skeene: "The voice Helen Furr was cultivating was quite a pleasant one. The voice Georgine Skeene was cultivating was, some said, a better one. The voice Helen Furr was cultivating she cultivated and it was quite completely a pleasant enough one then, a cultivated enough one then. The voice Georgine Skeene was cultivating she did not cultivate too much" (18). The passage may convey Stein's awareness that lesbian couples can replicate heterosexual sex roles, for in not cultivating her voice too much, Miss

Skeene plays the part of a "wife" to Miss Furr's "husband." According to these roles, only one voice speaks for a couple. In this case, Miss Furr makes the decisions: "They did some travelling, not very much travelling, Georgine Skeene would have liked to do more travelling, Helen Furr did not care about travelling." As with the ambiguous "very many," the voices of the anonymous speakers who feel that Miss Skeene's voice is "a better one" are summarized within a single speech act. There is little opportunity to hear what their words might have been; as a result, dissenting voices cannot be identified with a particular social group, remaining, instead, disembodied through abstraction. As Volosinov explains, "There is no wherewithal here for the speaker[s'] individuality to congeal into an image" (132). The repetitive structure of all four sentences ("The voice . . . was cultivating") suggests that the texture, too, has been transformed to conform with the authorial style. Character voices exist as mere traces, their message transformed to emphasize syntactical rhythm.

Elsewhere, however, one can discern a more overt interplay between a fictional utterance and its narration. When the narrator reports that Helen "said she would not stay where she did not find it gay," one assumes that the rhyme is not characteristic of her dialogue, especially since similar rhyme schemes appear in passages that have no indirect speech. But the same cannot be said for repetition. As I asserted earlier, here repetition intensifies Helen's unwillingness to remain in a place where she cannot cultivate her voice. Texture is equally expressive of the "stylistic physiognomy" of Helen's voice as the author's. The repetition signifies her insistence as well as the narrator's. Similarly, "telling them quite often, telling them again and again" captures the emphatic nature of Helen's speaking by dramatizing her need to teach others how to be gay in order to continue cultivating her voice. Repetition may be such an obvious trait of the authorial voice that its relevance to the character's summarized speech can be easily overlooked, yet the passage offers a clue to the formative changes that Helen undergoes by fusing Volosinov's two types of analyses. Because the referent is so ambiguous (the particular meaning of *gay*), any recognition of a meaning on the reader's part falls back on the stylistic texture. In such an onomatopoetic mode of narration, words create soundscapes rather than landscapes while character develops from sonic rather than psychological patterns. For a reader who cannot hear the character voices circulating beneath Stein's trademark style, the story of Helen Furr's cultivation goes undetected. Edmund Wilson's comments on "Miss Furr and Miss Skeene" in *Axel's Castle* dramatize what we might call the tone-deaf response since, for him, the "repetitive rigmarole manner is admirably suited to render the monotony and insipidity of the feminine lives which are being narrated."[20] For a reader who perceives a story submerged beneath the style, however, Helen's life is anything but monotonous and insipid. For Stein a stylistic device like repetition simply functions as a symbolic vehicle used for evoking the same emotional intensity that Wilson finds Rimbaud, Valery, and Yeats exploiting through their "medley of metaphors."

"Miss Furr and Miss Skeene" thus forces the reader to infer its manifold plot by recognizing that beneath the seemingly meaningless patterns of repetition and rhyme lies a very real struggle for self-expression. Apparently, however, the interpretive possibilities generated by Stein's style so disconcerted *Vanity Fair*'s editors that they decided to clue their audience to a single meaning that the text itself disallows. In its introduction, the magazine links Stein's "manner" to the plot with a stunning reductio ad absurdum: "It will be seen that the style, though queer, is exactly suited to the subject" (55). Connotations of *gay* may have been equivocal in the 1920s, but *queer* carried more obvious hints of same-sex relations. The note implies a connection between sexual preference and narrative technique, thus offering its readers a clue to interpreting the tale specifically as a lesbian love story. However oblique the reference to Stein's lesbianism, *Vanity Fair* attempts to yoke the narrative voice to the authorial body by calling upon the audience's perception of Stein as a *queer* figure.

An even more dramatic example of how the author function limits the story's interpretive possibilities is illustrated by a *Vanity Fair* parody of "Miss Furr and Miss Skeene" entitled "When Helen Furr Got Gay With Harold Moos: A Narrative Written in the Now Popular Manner of Gertrude Stein," credited to one "K. D."[21] As the title suggests, the satirist cannot simply reproduce Stein's voice in order to pinpoint the particular object of ridicule; K. D. must introduce new characters, a new plot, new words, and new inflections that tear the fabric of imitation. After Georgine Skeene leaves their home, Helen Furr takes up with Harold Moos, who, we are told, "was not a gay man." Despite Moos's apparent heterosexuality, Miss Furr becomes even more gay with him. She takes great delight in pulling his chair out from under him and knocking his hat off his head, indulging, in other words, in the very sorts of physical, scene-specific actions that Stein avoids narrating. To emphasize the revisionary plot, K. D. must ascribe motives that, in the original story, are ambiguous, as in the parody's most surprising plot twist: "One day when Helen Furr was being gay and Harold Moos was feeling dark and very heavy and very bald and not at all gay they were married."

Despite her nuptials, Miss Furr resists becoming Mrs. Moos, and her continued "gaiety" is ridiculed as both frivolous and irresponsible. In the original story, Helen wins independence both from her parents and her companion, but in the parody she remains a child who utters "baby-talk," a common, derogatory description of Stein's style. K. D. even invites a direct association with homosexuality by describing Helen as being "gay in lisping," a character trait not dramatized in the story. Harold Moos ultimately finds himself so oppressed by his wife's need to be gay that he turns violent: "I have been thinking up a way of making you less gay and of making myself more regularly gay and in a *wholly new way*; and, with that end in view, I hereby hit you three times regularly on the head with this walking stick." Just as Mr. Moos attempts to cure Miss Furr's sexuality, K. D. tries to rescue the word *gay* itself from the erotic significations that Stein invites it to assume. To make the point, K. D. must allow Harold Moos to speak, but the introduction of dialogue signals the end of parody and the assertion of a conventional moral authority. It marks the point at which K. D. stops imitating Stein in order to intimidate or threaten her. Direct speech becomes the explicit announcement of meaning and motive that Stein's indirect speech defers to the audience.

The violence with which this parody ends is shocking for its open display of hostility toward the author, yet its overall method is by no means unique. When reviewers and critics assumed Stein was indulging in nonsense, they ridiculed her style by amplifying its more obvious features. Yet many discovered that her techniques would not accommodate the communication of their intent. Indeed, parodies of Stein are notable because they often abandon all pretense of imitation. Instead they degenerate into rather puerile jibes about her size, her "mannishness," and her sexual orientation, thus dramatizing the resolute unwillingness of many readers to participate in the storytelling exchange in the manner that her narrative method asks. Like "Miss Furr and Miss Skeene," many of Stein's obscure short pieces can be read as emotionally profound stories. To do so, however, one cannot look to authorial intent but must assume responsibility for crafting what may be only one variation of the meaning of the story. In this sense, despite her anti-communicative narrative stance, Stein invites creative reception as much as realists like Davis, Jewett, and Gilman. By dismissing the standard repertoire of fictional techniques like dialogue that, for her, precipitate a more passive interaction with art, she asks the reader to recognize just how many voices can be cultivated within her own monophonic style.

8

Ernest Hemingway: Repetition, Stylization, and Dialogue in "Hills Like White Elephants"

In her autobiography, Stein launches a famously caustic attack on Hemingway, chiding him for "smell[ing] of museums" and being at heart more of a Rotarian than a modernist. Stein's "favourite pupil" responded by declaring that she was simply ungrateful for what he had taught her: "She could never write dialogue," he announced in *Green Hills of Africa* (1935). "It was terrible. She learned how to do it from my stuff. . . . She never could forgive learning that and she was afraid people would notice it, where she'd learned it, so she had to attack me." Even after admitting that his own penchant for repetition had been inspired by his Parisian mentor (but only after Stein died in 1946), he repeatedly claimed to have taught her dialogue to cancel the bothersome debt of her influence.

Yet whether Stein learned this art from him is doubtful, for, as we have just seen, she rarely employs it. As in "Miss Furr and Miss Skeene," she submerges her characters' voices within indirect speech acts that offer only a skeletal description of the fictional dialogue. When she does approach a more mimetic style of direct discourse, as in her autobiographical work, she omits quotation marks, accents, and other typographic cues that encourage the audience to segregate voices, thus peppering historical conversations with her own piquant inflections. (The only work in which she even comes close to using conventional dialogue, in fact, is *Three Lives*, published when her protégé was barely ten years old.) Hemingway, by contrast, often omits everything *but* dialogue. To borrow his famous image, verbal exchanges provide only the visible surface of the iceberg, leaving readers to infer from the characters' interaction whatever drama floats below. While Stein's use of indirect speech asks readers to distinguish the stylistic peculiarities of characters' voices from her more prominent authorial techniques, Hemingway supplies those peculiarities and asks that we reconstruct, from the pattern of dramatized talk, what inspires or provokes characters.

Conversational exchanges are most prominent in the stories gathered in *Men Without Women* (1927). While *In Our Time* (1925) and *Winner Take Nothing* (1933) employ a range of attributional devices, Hemingway's second story collection is nearly devoid of signs of narrative subjectivity, for few speech acts are summarized, and free indirect discourse appears in only two stories.[22] His reticence is so extreme that several stories, including "Hills Like White Elephants" and "The Killers," have become canonical examples of the behaviorist or objective style of storytelling in which the narrative perspective functions as a camera lens, recording events that pass before its eye without comment. As I argued throughout Part 2 of this study, cultural presumptions about gendered language allow direct addresses to be stereotyped as a feminine strategy because the appeal that they voice is "excessively" emotional and therefore different from a "rational, objective" (i.e. masculine) narrator. If reticence and understatement are presumably uncharacteristic of feminine speech, we should not be surprised to find Hemingway's severe economy of expression described as "masculine nudity of the starkest sort."[23] Unmediated, dialogue is the purest expression of a man-without-woman style.

One question the critic quoted above does not explore, however, is how a reader might be affected when exposed to "naked" dialogue, an issue that for Virginia Woolf, reviewing the collection in *The New York Herald Tribune*, was of paramount importance:

> A writer will always be chary of dialogue because dialogue puts the most violent pressure on the reader's attention. He has to hear, to see, to supply the right tone, and to fill in the background from what the characters say without any help from the author. Therefore, when fictitious people are allowed to speak it must be because they have something so important to say that it stimulates the reader to do rather more than his

> share of the work of creation. But, although Mr. Hemingway keeps us under the fire of dialogue constantly, his people, half the time, are only saying what the author could say much more economically for them. At last we are inclined to cry out with the little girl in "Hills Like White Elephants"[:] "Would you please please please please please please stop talking?"[24]

Jig, the girl of the story, actually says please seven times, not six, suggesting the sort of "violent pressure" Woolf apparently felt applied to her own attention. By "flood[ing] the page with unnecessary dialogue," Hemingway fails to offer the reader those "sharp, unmistakable points by which we can take hold of the story," leaving characters to talk without purpose.

Significantly, Woolf begins her review by criticizing the link between Hemingway's narrative reticence and his "self-consciously virile" public persona. Part of the essay is a response to an advertising blurb announcing that in *Men Without Women* "the softening feminine influence is absent—either through training, discipline, death, or situation," a line lifted without permission from Hemingway's correspondence with Max Perkins, his editor at Scribner's.[25] "The greatest writers lay no stress upon sex one way or another," Woolf replies. Far from being a measure of heroic restraint, reliance on dialogue belies artistic cowardice, a point that she emphasizes by appropriating an analogy dear to Hemingway's heart: "Though Mr. Hemingway is brilliantly and enormously skillfull, he lets his dexterity, like the bullfighter's cloak, get between him and the fact." A bullfighter too preoccupied with his style can "go through every sort of contortion so that the public thinks one is running every risk and displaying superb gallantry. But the true writer stands close up to the bull and lets the horns—call them life, truth, reality, whatever you like,—pass him close each time." The stories in *Men Without Women*, she adds, are "dry and sterile" because excessive dialogue allows the author to avoid grappling with the dramatic import behind the exchanges.

Whether one agrees with Woolf's judgment, her review highlights the interpretive difficulties that a reader might face when the narrative context is severely elided. The problem is further complicated because Hemingway's characters often sound like their author—or, rather, they sound like what an audience familiar with

Hemingway's style might expect *him* to sound like. Characters share his preference for simple sentences, abstract modifiers ("bright," "nice"), proper nouns, and, most important, the habit of repetition. The similarity between the voices of the author and his characters raises a question: What happens when a storyteller's stylistic devices perforate the fictional speech acts and call attention to themselves?

Bakhtin describes a similar phenomenon called "stylization," a type of double-voiced discourse in which the audience perceives two perspectives informing the same word, competing for recognition.[26] Typically, dialogue embodies the storyteller's "objectification" of a speech style associated with a certain "characterological type or profile." The audience recognizes a firm boundary between author and character voices; the storyteller's "semantic authority" is never threatened because character voices serve an overall authorial design. This is why, according to Bakhtin, the mere presence of dialogue does not automatically constitute a double-voiced discourse. In stylization, however, the audience recognizes the authorial style within the character's voice, impinging the autonomy of that objectified type or profile. A character "always speaks in earnest," Bakhtin writes, but when the values publicly associated with Hemingway's style influence how one interprets the dialogue, the character speaks *in Ernest*. When, for example, the reviewer who compliments Hemingway for his "masculine nudity" subsequently announces that "there is nothing about his prose or his subject matter that is effeminate," one wonders if he even read "Hills Like White Elephants," which asks the audience to identify with that "softening feminine influence" supposedly eliminated from the collection.

Despite this reviewer's judgment, critics concede that Hemingway is capable of "present[ing] a woman's point of view and attribut[ing] her plight . . . to a combination of male self-involvement and self-aggrandizement, a combination of which the text is aware and to which it is not sympathetic."[27] Jig serves as prime evidence of this sensitivity, for none of the ambiguity surrounding the "rich bitch" wives in stories such as "The Short Happy Life of Francis Macomber" and "The Snows of Kilimanjaro" surrounds her portrayal. Still, the presence of stylization in "Hills Like White Elephants" raises the issue of what happens when the audience is encouraged to identify with a woman's point of view expressed in a style that is culturally defined as masculine. Simply put, stylization may shift attention away from the drama by reminding one that a story is in the process of being narrated.

The distinction between the story and its telling may seem slight, but its importance can be illustrated by asking how a stylistic trait like repetition functions in these different narrative planes. Within the dialogue in "Hills," for example, repetition is a turn-taking gesture indicative of the imbalance of power in the couple's relationship. Jig cannot express her feelings because her companion revises the meaning of her words by making them sound childish and demanding. She can only mimic *his* language, thus challenging his control by parodying his conversational style. When mimicry fails to redress the imbalance, she adopts his strategy, and the conversation breaks off without resolution. Repetition is thus a key device of what Madeline Kahn calls "narrative transvestism . . . the process whereby a male author gains access to a culturally defined female voice and sensibility but runs no risk of being trapped in the [culturally] devalued female realm."[28] Yet repetition also appears in the author's style, where it functions as a literary device that conveys the aridity and bleakness of the theme. Its pattern on this plane offers readers potential clues to the unarticulated meaning of the story, the circumscribed depth that one must infer. Yet it does so by employing the same style of repetition that, in the dialogue, prevents Jig from expressing herself. In other words, the conversational strategy that the theme critiques provides the storyteller a key device of rhetorical emphasis.

The couple's first exchange illustrates how the companion controls the conversation by redefining key words to his own advantage:

> "They look like white elephants," she said.
> "I've never seen one," the man drank his beer.
> "No, you wouldn't have."
> "I might have," the man said. "Just because I wouldn't have doesn't prove anything." (211)

Jig insults the man's imagination when he refuses her invitation to join in the conversation. He responds by challenging her assertion. Substituting "might" for "wouldn't," he expunges the pungency of her inflections. Repeating the original phrase then allows him to dismiss the charge by intimating that she has no proof. Here the strategy works. Rather than carry on the conversation, Jig looks at the beaded curtain in the doorway of the bar. The exchange captures the asymmetry that provokes her to challenge his authority, for he assumes the right to define the terms in which they will talk.

When Jig repeats *his* words, she redefines his meaning by mimicking his authority. Assuming his voice, she can then reprimand him for his own failure in the relationship:

> "It tastes like licorice," the girl said and put the glass down.
>
> "That's the way with everything."
>
> "Yes," the girl said. "Everything tastes of licorice. Especially all the things you've waited so long for, like absinthe."
>
> "Oh, cut it out."

Jig describes the taste of the drink, which she apparently does not like, as she describes the hills as white elephants—the simile is an invitation to talk. Yet the American interprets the comment as a complaint blaming him for the flavor. He communicates his impatience by suggesting that she compares *everything* to licorice. Jig in turn interprets this as implying that she complains too much. She repeats his words, mocking his judgment to point out where he has failed her; apparently the companion has been promising absinthe for some time. Regardless of the symbolic importance of licorice and absinthe, the passage exemplifies how repetition empowers Jig, if only momentarily, by turning the companion's own standards against him and subverting his control. Recognizing this, the American can shore up his eroding authority only by commanding her to stop the parody.

Jig does not stop talking, however. She repeats her own words, transforming them from assertions to questions: "I wanted to try this new drink: That's all we do, isn't it—look at things and try new drinks?" Quoting Robin Lakoff's gender-coded theory of tag questions ("isn't it"), Pamela Smiley has suggested that Jig turns her assertions into questions because she lacks authority and self-confidence. Yet interrogatives also allow Jig to define the relationship through a more subtle form of conversational framing. In some cases, tag questions may signal a lack of self-assertion, but, as Lakoff has more recently argued, they also place a respondent into the speaker's conversational frame by limiting the range of reply to a yes or no, thus denying the opportunity to challenge implicit premises.[29] In this case, the companion concurs by echoing Jig's words. "I said the mountains looked like white elephants. Wasn't that bright?" she asks. "That was bright," he agrees, without attempting to re-frame the statement.

Jig maintains the advantage only momentarily, however, for the companion soon tries to convince her she should have the abortion: "That's the only thing that bothers us. It's the only thing that's made us unhappy" (212). Whenever Jig voices her suspicion, he reminds her that "if you don't want to you don't have to. I wouldn't have you do it if you didn't want to," a line repeated five more times. Yet Jig remains unpersuaded. The reason is that, as the American tries to sway her, she recognizes that his conversational style enforces her dependence upon him. As he assures her that "I know you wouldn't mind it," he implies that she should defer all decisions to him. She begins to understand that they will never be "all right and . . . happy" regardless of whether she consents to the abortion. To counter his argument, she asks a series of questions, attempting to re-frame the dialogue to address the inequality in their relationship.

> "And you really want to?" [she asked.]
>
> "I think it's the best thing to do. But I don't want you to do it if you don't really want to."
>
> "And if I do it you'll be happy and things will be like they were and you'll love me?"
>
> "I love you now. You know I love you."
>
> "I know. But if I do it, then it will be nice again if I say things are like white elephants, and you'll like it?"
>
> "I'll love it. I love it now but I just can't think about it. You know how I get when I worry."
>
> "If I do it you won't ever worry?"
>
> "I won't worry about that because it's perfectly simple."
>
> "Then I'll do it. Because I don't care about me."
>
> "What do you mean?"
>
> "I don't care about me."
>
> "Well, I care about you."
>
> "Oh, yes. But I don't care about me. And I'll do it and then everything will be fine."
>
> "I don't want you to do it if you feel that way." (213)

Smiley calls Jig's style in this passage a "direct attack [that] is very uncharacteristic of feminine speech" (294–95). The questions are uncharacteristic because they do not invite what Deborah Tannen calls "rapport talk" (conversation in which the discussion of similar experiences establishes the groundwork for mutual support), prompting instead simple yes/no responses or "report talk." Jig's use of repetition is likewise uncharacteristic. If, as Tannen argues, the conversational objective of feminine speech is to establish and maintain intimacy, repetition should ratify listenership; by incorporating her companion's words into her own talk, Jig typically would encourage him to continue participating.[30] Instead, she turns his responses into conditions, forcing him to agree or disagree. Repetition allows her to distill from his responses the source of his despair, which he finally admits is his worry. The phrase "If I do it you won't ever worry?" implies that a woman should accommodate a man's happiness, regardless of the sacrifice involved. But when Jig makes this the actual message ("I don't care about me"), challenging the companion to confirm what she infers, the admission is too direct for him. He must deny the implications of Jig's statement by again insisting that the decision is hers. Jig knows now what she suspected. He may indeed care about her, but his concerns define the relationship.

This passage marks the turning point in the conversation when Jig defers the caretaking to the American. Recognizing his selfishness and her lack of choice, she abandons face-to-face contact, leaving the table to walk to the other end of the station. How each interprets this gesture further marks the asymmetry of their conversation. As Tannen argues, women typically anchor their gaze on a conversant's face to show support, while men regard such an act as a threat employed only when challenging authority (83). However, Jig seems to disengage from the conversation as she recognizes the futility of trying to persuade him to keep the baby. "And we could have all this," she tells him with resignation, "and we could have everything and every day we make it more impossible." For the American, her leaving the table threatens his control of the conversation. The intensity of his gaze is part of his persuasive strategy, but now Jig distances him. Suddenly, he is in the position of maintaining the talk.

Yet Jig is not satisfied by her power. When she returns to the table, she recognizes that he will choose death over life. She now looks at the dry side of the valley, leaving him anchoring his gaze on her:

> "Doesn't it mean anything to you? We could get along." [said Jig.]
>
> "Of course it does. But I don't want anybody but you. I don't want any one else. And I know it's perfectly simple."
>
> "Yes, you know it's perfectly simple."
>
> "It's all right for you to say that, but I do know it." (214)

Frustrated by his presumptions, she mocks the affective force of his repetition strategy in order to halt the conversation completely: "Would you please please please please please please please stop talking?" But not even this dampens his need to persuade. He insists again that he wants only what she wants, and Jig makes her point even more emphatically: "I'll scream," she promises. The lengths that Jig must go to free herself from his conversational frame only traps her deeper within it, for by threatening to scream, she becomes a woman without an argument, a woman without language. As if recognizing this predicament, she adopts an artificial economy of emotion. Rather than reveal the mixed shade of her confusion, she speaks in primary colors. "Do you feel better?" he asks after carrying their bags to meet the oncoming train. "I feel fine," Jig replies. "There's nothing wrong with me. I feel fine."

As this reading suggests, the linear flow of the story gears sympathy toward Jig by dramatizing her disadvantage in the asymmetry of the conversation. The companion's empty repetition impedes the give-and-take of the dialogue by effecting an emotional stutter in which he states repeatedly what he wants Jig to believe. At two curious points in the narrative, however, the narrator employs the same repetition strategy that the story attacks. Both instances center on exchanges between the couple and the Spanish woman tending bar at the train station:

> "We want two Anis del Toro." [he tells the bartender]
>
> "With water?"
>
> "Do you want it with water?"
>
> "I don't know," the girl said. "Is it good with water?"
>
> "It's all right."

> "You want them with water?" asked the woman.
>
> "Yes, with water."

In the fictional world, the words "with water" are not repeated five times because the companion and the woman speak in Spanish, which Jig does not understand. The storyteller translates the passage into the narrative style, cuing the audience to the elemental significance of water in the dry valley by creating a pattern of emphasis audible only to the reader, not the characters.

A similar if less exaggerated incident occurs toward the end of the story, after Jig promises to scream if the American does not stop talking.

> The woman came out through the curtains with two glasses of beer and put them down on the damp felt pads. "The train comes in five minutes," she said.
>
> "What did she say?" asked the girl.
>
> "That the train is coming in five minutes."

Again, the storyteller translates the language of the characters' voices into English; as a result, a pattern of repetition is created on the narrative plane that is not heard in the fictional world. What do these secret patterns contribute to the story? One might suggest that they dramatize Jig's dependence on her companion, yet a reader may recognize that point without sharing the experience. Only if the passages were written in the "original" Spanish would the audience (at least those not fluent in the language) feel Jig's isolation. As we account for the translation, we break our identification with Jig. By calling attention to the storyteller's presence, the repetition relocates us from the sensory immediacy of the fictional world to the upper atmosphere of its telling. As a stylistic device, repetition here illustrates a central theme of the story, the death of communication, which a reader recognizes (if at all) only because, consciously or not, Hemingway has raised the volume of his own voice.

A common criticism of Hemingway's career after *Men Without Women* is that trademark devices degenerated into predictable mannerisms so that instances of "empty" repetition—patterns like those in "Hills" that contribute little to the development of the plot—appear more frequently. I would argue, however, that readers who imagine the increasing prominence of Hemingway's authorial voice do so in part because their responses are affected by the values publicly attached to his style. Such readings are not faulty; the identification may be inevitable since Hemingway promulgated the connection between art and artist. Yet judgments about the aesthetic purpose of his devices often evoke the author function to generate meanings that, if one tries to filter out Hemingway's voice, contradict what the stories imply.

"The Sea Change" (1931), for example, is often regarded as a poor cousin of "Hills Like White Elephants" not because it, too, asks the reader to infer the unspoken subject of a couple's conversation (in this case, the woman's sexual preference) but because the patterns of repetition in the dialogue fail to generate the tension so pronounced in Jig's story:

> "All right," said the man. "What about it?"
> "No," said the girl, "I can't."
> "You mean you won't."
> "I can't," said the girl. "That's all I mean."
> "You mean you won't."
> "All right," said the girl. "You have it your own way." (302)

If the rhetorical tension of "Hills" involves a power struggle between conversational styles, "The Sea Change" foregrounds the repetition strategy employed by Jig's companion. Yet here the female speaker refuses to allow the man to revise her meaning to his advantage; indeed, when he persists, she breaks off the exchange, and both speakers remain locked within their mutually exclusive conversational frames. Despite superficial similarities with "Hills" (a couple, a bar, an antagonistic exchange), the sex roles in the two stories are vastly different, for the repetition strategy that trapped Jig in speechlessness here empowers the woman. However clumsily Phil, the man, may try to dodge her rhetorical questions ("You don't believe I love you, do you?" "Don't you really believe I love you?"), she foregrounds her insistence that she is leaving him because she "has to," not because she "wants to." But if this woman succeeds where Jig fails, why is "The Sea Change" regarded as one of Hemingway's minor short fictions? One can argue the relative merits of each work, but I would again suggest that any aesthetic contrast evaluates this later story according to the widespread assumption that Hemingway's voice had, by the 1930s, lost its originality.

Nowhere is this belief more prominent than in Wyndham Lewis's infamous essay "The Dumb Ox" (1934), the most belligerent critical assault that Hemingway experienced in his lifetime. (He was so angered upon reading it in Sylvia Beach's Shakespeare & Co. bookshop that he shattered a lamp.) Though Lewis does not refer specifically to "Hills" or to "The Sea Change," his discussion of Hemingway's style is important for two reasons: first, he demonstrates how, despite its emphasis on impersonality, modernism often invokes authorial agency to define its standards of literariness. Equally important, he links these standards to a written rather than oral style of narration. Appearing in the wake of Stein's *Autobiography of Alice B. Toklas*, which revived a decade-old debate over Hemingway's debt to his mentor, "The Dumb Ox" is most notorious for the inexorable link Lewis perceives between the writers. Stein's "overmastering" influence destroys Hemingway's art because once readers recognize her voice within his, the style assumes the tone of an "infantile, dull-witted dreamy stutter." He wonders whether one can even appreciate Hemingway's writing after learning of this influence:

> If we blot out Gertrude Stein, and suppose she does not exist, does this part of Hemingway's equipment [his use of repetition] help or not? We must answer *Yes* I think. It does seem to help a good deal: many of his best effects are obtained by means of it. It is so much a part of his craft, indeed, that it is difficult now to imagine Hemingway without this mannerism.

Yet ignoring echoes of Stein's voice, especially as "near to communism as we all are," is an ethical failure on the part of the reader. If a writer assumes "lock, stock and barrel from another artist the very thing for which he is mainly known," the aesthetic individuality of art is threatened, and "such a practice must result, if universally indulged in, in hybrid forms or monstrosities."

While Lewis fails to develop this line of his argument—in part because he is far more interested in his slurs and insults—one can nevertheless explore its implications. He suggests here that readers are responsible for some knowledge of the authorial voice, for without an awareness of what constitutes their literary composition, words serve only pragmatic or narrowly rhetorical functions. Style without a stylist does not sufficiently remove language from commonplace usage; instead, it echoes the speakerless appeals of advertising and the news. What makes Hemingway's writing "dumb art," finally, is his failure to establish a singular perspective, for "with Stein's bag of tricks he takes over a *Weltanschauung*, which may not at all be his, and does in fact seem to contradict his major personal quality." In other words, far from conveying "masculine nudity of the starkest sort," Hemingway's economy suggests a passivity that Lewis associates with the anonymity of folk culture, the "masses, who are the cannon-fodder, the cattle outside the slaughter-house . . . *those to whom things are done*, in contrast to those who have executive will and intelligence."[31]

The criticism leads to the second objection: Hemingway's style, if not read in deference to his public stature as an author, is "valueless as writing" because "it is not written." Rather, "it is lifted out of Nature and very artfully and adroitly tumbled upon the page: it is the brute material of every-day proletarian speech and feeling" (201–2). One can detect here an echo of Woolf's criticism. Excessive dialogue erodes perceptions of authorial agency resulting in writing that seems transcribed from everyday speech. Significantly, Lewis suggests that the executive will and intelligence that literary writing conveys are incompatible with American English, whose penchant for colloquialisms or "*pidgin* tongue" is the essence of "the prose of reality—the prose of the street-car or the provincial newspaper or the five and ten cent store"—the prose, in other words, of mass culture. By linking stylistic economy to the "national underdog dialect," he implicates Hemingway in the destructive sort of brevity that Canby, Cory, Pattee, and O'Brien all associate with the formulaic efficiency of short-story telling.

However extreme, Lewis's essay reveals how Hemingway's economy was pejoratively defined by the 1930s. What for early reviewers was naked art became, for Lewis, an "art of the surface" whose simplicity evoked the concise gimmickry of cultural rhetoric. While such an oversimplification does a vast injustice to later stories like "The Short Happy Life of Francis Macomber" and "The Snows of Kilimanjaro" (both of which experiment with multiple perspectives and a lyric density uncharacteristic of his earlier fictions), Hemingway himself recognized that the ideological significance attached to his style had overdetermined his art. In the preface to *The First Forty-Nine* (1938), he concedes that his techniques had lost their luster: "In going where you have to go, and doing what you have to do, and seeing what you have to see, you dull and blunt the instrument you write with." He then defends himself: "But I would rather have it bent and dull and know I had to put it on the grindstone again and hammer it into shape and put a whetstone to it, and know that I had something to write about, than to have it bright and shining [with] nothing to say, or smooth and well-oiled in the closet, but unused" (3–4).

The passage is vintage Hemingway, celebrating the author as craftsman in a manner not dissimilar to Benjamin's evocation of the storyteller, written two years previously in 1936. For both writers, the ethos of craftsmanship means that "traces of the storyteller cling to the story the way the handprints of the potter cling to the clay vessel" (92). Yet Benjamin describes such traces as merely another layer of meaning that accrues through the circulation of the story. What Hemingway puts to the grindstone, by contrast, is less his style than this public persona in order to mollify complaints about the dulling of his "blade." The purpose of storytelling for Benjamin is to render the teller's presence obsolete so the implicit plenitude of a tale can be realized. By contrast, Hemingway's narrative agency limits potential significance as public familiarity with the author's trademark techniques establishes an ideological matrix of intent. As both "Hills Like White Elephants" and "The Sea Change" reveal, the interplay between dialogue and repetition generates multiple interpretations depending upon the degree to which a reader perceives the authorial voice in the exchange. Unlike Stein's style, which foregrounds narrative presence yet refrains from articulating *a* meaning to the story, Hemingway's mannerisms reveal his agency precisely at the moment that they try to deny it.

9

Djuna Barnes: Free Indirect Discourse and Parody in "Run Girls, Run"

The same newspaper that celebrated *Men Without Women* as naked art had, four years earlier, dismissed Djuna Barnes's first story collection, *A Book* (1923), as decadent "cesspool literature." Another reviewer suggested that "after finishing this book, one finds it necessary to stick pins in oneself . . . to see if there is anything real and normal in the world." Forty years later, still another critic complained that *Spillway*, a collection of radically revised stories from the 1920s, manifests "egoism and emptiness," full of moments that "reveal little in themselves, dealing as they do, with attitudinising [*sic*], oddly clad, unreal figures like nineteenth-century fashion plates."[32] The criticism is not atypical; for readers past and present, Barnes's short fictions are less successful than her novels because they contain too much rhetoric, too many flat characters, and the plots are too bizarre to stomach. Perhaps Julian Symons, perceiving Poe's influence in the odd commingling of macabre scenario and erudite language, phrases the consensus most kindly when he says that "in [her] stories nothing may be reasonable, but everything is explained." Whereas Hemingway's reticence complemented a hard-boiled public persona, Barnes's lyrical, idiomatic style suggested to resisting readers a haughty, aloof bohemian interested in affectation rather than audience appeal.[33] Her manner even inspired jokes as derisive as the "baby talk" jibe leveled at Stein: Ezra Pound, whose appreciation for her work dimmed when she declined to sleep with him—she "weren't too cuddly," he complained—wrote a scurrilous invective announcing that "her blubbery prose had no fingers or toes."[34]

Accusations of "blubbery prose" presuppose an artificial distinction between expression and content in which words are devices that veil the clarity of meaning, an interpretive stance that, according to feminist critics, manifests a barely disguised misogyny. As Shari Benstock suggests in *Women of the Left Bank,* "The text [is] likened to a woman's body whose envelope (style or code) must be broken in order for the substance to be recovered and explained. Reading is rape, a submission of the text (woman) to patriarchal (critical) priorities" (246). Barnes's stories are, arguably, more vulnerable to this abuse than her longer works since the novel arises from a tradition of rhetorical luxuriance; encyclopedic prose forms, in fact, demand what is often derogatorily called "digression." If one reads her longer works *Ryder* and *Nightwood* as anatomies (Burton's *Anatomy of Melancholy* was one of her favorite books, and *Nightwood* was originally subtitled "Anatomy of Night"), accusations of rhetorical excess are as misinformed as they are misogynistic. The compact space of the short story, by contrast, enhances this illusory split between style and subject, leading to oversimplified readings in which Barnes's lyricism is said to rob characters of mimetic life by reducing them to a gimmicky, "attitudinising" body of phrases.

Exploring the function of free indirect discourse in her short fiction should alert us to the faultiness of the link between her voice and her identity as an "aloof, decadent" modernist exile. Just as Stein uses idiosyncratic expressions to undermine enculturated interpretive habits (she collapses the difference between speaking and listening), Barnes forces the reader to confront words wrested away from their typical referential function. Yet as Stein defamiliarizes language by subjecting it to a familiar set of authorial habits like repetition and rhyme, Barnes nearly evaporates from her texts. As Karen Kaivola suggests, her techniques prevent us from speaking of a single authorial "style" because "many voices speak" in her prose, thus "undermining the authority of any one position and producing a contradictory and heterogeneous discourse composed of an amalgam of styles."[35]

What makes the rhetorical potpourri of "Run Girls, Run" so contradictory are modern inflections that seem to satirize the Elizabethan and Jacobean vernacular of its half-dozen vignettes, all of which focus on female sexuality: "Hazel fainted on the milk-white knob of her father's door. . . . Why? because Hazel had been caught hot-footing it down the paternal ivy facing Main Street at all hours of the night."[36] With this often bewildering brew of archaisms and twentieth-century slang, Barnes dramatizes how folk tales, mythology, and history all constrain sex for women into oppressive plot lines like rape, illegitimate birth, adultery, and jealousy. Her wildly multi-voiced approach disrupts these traditional forms by exploding their pretensions to linearity and unity. Yet Kaivola's claim that her willful dissonance leaves the reader stranded in a sea of sociolects ignores a more probable effect; for as Barnes undermines the voice of authority that shapes representations of female desire, we must perforce ascribe a greater amount of authority *to her.* Because one cannot infer irony without ascribing intent, the author function, by necessity, plays a more overt role in our reading. The result is a paradox: To make sense of the story, we must presume the same centralized narrative presence that Barnes's disparate styles disrupt.

Yet the influence of the author function on our reading is problematic here because the story is relatively obscure. Originally discarded as the opening chapter of *Nightwood*, "Run Girls, Run" was first published in March 1936 in a short-lived periodical called *Caravel* (co-edited by Barnes's long-time friend Charles Henri Ford) where it promptly disappeared for almost forty years. Barnes unsuccessfully tried to republish the story in the early 1970s in *Poetry Magazine*, but only when Frank Hallman reprinted it in 1974 with a lost journalistic piece on Paris, "Vagaries Malicieux," would it gain anything resembling a wide circulation. (As Hank O'Neal mentions in his "informal" memoir of Barnes's later years, this edition was pirated; the author claimed that she never saw a copy of it.)[37] Despite its recent availability, no biography or scholarly article to date has discussed the story. Without the typical interpretive accouterments (critical commentary, letters, journals) that shape an audience's awareness of the storyteller's relationship to his or her work, "Run Girls, Run" is as authorless a text as one can find by a recently canonized modernist.

Despite this limitation, one can recognize an obvious pattern of parodic double-voicing in the narration that centers around Barnes's use of free indirect discourse. As Charles Jones has argued, the ironic effect of free indirect discourse often arises from a juxtaposition of informal and formal styles: Because direct speech evokes oral conversation, colloquialisms typically distinguish character voices from the narrator's "literary" voice as the sudden air of informality within formal narration creates a satiric dissonance. Hypothetically, the greater the juxtaposition, the more obvious the "register of irony."[38] Yet by associating speech exclusively with colloquial language, Jones ignores the sorts of formal oral discourses like epic poetry, opera, and oratory that fascinated Barnes. Once a playwright and actress with the Provincetown Playhouse, her work often draws from what biographer Andrew Field calls the "ritual folk music-theatre in which characters give disconnected recitatives (sometimes in mime, sometimes playing instruments, speaking, singing)" (183). Both *Ryder* and *Nightwood*, in fact, incorporate oral discourses like the lullaby, the sermon, and the riddle into their *sui-generis* textures; "Run Girls, Run" likewise contains several soliloquies, perhaps the quintessential "disconnected recitatif." The juxtaposition that Jones posits is operative, but its parody emerges as devices associated with writing interject an unspoken irony into its spoken-word style, not vice versa.

The opening lines suggest how this double-voicing reveals itself: "In the days when three sorts of nature but made a man; when the Marquis had no Seningalt, and the Chevalier d'Eon had yet to raise his petticoat to posterity; when . . . the night covered all for the gossips of dawn . . . we had this story—the first of its kind, though those that followed were as like as the links in the ankle chain of a convict" (31). The epic register speaks with the authority of tradition; the oral formula that defines the scope of history ("in the days") minimizes the "unmanliness" of the Marquis and the Chevalier by consigning them to the "night," out of the glare of history where they are subjects of "mere" gossip. The second voice speaks for those excluded, revealing how history perpetuates itself by repeating narratives until they become myth, lore, and other links that shackle identity. The first voice, which defines tradition as "the days of our fathers," assumes a decidedly masculine air, while the secondary voice identifies the convicts as those women, mothers and wives, who become the subject of (or are subjected to) history. The adulteress, the ingénue, the prostitute, the hag, the libertine, and the jealous wife all embody female desire in male narratives. One by one, the dialogue instigated by this second voice rewrites these stories.

The first scenario, an adultery narrative, introduces a pattern of recurring print inflections. The first father is identified with Christ by a capitalized "He," but any air of divinity is quickly undercut by a parenthetical insertion that links him to Othello; he has "a bit of a Moor" in him, and his nightshirt is "bespattered with the wine of thanks-giving." The equation of masculine sexuality and divine right is further undermined by the husband's name, "Don Juan B.C.," which is at once an anachronism (dating from the 17th-century, long after Christ) and an anomaly; this Don—Barnes transforms titular status into a proper noun—is neither dandy nor seducer but an impotent cuckold. His wife "had borne him no sons but a thundering head brace of thorns, having diddled and horned him on every one of his fleecy temples . . ." The subtle substitution of *thorns* for *horns* links crucifixion with adultery. With his "fleecy" temples, Don is the lamb of God, his pride martyred in the name of monogamy.

An epic catalogue lists the wife's adulterous liaisons: a soldier, a senator, a huntsman, a headsman, a carpenter, a bishop, and "the power behind the Throne," to name just a few. The severity of her "sin" is deflated both by the exaggerated length of the list (at least eleven lovers, not including an unspecified number of "stew boys") and mock-judgmental aphorisms offered in parenthetical asides such as "women love the stoop in conquer" and "a woman will sidle up to a climax." The first phrase echoes both Goldsmith's play and Eliot's *The Waste Land*, in which the typist "stoops to folly" with a "carbuncular" lover. In those scenarios, the women are seduced, but here the wife is the aggressor. The lover with whom she stoops is a "galley-slave without an oar," his phallic inadequacy symbolic of his social inferiority. For Don Juan, it is bad enough that his wife is unfaithful; she sleeps across the very class boundaries that define his status as a gentleman. Adultery doubly insults his authority.

Throughout the story, parenthetical asides signal what might be called "phallic deflations." Another lover, a priest, is "nowhere to blame had his breviary been bigger." The thinness of his hymnal not only fails to prevent his seduction; it alludes to his sexual inadequacy, much as the absent oar handicapped the galley slave. As Don sneaks upon his wife's bed chamber, he doffs his "ton of Toledo cod-work (protecting what she had never respected)," the aside asserting and lampooning his supremacy. Without his cod piece attached, Don's masculinity literally withers. He transforms into Richard the Lion-hearted, "crying like a gosling," but his self-pity is self-serving: His wife's sexuality threatens his identity, but "his man's eye," as another parenthesis reveals, "was embroidered all over with vestal lace making his grief slightly dubious" (33). Draped suddenly in women's clothing (the vestal lace), he is less than a cuckold, for her adultery has reduced him to a state of virginity. Don knows that killing his wife with an Othello-like smother is part of a long tradition. "Jump back into folk-lore, that old rhyme-makers may toughen their teeth on you," he cries as he suffocates her. He shouts, "the sooner I'm done with you, that sooner will you be sung of!"

But even murder cannot assuage Don's lost power; he breaks down "in the classic manner" and begins a long soliloquy meant to justify his crime as a preservation of tradition. His speech is notable for its declamatory style:

> Hey nonnie, I weep like a tiger in stripes for a whelp crying "Mother!" high on a spear's end, in doing away with your habits, which were, God knows, of the worst! . . . right or wrong, payment of sin always finds a head-under-pillow! So, when I marry again at ninety, my other daughter will be a fin from another fish, blind of an eye for the generation's sake. And will she fore-fear the blood! She will, when she learns that you were cooled with a pillow! (34)

Barnes parodies here the long tradition in Elizabethan theater of the *ars moriendi*, the art of dying well, through which heroines such as Ophelia and Desdemona as well as the titular character of Webster's *The Duchess of Malfi* maintain heavenly virtue and feminine dignity in the midst of their violent deaths. This "poor slut," however, literally goes kicking and screaming, and even after a long round of suffocation is "not dead yet by a damned sight." Only after she strikes a series of tragic poses, her voice reduced to "Nay! Nay! Nay!" does she succumb: "her hands went as high as her crown, and her hands went as high as her eyes, and her hands went as high as her mouth . . . and with that her hands had no more ways, and her soul roared from the portal." Exaggerating the iconography of death, the ironic voice transforms tragedy into farce. If deathbed scenes in the Elizabethan theater were cathartic spectacles, Barnes turns them into slapstick. But while the gestures of the dying adulteress are no more exaggerated than Don's exclamatory speech, it is her corpse that occasions the public reaffirmation of social authority. As the "many faced populace" tosses "shock-blossoms" upon her funeral procession, they are "never so pleasantly pleased as when pelting history new made in its own courtyard." Don accompanies the casket, still striking wounded poses so he now resembles Little Lord Fauntleroy, "shaken with a lad's grief, though of course a man among MEN" (34). Here Barnes's habit of random capitalization asserts and deflates titular status as Don's absurd minions (including the "Lord of the Breeches" and the "Lady of the Hose") offer condolences.

The description of the corpse is a bitterly ironic passage that introduces another parodic touchstone. Susan Snaider Lanser has noted the presence in Barnes's writing of a "gynocentric sexual rhetoric . . . [in which] terms for the female body—furrow, nook, path, keyhole, whorl, crevice, conch shell . . . are clearly designed to counteract emerging Freudian notions of phallic supremacy and clitoral insufficiency."[39] Similar imagery pervades "Run Girls, Run," but with a less certain revisionary emphasis. Because the narrative voice assumes the tenor of history, vaginal imagery, on the surface, evokes fear of the unknown: "They snatched her up and sealed her with wax (better for her had it been done in her lifetime)." The custom of sealing the corpse's orifices provides a startling metaphor for cultural strictures on female sexuality. The parenthetical utterance has two meanings: According to the primary voice, a woman's chastity must be enforced by whatever means necessary. But the ironic voice implies that unexpressed desire results in a death-in-life predicament. With its sexual sites waxed over and plugged, the corpse becomes a figurine. (Doll imagery is prevalent throughout both *Nightwood* and the bulk of Barnes's short stories, in fact.) Swathed in "trumpery satin," the dead wife is "a fright of a gaud," attractive because "a woman packs close [draws a crowd] when she has died of suspicion." Parodying the lure of sexual scandal, the ironic voice suggests that the spectacle of her now immobile body is enough to distract from the fact she was murdered.

The second vignette introduces another parodic device, the deliberative question, which voices the mystery of nature, associated here with female sexuality through fertility myths. The "next [convict] in line" is Nancy, who, despite her family's best efforts, loses her virginity and is impregnated without her knowledge. For the primary voice, the ambiguous borderline between the asexual girl and the sexual woman is a mystery of cultivation: "What had been up to her nines that controversy roved her marrow at such an early age? Was she a child, or was she not, when she first ate her porridge? Was she a woman, when a woman, she split to the harvest? . . . Or was it ignorance, plain and simple, that reaped her eye-sockets of trouble?" (34–35). The ironic voice subtly answers the mystery by alluding to pseudo-incest narratives, from Greek mythology (Zeus's numerous seductions) to Christian doctrine (the immaculate conception). Nancy's troubles begin when she discovers a plover's egg; the parenthetical voice underscores the persistence of this seduction narrative by admitting that "I may have the wrong egg." As the father/seducer figure goes unaccused, his identity unknown, the moral weight of the illegitimate birth falls upon the woman's shoulders. If Don Juan recovered his threatened masculinity through blustery exclamations, Nancy's soliloquy is marked by deliberative questions. Each night she asks herself: "Now how was it? And why was it? And *who* was it, by damn?" (35). According to the primary voice, a man regards female sexuality as a devious, subversive force. For a woman herself, however, it is not even a power consciously wielded.

The funeral fineries draped upon the murdered adulteress transform her into a child-like doll, but Nancy's costume is meant to ensure her chastity. The mystery of the pregnancy rests on how the unknown father was able to "plough up the borders of [her] caution" while she harvests the family fields. Her clothes are meant to be a protection against such a fate, but "tucked up as neat as a hen's pinions," they are a form of imprisonment, "pinioning" her. Moral traditions established by patriarchal rule should curtail illicit passions; at Nancy's home, however, "every fire in the house," the passions of the family romance, are "kept burning and roaring away with leaves snatched from the Bible and The Book of Creation, the Zend Avista, and the Zohar." While her mother "darn[s] maxims . . . into hosen," weaving a moral chastity belt, the very "thou-shalt-nots" sewn into the "family crotch work" provoke the threat of incest that controls women's sexuality. Nothing better dramatizes the need for taboos, Barnes implies, than a broken one. The sense that female sexuality should serve only reproductive ends is both asserted and ridiculed: "Was she perhaps noosed in a caul?" The narrator alludes to the superstition that the caul, the membrane that covers the head of a fetus, is a sign of good luck. Here, however, the word *noose* makes the phrase less prophetic than fateful, for Nancy has no power to question it (35). Incest is a disturbing subtext throughout Barnes's writings; here she dramatizes the victim's awareness that her inability to name the father turns her into the criminal: "I'll be called a witch at the weather, be tarred for a warning and feathered for fear's sake, be burned in the market, or ducked in a pond" (36).

The third vignette makes the strongest connection with *Nightwood* by drawing an extended analogy between women's cultural marginality and the Jewish Diaspora. Nell assumes the identity of a Saxon, with a "saxe-blue bonnet" and a "breastful of bosoms strapped into a keel-shaped corset from old Spitzburgen." Here orthography marks the irony: The name of the Norwegian Islands (Spitsbergen) is Germanized, alluding to the Nazi propaganda of Aryan beauty and purity circulating through post-Weimar Germany, a subtext of *Nightwood* as well. Despite the disguises, Nell remains "a wandering Jewess, ladled up handsomely from the vat of the Hebrew," with gloves of "plausible suede from Mount Sinai" and a dress made from "ten good yards of Ghetto taffeta" (36). Homeless, Nell becomes a "heathen," her tragedy another spectacle worthy of Thomas Gainsborough, the English painter: "Observe her poses. Impressive!" The ironic voice parodies fascination with the prostitute who stands with "her hand on her hip, her hip on a tilt, on her arm at the full, a reticule bulging with scraps swept from Parliament Street up Sinister Lane" (37). The bulging purse becomes the synecdoche of her social identity, dramatizing the connection between her sexuality and economic survival. Stuffed with remnants of her subsistence living, its "bulging" evokes masculine genitalia as well, so the reticule symbolizes the occupation of the vagina, the penetration that Nell must promise the "sailors closing in on her from all seas" if she is to stay alive. Parenthetical insertions again signal a parodic undercurrent as Nell sings "in falsetto (the voice we all come to) 'Only A Bird In A Gilded Cage' (God, what a voice!), changing from largo to largo retardo as she breaks into the strains of 'You Would Not Dare To Insult Me If My Brother Were Here.'"

A deliberative question voices the voyeurism of that attraction: "So did she, holding on to the hand of her illegitimate daughter, on the instant of passing a beautiful deep-seated cistern, throw herself in by mistake? . . . She did and was a wet sighing sea-work in less than a month." The suicide passes unquestioned, however; Nell's body decomposes, absorbed in vapor and sent down in rain. In the most surreal vignette, Nell's daughter gains celebrity as "the ugliest woman in history (dating about the Voltaire period)," the parenthesis parodying the arbitrary dating of tradition. As a homeless, nameless orphan, Nell's daughter evokes an older tradition of the female grotesque, which Barnes knew from her reading of Rabelais. As a "dog-faced Girl" who grows "fat as a pudding" and takes "to loud barking [like] a beagle pointing herself by the scruff of her neck," she embodies the paradox of the grotesque body as she transgresses the idealized feminine beauty that her mother symbolized. Yet her indifference to beauty itself becomes the focus of male obsession, for "men hunted her in the spring like hounds; they plunged through the snow, sleet, rain, all for a word with her about it . . . in the end she was traced back into Perugia by fools-cap and urine, all the way out of Egypt and over the Andes into Peru" (28). In a scene that evokes the imagery of "pregnant death" from *Ryder*, she gives birth not to a child but to "the Bird of her Soul, which pecking on a long seam came out at her navel, and on flat wings flew straight into the Face of Convention."[40] The "bird" or child astonishes "the Elders" of heaven by rewriting mythology, for she is virile rather than passive. Indeed, Leda turns out "to be a boy with a Greek face." The gender roles are reversed here as the bird is a woman whose Zeus-like sexuality astonishes the gods. Stunned to discover the shape and contours of his own body, Leda contorts himself into a mock-erotic position, "never having heard there's nothing much on the back" (38). By reversing roles in the rape scene, the ironic voice transforms death into liberty. Free from the body, the androgynous soul obtains a fuller identity.

The final vignette offers two visions of a bestial woman, Hazel the sexual libertine and Frampucca the jealous, devious virago. We first see Hazel fainting at the "milk-white knob" of her father's house. A parenthetical aside distinguishes her from the other women: "no babe whimpered at the breast bone nor was there snow in the air." Instead, Hazel has been "hot-footing" with her boyfriend. Her father accuses her of "setting her chin out from the family" and promptly tosses her out, but not before "beard[ing] her night trick," again, an ambiguous reference to incest. The Lord offers Hazel to Frampucca's frazzled butcher-husband, Gonzales, as an extramarital gift for "having taken in marriage a Christ day resenter, a terrible creature who walked on her two feet as if they were four, whose one eye was dour for the sake of the other" (39). To hide their liaison, Hazel dresses as a boy in galligaskins and calls herself Gavin, but the body cannot be hidden beneath clothes. Frampucca recognizes that she "was no more girl than the pout of her breeks [breeches] would suggest" (39). But Gonzales and Hazel are hardly discrete. They take to "sweet kissing" under a "mythically roving moon" in "gall-spotted" pastures. "Could matters so stand?" the narrator asks with an air of inevitable destruction.

The jealous wife murders Hazel because "lore *must* be served; tragedy must come from all points of the compass. The Hellenic gesture, Epic injustice, were in those days, things that did not see the brains of scholars alone; oftimes the exceeding small inch of damnation called a feminine skull could catch out scorpions, and such an inch had Frampucca" (39–40). Barnes dramatizes the murder as a parodic aggression against female sexuality. Unlike Don Juan B.C., whose revenge is a spontaneous, momentary but justifiable loss of control (a crime of passion, in other words), Frampucca concocts a grotesque, premeditated demise for her rival: Hazel is roasted alive "like a queen in her chamber" in the belly of Gonzales' best white ox.

Frampucca's bestial nature is an affront to Gonzales' masculinity. "Scattered and harried by the hell in his wife," he recalls Don Juan B.C. with his head of "fleecy thorns" (40). He hardly seems worthy of the bull, "the hero of the herd," whose fertility is figured into the arch of its horns. While the ox models "a gibbus [a rounded bulge] of plenty against the night sky," Gonzales scurries about in an apron, his tapes "stiff as the switch in the tail of an ass, what with hurrying hither and yon at her bidding." Yet Hazel's murder, far from further diminishing his phallic power, confers upon Gonzales a tragic status. No longer an ass, he assumes the imagery of a soldier: "Who was it gave out that long wailing cry like a bell torn from the arms of the hour? Gonzales going head forward, headlong, at battle alone" (41). While the murder bears an obvious negative effect on the two women, it inspires the masculinity Gonzales has long lacked, much as the funeral possession confers upon Don Juan B.C. the public respect that he privately lacks in his marriage. The transformation is the most egregious display of the bias of history: If the primary voice is masculine, as the opening invocation suggests, Barnes implies that, whatever its truth, history is told to the advantage of its authors. She caps the point by ending the story with a one-line memorial to these victims borrowed both from *Hamlet* and Eliot's *The Waste Land*: "Farewell, Ladies, farewell! farewell!" (41). The phrase implies less concern with the tragedy of the women than their value as tragic figures. It also brings the text to an ironic full circle by inverting the story's title. "Run Girls, Run" urges women to escape history, but the farewell suggests that, simply for their lives to make the official record, they must submit or bow down to the roles dictated by myth and legend.

Even more than Stein then, Barnes depersonalizes narrative addresses by locating the writtenness of her style in typographic cues that serve as visual rather than vocal markers of authorial presence. Parentheses, random capitalization, and spelling inflect into speech genres a dissonance that circulates without reference to a physical speaker, thus freeing the parodic voice from the sorts of limiting story lines that confine the voiceless "convicts" in the vignettes. Because the opposition between orality and writing here reverses the values ascribed to each medium by Romantic storytellers, Barnes's style exemplifies the expressive freedom that print offered modernists. For Irving, orality erodes the anonymity of address in written discourse by dramatizing the circulation of his legend among at least three simultaneous audiences. For Barnes, however, the spoken word signifies the conformity of history and tradition, which can only be ruptured by graphic gestures that confound the illusory univocality of the narrative speech act. Like "The Legend of Sleepy Hollow," "Run Girls, Run" dramatizes how retellings inform stories with multiple perspectives. But while Irving layers the text with storytelling frames that subtly preclude attribution to a single speaker, Barnes suggests that these single voices themselves strain to hide the contradictory resonances that arise in their articulation. Crafting a style that amalgamates various rhetorical modes, Barnes allows these resonances free play in her voice, resulting in a continuous juxtaposition of idioms that parodies the authority by which speakers invoke myth and history.

10

Richard Wright: Free Indirect Discourse, Dialect, and Empathy in "Almos' a Man"

"Run Girls, Run" illustrates how free indirect discourse can undermine the deceptively unified voice of a storyteller by exposing the whispering contradictions repressed in the rhetorical modes and styles she/he employs. The paradox of the story lies in the fact that to recognize the cues by which the stereotypical representations of women are ridiculed and rewritten we must presume a central authorial presence actively parodying them. In effect, we must reinstitute the textual authority of Barnes's voice that, within the work itself, is rigorously disassembled. Richard Wright's "Almos' a Man" (1940)—better known in its revised form as "The Man Who Was Almost a Man," published in the posthumous story collection *Eight Men* (1961)[41]—offers an equally complex example of the ambiguous interplay between character voices and authorial styles in modernist stories. Although it is Wright's best-known short fiction, it has attracted surprisingly little critical attention. The isolated commentary that exists treats the tale as a comedy of errors staged at the expense of its adolescent hero, Dave Saunders, whose intense desire to be recognized as a man has been interpreted (at best) as naïve and (at worst) as immature. Edward Margolies summarizes the critical consensus when he writes that "the pathos of the story lies in the poverty of Dave's dreams. For him, as for most adolescents, manhood is the highest order of achievement—but his paucity of social and emotional experience makes him view that goal in the image of a gun."[42] Because Dave accidentally shoots his employer's mule the first time he fires the weapon that symbolizes his masculinity, critics assume that Wright is satirizing the desire for power.

My reading challenges this conventional interpretation by analyzing the relationship between the narrating voice and Dave's internal thoughts and feelings. Rather than parody the quest for manhood, the storyteller endorses it by strategically revising the black dialect in which Dave expresses himself into an objective, omniscient style that (ostensibly) universalizes his longing. Free indirect discourse for Wright is not a device for inflecting contradictory voices into the text, as it is for Barnes. Instead, it allows him to lend the authority of his own narrative voice to Dave's desire and to validate it through strategic acts of repetition that encourage readers to empathize with Dave. As we shall see, when we read "Almos' a Man" in the context of Wright's ambivalence toward black vernacular traditions (which he felt too easily succumbed to racial stereotyping), a parodic interpretation of the story contradicts the author's intent as it can best be reconstructed. The degree to which one senses that Dave is worthy either of pity or compassion depends finally upon the degree to which one associates the beliefs of Richard Wright with the voice telling the story.

The mesh of voices in "Almos' a Man" is obvious from its opening passage: "Dave struck out across the fields, looking homeward through paling light. Whuts the usa talkin wid em niggers in the field? Anyhow, his mother was putting supper on the table. Them niggers can't understan *nothing*. One of these days he was going to get a gun and practice shooting, then they can't talk to him as though he were a little boy. He slowed, looking at the ground. Shucks, Ah ain scareda them even ef they are biggern me!" (356). Three attributional forms are juxtaposed here: (1) the narrative voice that records exterior actions and events ("he slowed"); (2) free indirect discourse, in which Dave's thoughts are expressed in the style of that unmarked voice ("one of these days"); and (3) interior monologue, in which Dave's thoughts are expressed in his own black idiom ("Ah ain scareda"). The co-presence of the final two styles is curious. Interior monologue is defined as a more descriptive style of free indirect discourse meant to represent a character's unspoken thoughts without a narrator's intervention. Distinguished by first-person pronouns and the present tense, it is the equivalent of dialogue without the quotation marks. Because it is a less-mediated style of representation that submerges us in a protagonist's consciousness, interior monologue has long been regarded as the quintessential device for prompting reader empathy. In "Almos' a Man," however, the juxtaposed sentences of free indirect discourse diminish the immediacy credited with encouraging this response. Side by side, the two modes create a perspectival uncertainty, for the storyteller allows certain thoughts to be heard in Dave's own voice but assumes responsibility for articulating others.

Understanding why Wright would mingle these attributional forms necessitates recognizing his long running resistance to incorporating black dialect into his own narrative voice. Wright *did* speak favorably of some representations of black speech, most memorably in a review of Stein's *Wars I Have Seen* (1945), in which he describes reading her short story "Melanctha" (published in *Three Lives*) in the early 1930s: "My ears were opened for the first time to the magic of the spoken word. I began to hear the speech of my grandmother, who spoke a deep, pure Negro dialect. All of my life I had been only half hearing, but Miss Stein's struggling words made the speech of the people around me vivid. From that moment on, in my attempts at writing, I was able to tap at will the vast pool of living words that swirled around me." Suspicious that he might be "worshipping decadence" by admiring the mere literariness of Stein's style, he decided to conduct an experiment to test the realism of her prose: "I gathered a group of semi-literate Negro stockyard workers . . . into a Black Belt basement and read 'Melanctha' aloud to them. . . . Enthralled, they slapped their thighs, howled, laughed, stomped and interrupted me constantly to comment upon the characters."[43] Several commentators have questioned the veracity of Wright's account, for one need not dive too deep into the "vast pool of living words" in "Melanctha" to recognize that it is hardly authentic black dialect. The scene is nevertheless a central motif of minority literature, dramatizing the community and mutuality of an audience sharing in its folk traditions.

Yet such scenes of intraracial, communal identification are rare in Wright's fiction, for, as John McCluskey, Jr., suggests, he was "bound to a rhetorical strategy that precluded a sense of supporting [folkloric] traditions."[44] The strategy to which he committed himself can be reconstructed from a number of essays and reviews in which he sketched the limitations of the vernacular tradition. In the 1940 essay "How 'Bigger' Was Born," he describes how he forged his style with mainstream modernist strategies to create a character in *Native Son* whose tragedy transcended race, for "Bigger Thomas was not black all the time; he was white, too, and there were literally millions of him, everywhere." To make Bigger a symbol of a broader "behavioristic pattern which grew out of a more subtle and broader [social and economic] frustration" than racism, required him to look beyond black traditions toward the literary styles of the dominant culture. Wright explains, "I took these techniques [of 'white writers' that he knew], these ways of seeing and feeling, and twisted them, bent them, adapted them, until they became my ways of apprehending the locked-in life of the Black Belt Areas. This association with white writers was the life preserver of my hope to depict Negro life in fiction, for my race possessed no fictional works dealing with such problems, had no background in such hard and critical testing of experience."[45]

In Wright's mind, appropriating modernist storytelling strategies allowed him to free black writing from the dialect that, in a well-known 1937 review of Zora Neale Hurston's *Their Eyes Were Watching God,* he dismissed as a "minstrel technique that makes 'white folks' laugh . . . [by] exploit[ing] that phase of Negro life which is 'quaint,' the phase which evokes a piteous smile on the lips of the 'superior' race." The use of black dialect by Hurston and her Harlem Renaissance contemporaries allowed the existing African-American literary tradition to be stereotyped as "humble" and "decorous," thus crippling its incipient power as an agent of social change. As he suggests in "Blueprint for Negro Writing" (1938), only by turning to the devices of "Eliot, Stein, Joyce, Proust, Hemingway, and Anderson" could a writer express the "deep, informed, and complex consciousness" heretofore absent in black writing.[46]

Wright's unwillingness to incorporate black vernacular into his style has long condemned him to an ambivalent place in the African-American literary tradition. From Ralph Ellison and James Baldwin to Robert Stepto and a host of contemporary critics, his failure to experiment with black folk expression the way Harlem Renaissance writers like Hurston did marks the limitations of his naïve polemicism, his inability to imagine an authorial voice that could blend modernist poetics and the African-American idiom rather than reject one in favor of the other. Of such criticism, the most relevant is Henry Louis Gates's *The Signifying Monkey,* which contrasts the narrative strategies of *Native Son* to those of Hurston's *Their Eyes Were Watching God.* Hurston's narrative voice, first cast in standard English, gradually absorbs the speech style of various characters, including the book's protagonist Janie, until it speaks for an entire community by mingling multiple perspectives in her idiom. Free indirect discourse provides Hurston a tool for fashioning an "authentic narrative voice that echoes and aspires to the status of the impersonality, anonymity, and authority of the black vernacular tradition, a nameless, selfless tradition, at once collective and compelling." Wright's style, by contrast, displays an inveterate individualism, for he refuses to relinquish "what Roland Barthes calls the 'proprietary consciousness,' the constant sign of his presence and of some larger context, which the third-person voice inevitably entails." While he employs free indirect discourse in *Native Son,* Bigger's thoughts are transcribed into standard English, not black dialect, which appears in the novel only between quotation marks.[47]

As we have seen, black dialect *does* appear in sentences of interior monologue in "Almos' a Man," although they are framed by free indirect discourse. But the odd interplay between the character and authorial voices represents less of an unhealthy individualism than an early struggle to resolve the stylistic issue that, in "Blueprint for Negro Writing," Wright describes as "the problem of perspective." If African-American literature is to transcend its cultural status as primitive and simplistic, it must reach beyond its immediate audience to force all readers to recognize the complexity and meaningfulness of black life. To do so, a storyteller must speak from a "fixed point in intellectual space where [he] stands to view the struggle, hopes, and sufferings of his people." This perspective is a "pre-conscious assumption," an intuitive, informed angle of vision by which the minority writer can "create in his readers' minds a relationship between a Negro woman hoeing cotton in the South and the men who loll in swivel chairs in Wall Street and take the fruits of her toil." Although Wright's definition of the term is exceedingly impressionistic, one can extrapolate to suggest the effect he intended. When he claims that perspective allows African-American writers to compare "the harsh lot of their race" with "the hopes and struggle of minority peoples everywhere," he implies that it is a force of empathy. As it immerses us within the "complexity, the strangeness, the magic wonder" of black life, it seeks to overcome alienating racial differences by challenging readers to recognize the psychological depth that they may have presumed minority characters incapable of experiencing. What Gates sees as the "proprietary consciousness" of his style, Wright would argue is the "functional autonomy" of perspective; as a dialectical agency, it conveys the "the fluid state of [African-American] daily speech" while transcending the stereotypes by which the surrounding dominant culture minimizes its affective power. In "Almos' a Man," the juxtaposition of interior monologue and free indirect discourse realizes this prerogative, for as the former expresses Dave's idiomatic longings, the latter encourages empathy by revising them into standard English.

The need to establish the autonomy of one's perspective is a central theme of "Almos' a Man." This theme is realized through a matrix of thematic oppositions—not only black vs. white, but child vs. parent, interior vs. exterior, psychology vs. sociology, and, most important, man vs. boy, all of which illustrate how cultural connotations restrict the healthy development of black self-image. *Boy*, for example, has two obvious meanings, identifying Dave both as an adolescent and a black male. When whites like Joe the store owner and Jim Hawkins, his boss, speak of Dave as "nuthin' but a boy," both meanings are inevitably invoked. For Dave to achieve manhood, the story implies, he must see himself outside of the restrictive, pejorative terms of white culture.

Especially for critics of Wright's individualism, the dominant culture also shapes meanings within the minority community of "Almos' a Man" as racial markers like *boy* determine relations between blacks. Dave refers to the other field hands as *niggers*. When he asks his mother if he can buy a gun, she says, "Nigger, is yuh gone plumb crazy?" Regardless of who speaks, language is a force of deception and manipulation. When Dave reminds his mother that she promised him a gun, she disowns her words: "Ah don care whut Ah promised! Yuh ain nothing but a boy yit!"[48] Dave himself lies repeatedly, telling his mother that he has been talking with other boys when he was borrowing Joe's catalogue, and later, telling his father that he threw the gun into the creek when he actually buried it beside a tree. His most egregious lie comes, of course, when he claims that Jenny the mule impaled itself on the plow after he accidentally shoots it. Knowing that the lie will fail, he realizes that the truth is too humiliating to confess: "He could not tell Jim Hawkins he had shot his mule. But he had to tell something. Yeah, Ahll tell em Jenny started gittin wil n fell on the joint of the plow. . . . But that would hardly happen to a mule" (365). In an environment in which words are a force of oppression, not even lying affords one sanctuary from humiliation.

The scene in which Dave confesses to shooting Jenny is the most dramatic rendering of the text's thematic oppositions, suggesting why he must ultimately jump a northbound train to that ambiguous "somewhere" where he can be a man. Unlike a contemporaneous Wright story like "Big Boy Leaves Home," in which the hero also escapes by train, the minority community in "Almos' a Man" offers neither support nor encouragement. The crowd that gathers to gawk at the dead beast, which includes Dave's parents and Jim Hawkins, is biracial. Dave, reduced to tears, "see[s] blurred white and black faces," the color line blended by his humiliation. The individual voices in the crowd are not distinguished by variations in dialect; the community acts uniformly in ridiculing Dave's attempt to lie:

> Somebody in the crowd laughed. Jim Hawkins walked close to Dave and looked into his face.
>
> "Well, looks like you have bought you a mule, Dave."
>
> "Ah swear fo Gawd, Ah didn't go t kill the mule, Mistah Hawkins!"
>
> "But you killed her!"
>
> All the crowd was laughing now. They stood on tiptoe and poked heads over one another's shoulders.
>
> "Well, boy, looks like yuh done bought a dead mule! Hahaha!"
>
> "Ain tha ershame."
>
> "Hohohohoho."
>
> Dave stood, head down, twisting his feet in the dirt. (367)

Conflating the response of the townsfolk into collective speech acts such as "ain tha ershame" and "hohohohoho," Wright implies that the homogeneity of the community perspective takes shape as a force that must be resisted.

Precisely how the odd shifts between interior monologue and

free indirect discourse convey this theme of manhood and individualism can be illustrated through the evocative metaphor of "black (w)holeness" that Houston A. Baker argues is the central trope of Wright's writing. What prompts Dave to retrieve the gun and re-fire it after his scene of humiliation is an intense awareness of his minority status in the community: "Dam em *all!* Nobody ever gave him anything. All he did was work. They treat me lika mule. . . . N then they beat me. . . . He gritted his teeth. N Ma had t tell on me" (368). The moment evokes what Baker describes as the black self's sudden awareness of his or her "zero image" in the "perceptual schemes of the white, dominant culture." The realization prompts the first stage of the "rites of the black (w)hole," a ritual passage into a self-defined identity, which, as his pun implies, Baker illustrates with the metaphor of the collapsed star whose intense concentration of mass reverses gravitational fields, drawing all light to its core.[49] "Almos' a Man" is wholly compatible with this ritualistic passage since, as the title suggests, what Dave desires is an escape from the dependency of adolescence to the self-sufficiency of manhood. "The trope of the black hole," writes Baker, "suggests a 'squeezing' of matter of zero sum." The individual, having absorbed the "zero image" that he or she embodies in the dominant culture, appropriates and compresses it to a zero mass, nullifying it by the sheer force of his or her unrealized desire.

In "Almos' a Man," the act of squeezing the gun's trigger symbolizes this moment of compression. In both shooting scenes, the firing of the gun is the pivotal moment of transformation, the line that Dave momentarily hesitates to cross. Although he associates its power with manhood—"if he were holding his gun in his hand nobody could run over him; they would have to respect him" (362)—it is a force that nevertheless frightens him. In the first scene, when he fatally wounds Jenny, the firing knocks him to the ground, where he finds "himself on his knees, squeezing his fingers hard between his legs" (363). But after the crowd humiliates him, the gun becomes a more attractive object of desire as he convinces himself that "ef other men kin shoota gun, by Gawd, Ah kin!" As he empties the chambers, the storyteller repeats this line in free indirect discourse: "With effort he held his eyes open; then he squeezed. . . . *Bloooom! Bloooom! Click, click!* There! It was empty. If anybody could shoot a gun, he could" (369). The recasting of these thoughts into the unmarked style establishes that Dave—at least in his own mind—has passed into manhood, for he has killed the community's image of him as a beast of burden, as someone who would allow them to "treat [him] lika mule."

By delineating Dave's discovery of his potential "black (w)holeness" in the face of oppression, "Almos' a Man" dramatizes the spark of desire that transforms the unshaped consciousness into the autonomous individual. The internal struggle of this formation suggests why Wright used the more experientially immediate mode of interior monologue, because direct access to Dave's thoughts signals what Baker calls the "code of desire" whose energy traps and collapses cultural stereotypes. Yet the very dialect in which Dave's desire is voiced is itself a social discourse subject to stereotyping, namely the minstrel-show versions of black vernacular to which Wright linked Hurston's style. As a literary convention, dialect can perpetuate the same distribution of authority to which the African-American community in "Almos' a Man" has fallen prey. The shifts between private monologue and free indirect discourse thus mark Wright's effort to capture the private intensity of Dave's struggle for expression without allowing his own language to evoke conventional styles of African-American dialect.

Baker's reading of Wright's autobiography *Black Boy* (1945) suggests just how the unmarked narrative voice might inspire readers to identify intuitively with Dave. Describing the books that shaped his desire to flee the South as a youth, Wright offers an intriguing passage in which he claims to have cared little for "plots and stories," reading instead for the perspective that they offered: "I hungered for books, new ways of looking and seeing. It was not a matter of believing or disbelieving what I read, but of feeling something new, of being affected by something that made the look of the world different" (272). According to Baker, here Wright extracts from his reading "correlative structures" of desire that supply "an equivalent to that 'terribly important' *something* found absent" in his own life: "What he seeks, one might say, is a *difference* that will fulfill desire" (146). As a writer, Wright's own literary project aims to inspire in his audience a similar recognition of this absence. His goal is analogous to Roland Barthes's vision of "zero-degree writing," for by universalizing perspective as a quest for the "trace of desire," he inverts and nullifies the "fixed discursive norms" that define a particular moment in literary history. As Baker writes, "A beautifying, 'literary' language is a restrictive array of conventions preserving class division, maintaining the status quo surfaces of life, *creating desire* rather than elaborating its transcendence" (148). In other words, a dialect that emphasizes racial difference creates sympathy or pity, not empathy. Only by crafting an objective style can Wright inspire readers to identify intuitively with his characters.

The pattern of perspectival shifts in "Almos' a Man" exemplifies how Wright attempts to encode desire into an anti-literary language, for free indirect discourse serves as a rhetorical hedge that extinguishes lingering stereotypes of black vernacular by transmuting Dave's desire, expressed in interior monologue, into non-linguistic structures of vision and feeling. Predominantly cast in the form of exclamatory utterances, interior monologue emphasizes the intensity of Dave's desire: "Ahma git some money from Ma n buy me a gun! Only *two* dollahs!" Free indirect discourse repeatedly revises such statements, shifting the narrative perspective away from its expression to its perception. As Dave stares at Joe's catalogue, the feeling of desire moves from the cognitive to the tactile realm: "Lawd, ef Ah only had tha pretty one! He could almost feel the slickness of the weapon with his fingers. If he had a gun like that he would polish and keep it shining so it would never rust. N Ah'd keep it loaded, by Gawd!" (360). In such moments, desire takes shape as a prayer-like invocation—many of the interior-monologue fragments either begin with "Lawd," "by Gawd," or some variation of the two—that is then answered by the narrative voice, which both emphasizes and validates Dave's growing self-consciousness.

One of the minor revisions that Wright made shortly before his death in 1960 further illuminates the unfolding pattern of these shifts. In the 1940 version, Dave awakens the morning after he buys the gun: "In the gray light of dawn he held it loosely, feeling a sense of power. Could killa man wida gun like this. Kill anybody, black er white" (362). In the *Eight Men* (1961) version, however, the last sentence of the passage is rewritten into standard English. In the first case, the desire to murder dramatizes the lengths Dave is willing to go to "collapse" the community's image of him. In the revision, the narrator endorses the impulse, ostensibly universalizing it by lifting the desire out of Dave's dialectically marked perspective into the non-linguistic realm of intuitive, communal feeling. The new title likewise suggests a revisionary staging of the quest for "black (w)holeness." While "Almos' a Man" is a direct quotation of Dave's longing, "The Man Who Was Almost a Man" renders that desire tautological, for this *boy* only needs to realize that he is already a man to be one.

There are several explanations for why Wright stopped incorporating dialect into his narrative voice sometime between "Almos' a Man" and *Native Son*. In "How 'Bigger' Was Born," he describes his dissatisfaction with the reception of his 1938 story collection, *Uncle Tom's Children*, as his own failure to render the rebellion of its protagonists without provoking pity: "I found that I had written a book in which even bankers' daughters could read and weep over and feel good about. I swore to myself that if I ever wrote another book, no one would weep over it; that it would be so hard and deep that they would have to face it without the consolation of tears" (874). To rephrase this in Baker's terms, Wright finds that his stories inspire condescending sympathy or pity, not an empathy that transcends racial difference. To ensure the right sort of identification, Wright must resist blending other voices with his own so his point will not be ambiguous. He must try to "*render, depict,* [and] not merely tell the story" by stylistically foregrounding his "way of apprehending"—a task whose difficulty he openly admits: "Sometimes I'd find it necessary to use a stream of consciousness technique, then rise to an interior monologue, descend to a direct rendering of a dream state, then to a matter-of-fact depiction of what Bigger was saying, doing, and feeling. Then I'd find it impossible to say what I wanted to say without stepping in and speaking outright on my own" (878).

A storyteller's ability to speak "outright" and limit possible interpretations of his tale depends upon an ideologically compatible audience attuned to his motives, or at least one that can decode them in his style. Free indirect discourse may actually discourage this compatibility rather than enhance it because it complicates perceptions of narrative address, making it difficult to determine who is speaking. In the absence of an explicit storytelling exchange, audiences will choose between an empathetic or ironic reading according to their opinion of the subject rendered, one inevitably formed by *their*—not the writer's—belief system. The ambiguity of interior monologue and free indirect discourse helps explain why their interplay in "Almos' a Man" seems to distance most readers from Dave's quest rather than persuade them to identify with it. Especially for those who do not share Wright's equation of individuality with masculinity and violence, the unmarked narrative voice is powerless to legitimate Dave's exclamations. Because we inflect our own values into its seemingly objective tonality, we can easily assume that it speaks for what we take to be the voice of communal common sense, which judges the masculine individuality Dave desires as childish and immature. The fact that the narrative voice does not explicitly parody Dave's quest should caution unsympathetic readers to question just how they arrived at that interpretation. Unfortunately, the story's critical history reveals that audiences rarely recognize this imperative of self-interrogation.

James Baldwin's reading of "The Man Who Was Almost a Man" reveals how this tendency works to Wright's disadvantage. Baldwin describes how its "dry, savage folkloric humor . . . made [him] think of human loss and helplessness." He places the tale in the context of those folk traditions that Wright felt lacked expressive power, thus undermining the seriousness of Dave's desire for a self-fashioned "black (w)holeness" by receiving him an as inept figure. As "Alas, Poor Richard" (1963) makes clear, Baldwin's antipathy for Wright's polemicism prevents him from identifying with the authorial voice; indeed, he willfully does away with Wright's presence in the text. The death of the author—in this case, not an interpretive tactic but a biographical fact—means that "the baffling creator no longer stands between us and his works," and the reader is free to perceive "the genuine Richard Wright, who was being recorded all along." Whether his author figure is genuine is certainly questionable, for Baldwin imagines a storyteller who self-consciously contradicts the very intentions that Wright publicized through manifestos like "Blueprint for Negro Writing" and "How 'Bigger' Was Born."

Yet one need not share Baldwin's disdain for "militant" black literature to interpret the narrative voice in "Almos' a Man" as ironic. Many college anthologies, for example, eschew questions of authorial intent in favor of purely formalist readings in which Dave's quest for manhood is again presumed ironic:

> So accustomed is Dave to the invisibility of his race (that is, blacks are disregarded as men, as legitimate human beings with full rights) that he inadvertently undermines his own credibility when he acts irresponsibly, hiding the gun and shooting it. . . . From a psychological point of view, one could regard this scene [Jenny's death] as symbolic of Dave's fear of his own manhood. . . . Dave's limited self-perception results from a combination of immaturity and the low self-esteem he struggles to rid himself of, primarily through *a misconception of the power of violence*.[50]

From a different psychological point of view, as Baker's "black (w)hole" theory suggests, the shooting scenes can be read as expressing a commendable desire for manhood, not the fear of it, and "the power of violence" would only be a misconception for readers who perceive Dave's quest as ironic.

Successful or not, Wright's efforts to establish a voice that would lead readers to identify intuitively with the dramatic perspective illustrates the degree to which the singularity of the authorial style had become a form of textual authority in modernist styles by the 1940s. If the aesthetic demand for immediacy in short stories precluded employment of the traditional storyteller figure, then idiosyncratic styles allowed writers and readers to reinstate, knowingly or not, the very personality that strategies like indirect speech, dialogue, and free indirect discourse silenced. Wright is unique among the authors examined here, for he foregrounded his intentions to a greater degree than Stein, Barnes, or even Hemingway, whose styles, in a sense, spoke for them, engendering ideological significances in the public domain that often contradicted or subverted the meanings created by conflicting voices in their work. In this sense, the prominence of the narrative voice that revises Dave's interior thoughts into a non-vernacular language has the potential to recuperate the brevity of consumption that modernist devices impede by offering audiences the security of a centralized perspective. Yet the relative influence of the author function on the contradictory readings that "Almos' a Man" accommodates, suggests that a reader's perception of the writer's presence is ultimately determined by his or her individual desire for interpretive guidance.

Epilogue

Though typically regarded as a naturalist, Wright occupies a transitional place in the evolution of modernist styles. With techniques he claims to borrow from white writers like Stein and Hemingway (among others), he delineates the complexity of the black consciousness that he felt the African-American literary tradition failed to convey. As Baker argues, Wright's vision of a universal narrative voice impervious to racial stereotypes is analogous to Roland Barthes's description of a "zero-degree" language that studiously does away with literary affectations. By avoiding stylistic traits like dialect that can invoke readers' prejudices, storytellers transform writing into "a sort of negative mood in which the social or mythical characters of a language are abolished in favour of a neutral and inert state or form." Yet as Barthes admits, neutral styles always succumb to stereotyping as their objectivity erodes into cliché and a trademark form of literary expression "appears afresh in lieu of an indefinite language."[51] In other words, readers inevitably inflect tones into uninflected narrative voices and attribute attitudes to them even as those voices strive to present themselves as pure and unmarked. Like Stein, Hemingway, and Barnes, Wright employed modernist techniques like free indirect discourse to depersonalize his style only to find that his audience inferred a personality.

The complexity that modernist devices create ideally focuses our attention on internal criteria like psychological portraiture and symbolism instead of the storytelling exchange. What defines the stereotypical modernist short story is the self-conscious absence of address. By the 1980s, however, a new style of brevity quickly dubbed "minimalism" arose that reversed the bias toward content over contact. Rather than elide the narrative act, these stories foreground their own internal emptiness, challenging readers to supply the motives for actions and events sketched only in outline. To borrow a phrase from John Barth, the style transforms "the artist's mode or form into a metaphor for his concerns" as stories about the uncertainty of communication call attention to the reticence of the narrative acts articulating them.[52] While critics have debated the literary value of minimalism, few have noticed that its brevity restores storytelling to the prominence with which Romanticism treated it. Indeed, like nineteenth-century tales, minimalist stories evoke oral narrative traditions. But whereas in tales resonances of speech undermine the authority invested in writing, this minimalist economy erodes the temporal distance by which audiences are typically removed from the immediacy of the story. By heightening the reader's perception of his or her temporal participation in the storytelling event, the style solicits a form of creative reception charged with structuring texts that, on the surface, seem resolutely chaotic.

Part 4

The Talking Heads: Time, Tense, and the Minimalist Short Story

Prologue

In July 1984, *Harper's* launched an assault on its closest rival in the periodical fiction market by publishing "The *New Yorker* Story," by Martha Bayles. A writer named William, "striving for an atmosphere of depthless banality," invents a character named Betty, a cashier at J. C. Penney who lacquers her Honeybee Pink lips with Vaseline Lip Balm while daydreaming of meeting her boyfriend for patty melts and shakes at the local Denny's. William experiences an odd mixture of relief and superiority as he describes the "plastic, meaningless shopping mall" where Betty labors. Dropping brand names in a laborious effort to document the consumer obsessions and anxieties of American culture, he secretly knows that he escaped this "palace of materialism" only through the good graces of the *New Yorker*, which first recognized his talents. Had his short story "Fred," about "a middle-aged, Midwestern Middle American who pumps gas, regular and diesel, at a 76 truck stop" not made the pages of the prestigious magazine, William would have remained trapped in this "heartland without a heart to which his imagination keeps returning."

Yet once the author begins delineating the ennui of the breadbasket states, Betty starts taking on airs. She wears diamonds, demands fancy liqueurs, and converses like a heroine from a Fitzgerald story. Shocked, William tries to remind her just who created whom, but Betty complains of the drab existence that she has been bequeathed. "I merely describe. I don't judge," William replies defensively, "you can appreciate that." Betty has a complex story that she wants told. Her boyfriend is abusive, but she loves him anyway; she blames her masochism on her father, who ran off when she was young, but her mother thinks that all she needs to be happy is a friendly chat with the local priest. "Please!" William interrupts her, "I'm a postmodernist writer! No epiphanies, no romanticism! You have to realize, I've accepted the void!" The story ends in a stalemate—Betty pining for a fuller future, William insisting that she return to her cash register. Without recognizing the irony, he rebukes her upper-class pretensions: "Maybe someday you'll figure out that a character is more than a collection of possessions. . . . People are more than the sum total of their commercial surroundings."[1]

As a parody, Bayles's sketch is neither as humorous nor as vituperative as "When Harold Moos Got Gay with Helen Furr," the *Vanity Fair* lampoon of Gertrude Stein. Yet it does take aim at the most identifiable traits of the minimalist short story: There are the clipped, brittle sentences that convey alienation, fragmentation, and attenuated angst and the obsessive devotion to surface detail, including brand names, that creates a paralyzed sense of passive observation. There is also the conspicuous lack of growth or development in both character and plot that would otherwise justify the telling of the story. Finally and most obviously, "The *New Yorker* Story" projects the intense, almost suffocating immediacy engendered by the use of the present tense, whose effects will be the particular focus of this final section of my study.

Two years after the parody, *Harper's* featured an essay by Madison Smartt Bell, a fiction writer himself, which more directly articulates the critical animadversions to these stylistic characteristics. According to Bell, modernist brevity forces readers to infer implied details and imagine the expansive depth floating beneath the circumscribed surface. In a Hemingway story like "A Clean, Well-Lighted Place," the absence of ulterior motive solicits speculative intensity. Hemingway's abbreviated quietude seeks to soothe the wounds of modernity through the epic gesture of reticence; it attempts to shore the ruins of a crumbling ethical code by a conscientious withholding and suffering that, however tragic, strives to be cathartic and purifying. By contrast minimalist economy is superficial. Contemporary story writers like Bobbie Ann Mason and Raymond Carver indulge in an unearned emptiness, creating "people . . . as facelessly uniform as the people on television" while proliferating a "studiedly deterministic, at times nihilistic, vision of the world." Although minimalism requires a certain technical skill, it too frequently effects a "relentless leveling" of nuance through which characters are reduced to a "gee-whiz, *faux-naif* comportment [that] is not always convincing." Like Bayles, who implies that William boils down Betty's life to a list of consumer goods as a way of alleviating his own inferiority complex, Bell finds such portraits disingenuous. He argues that the overwhelming tone of "dime-store determinism" is contrived to draw in the reader "not by identification but by a sort of enlightened, superior sympathy: *I understand the nature of your difficulty; how is it you don't?*"

Bell concludes his critique by facetiously crediting minimalism with compensating for the short story's inability to compete against the novel for status and sales in the marketplace. The sing-song sameness of the style allows publishers to overcome the miscellaneity of the traditional story collection and publicize the product not only to book-buying readers but to a mass audience long distracted by audio and visual media like television, radio, and the cinema: "Because an effective strike at the lowest common denominator appears to require a drastic simplicity of presentation, contemporary big-business publishing places a heavy emphasis on packaging." He quotes a blurb on the cover of Mason's first collection, *Shiloh & Other Stories* (1982), to illustrate the pejorative influence of this "effective strike": "Like O [type] Blood, Bobbie Ann Mason's stories can be given to almost anyone." For Bell, this is a sales pitch masquerading as *faux* populism, an appeal to disposable dollars that suggests that, at heart, minimalism is more of a marketing strategy than an aesthetic style. "Literature might well undertake certain responsibilities abandoned by the rest of the entertainment industry," he concludes in a hopeful passage on repositioning art as cultural criticism. "Against the increasing homogeneity of our society, any strike for individualism made in fiction is useful. If our lives do in fact lack variety and meaning, maybe we had better make haste to invent some."[2]

If minimalism in the 1980s was a capitalist venture rather than an artistic pursuit, minimalist bashing quickly became its cottage-industry counterpart as critics trained in modernist aesthetics fired off increasingly virulent attacks on the style, its artists, and even the short story itself. In *Talents and Technicians: Literary Chic and the New Assembly-Line Fiction* (1991), John W. Aldridge quotes Bell's essay extensively, even revising his succinct title, "Less is Less" (a play on the minimalist battle cry "Less is more") into a more emphatic "Less is a Lot Less" to head one chapter. Minimalism, as another chapter title intones, is a "medium without message," a style in which "technique is paramount and content is as negligible as it is lacking in thematic point."[3] For Aldridge, this absence of thematic substance highlights the most baleful influence of minimalism, its widespread popularity in university-sponsored creative-writing programs, in which parvenu writers bereft of a singular subject matter can gain a semblance of professional proficiency without ever discovering and crafting their own unique literary vision. While the vogue for an essay entitled "Less is Really a Lot Less" may have passed, the so-called "style wars" continue to rage in the mid-1990s. A 1993 issue of the *AWP Chronicle*, the newsletter servicing campus writing programs, features an article by Bob Shacochis, the award-winning short-story writer, which chides students for adopting minimalism as their "official voice" and "official language" to the detriment of local color.[4] As his argument implies, the seeming generic simplicity of the mode threatens the stylistic singularity by which modernism defines the literary voice. Because minimalist stories flout internal complexity, they are too simplistic, too unambiguous, and too easy to read to be literature.

A striking feature of the one-sided debate over the merits of minimalism is how liberally complaints against it borrow from the traditional canon of complaints against the short story itself. William O'Rourke summarizes much of the critical dissatisfaction with the mode and the marketplace in his discussion of the "special economics of the short story form." A short story, he claims, is "capital intensive" because the time invested in its composition is greater than the time required to consume it. Of course, the consumption of any type of writing would logically seem less than its production, but the novel, according to O'Rourke, is "labor intensive" because the investment ratio between production and consumption is more proportional (though hardly equal). What makes the short story fashionable in an age of instant gratification is the quicker return on the investment—a stance recalling Fred Lewis Pattee's argument in 1923 that the short story promised "instant returns." O'Rourke quotes from a 1985 interview with Roger Angell, Mason's one-time editor at the *New Yorker*, to summarize his argument:

> "There's a great national factory out there. If you open the windows, you can hear the sound of typewriters driven by people writing stories all over the country. It may tell something about the state of the novel that this seems to be a particularly good time for the short story." What the sound of typewriters should tell Angell is that the writing of novels in the "national factories"—serious, literary (written, rather than oral) novels, macro-form, labor-intensive, vertebrate as they are—is an unprofitable enterprise, a fact which the newest generation of writers has (unconsciously, at least) assimilated, and that is why all those typewriters are pounding out micro-form, capital-intensive, exoskeletal short stories.[5]

In a market-oriented society in which the novel, as "serious" literature, is a long-term investment, the brevity of the short story tempts with the possibility of instant gains. The lure of easy money and inflated reputation cripples the growth of the fiction economy by opening the market to get-rich-quick schemes. From this perspective, minimalism, requiring even less capital than most styles because it is presumably easy to write, might be described as the literary equivalent of a junk bond. But to reverse the metaphor, the collateral that finances many anti-minimalist arguments is the same portfolio of critical prejudices against which Poe defined the tale, including the truism that bulk is totemic of aesthetic value. If Poe reacted against the belief that American literature had to be culturally bigger than its British competition, Bell, Aldridge, and Shacochis all invoke the "larger-art" criteria of modernism (depth of characterization, formal ambiguity, resistance to consumption) to dismiss minimalism's simplicity.

By the mid-1980s, in fact, minimalism had become such a negative label that Mason and Carver, not to mention the majority of their contemporaries, refused to be associated with it. "I don't like the term 'minimalism,'" Carver told one interviewer. "I don't like that term at all. Like a lot of other things in life, this too will pass. A few years from now all the writers being labeled 'minimalist' will be labeled something else, or not." Mason's disdain is equally laconic: "I'm not sure what's meant by minimalism. I'm not sure if it means something that is just so spare that there is hardly anything there . . . or if it's just a misnomer for what happens in any good short story, which is economy."[6] While John Barth defended the style in the *New York Times Book Review* in 1986, and Frederick Barthleme volleyed back at critics with an essay glibly subtitled "Convicted Minimalist Spills Bean," most writers associated with Carver and Mason placed themselves squarely in the realist tradition, leaving academic critics to develop Mason's suggestion that minimalism is a "misnomer" for an element universal in all short stories (and all narratives)—economy.

The prevailing strategy for resuscitating minimalist fiction after the initial flood of critical opprobrium has been to describe its affinities with the canonical postmodernism of Barth, Robert Coover, and Thomas Pynchon. Thus Carver and Mason, like postmodernists, "are suspicious of 'depth,' seeing that the (by now) traditional models of depth are unsupportable; instead they present a play of surfaces"; they "accept the effacement of the border between 'high' culture and 'popular' or 'commercial' culture, and they use the merging of the two for establishing wider cultural possibilities."[7] Their style manifests a "highly self-conscious response to the postmodern critique of representation, one which knowingly simulates a 'return' to plain style while remaining properly ironic about the discredited representational conventions on which plain style rests." Ultimately the "debate surrounding minimalist fiction has served much the same function within the writers' community" as the debate over post-structuralism within "academic scholarly circles" by calling attention to the basically fictive nature of all strategies of mimetic representation.[8] These arguments are certainly convincing, but as the last quotation implies, the aim to date has been to justify minimalist fiction as a valid area for research within the academy rather than exploring why it might arise at this point in the development of the American short story.

I argue that the controversy over the literary value of minimalism—essentially a formalist debate—loses much of its relevance if one substitutes Benjamin's theory of the cultural function of storytelling for the aesthetic paradigms of modernism. To be sure, the slacker bonhomie sometimes suggested by the radical economy of the mode may seem contrived and pretentious, just as the modernist angst of a collection like Barnes's *A Book* could strike reviewers as "cesspool literature." In many cases, however, minimalism's verbal sparsity marks an open embrace of storytelling after the hostility that modernism reserved for it. Here the analogy to Hemingway's economy is insightful. If he identifies himself as a consummate modernist by minimizing traces of his authorial agency so that his narratives are (ostensibly) self-contained, Mason and Carver tend to efface everything *but* the narration, for the surface upon which their stories glide is the moment of performance, which imbues their texts with a confessional aura. Depth in modernist stories is analogous to what Benjamin describes as "information," the psychological analysis and explanation that block creative reception by bloating the audience with facts that must be digested. Minimalist narrators, by contrast, take to heart Benjamin's imperative that "half the art of storytelling is to keep a story free from explanation as one reproduces it." The resulting works require what Karl Kroeber calls "contributory feedback" through which audiences must "create something out of the telling."[9] Despite the claims of aestheticians, many minimalist stories are not too easy to read; the slice of life that they offer may be profoundly depressing or even nihilistic, but their sparsity is a reticence not unlike Jewett's conspicuous silence in "A White Heron" that encourages active participation in the narrative exchange.

The device most responsible for emphasizing the function of storytelling in minimalist stories is the present tense, which redefines the narrator's traditional temporal orientation toward his or her material. As my reading of "Bartleby" implies, the most common temporal stance in written narrative is retrospective, a remembrance of things past in which a story and its telling are separated by some degree of time. The traditional past tense conveys the authority of experience, endowing the discourse with the authenticity of history so the narrative voice assumes a testimonial function. Retrospection and testimony in turn influence structure. Because most Western cultures measure time linearly, the traditional narrative norm is a chronological sequence. Though the order of presentation may not replicate this chronology, time's one-way movement implies a logic of cause and effect that rationalizes the plot of a story. Most theories of narrative development, in fact, model the structure of a story on the forward flow of linear time.

Yet time's influence on structure is itself subject to time and place. The rise of alternative temporal modalities promotes narrative strategies that challenge the conception of a story line as a causal chain. Stephen Kern has shown how innovations like the wireless telegraph, the telephone, and the cinema redefined perceptions of time between 1880 and 1918, raising two important issues that influenced modernist storytelling styles: whether the present was "a sequence of single local events or a simultaneity of multiple distant events, and whether [it was] an infinitesimal slice of time between the past and future or of more extended duration."[10] Amid this debate, Stein began writing in the "continuous present," known to grammarians as the habitual or iterative present tense, which expresses repetition and cycles. Such non-traditional forms have a revolutionary effect on narrative time since a moment is no longer an event in a sequence but an experience contained within itself.

Yet if Stein and other modernists write during an age when technology thickened cultural perceptions of time, minimalists bear witness to its virtual evaporation. As Fredric Jameson argues, the postmodern age is experiencing "the disappearance of a sense of history," for "our entire contemporary social system has little by little begun to lose its capacity to retain its own past, has begun to live in a perpetual present and in a perpetual change that obliterates traditions of the kind which all earlier social formations have had in one way or another sought to preserve."[11] To convey the resulting sense of impermanence, minimalists employ the punctual or instant present tense, the register of momentary experience, as in the opening sentence of Mason's "Shiloh": "Leroy Moffitt's wife, Norma Jean, is working on her pectorals. She lifts three-pound dumbbells to warm up, then progresses to a twenty-pound barbell."[12] Despite the hint of causal sequence that *progresses* brings to the sentence, the tense creates an aura of immediacy that does not accommodate the deeper reflection necessary to determine the logic structuring her actions. Instead, like Leroy, we find ourselves captive spectators bearing witness to the flow of events.

As Mason remarks in at least one interview, the static, episodic world that the present tense projects "obviously came from television" (qtd. in Lyons and Oliver 459). For many critics, television's influence is destructive because it promotes surface over substance, technique over texture, the visual over the visceral. Yet the analogy to electronic media deserves serious exploration, for it highlights two positive revisionary facets of the minimalist short story's structure of address, one structural and the other rhetorical. In the first case, as Raymond Williams has argued, broadcast media have transformed the "structure of feeling" that a sequence invokes. Whereas "a book or pamphlet was [once] taken and read as a specific item," electronic media overwhelm the idiosyncrasy of the single event by assimilating it into a continuous "flow" in which one program bears no more emphasis than what follows.[13] In present-tense narratives, the effect of this structural flow can be unsettling because it flouts expectations for plot development. As time passes, nothing seems to happen because events fail to culminate in significant conclusions. Instead, they pulse and flicker as montages of overlapping, intermingling images and moods.

William Gass, who gives contemporary writers a "failing grade" for their use of the present tense, is correct to say that, like television, minimalist short stories lack dimension. The absence of depth is readily observed in the repetitive sentence structures: "Kept simple, short, direct, like a punch, the sentences avoid subordination, qualification, subtlety. Subordination requires judgment, evaluation; it creates complexity, demands definition."[14] But judgment, evaluation, and definition also require time. By closing the temporal gap that separates the story and its telling, the present tense negates retrospection and limits omniscience to perception, making these evaluative acts impossible. As a result, minimalist stories project a narrative vulnerability in their presentation. As Mason remarks, "If the author is writing in present tense then you get the impression he doesn't know any more than you do about what's happening" (qtd. in Lyons and Oliver 460).[15]

This "impression" is most observable in the texturing of the text, the evaluation of narrative components that linguists call "grounding." Again, because the western narrative norm is sequential, events or actions that advance the plot are traditionally judged more important than the description and commentary that enhance them.[16] In many narratives, a switch from the simple past tense ("I ran") to the progressive past ("I was running") distinguishes a foregrounded event of some plot importance from descriptive background commentary. But in the present tense ("I run"), the difference between these two structural functions can be unclear. As a result, individual reading acts must texture the story as the audience decides, privately, what details should bear more emphasis than others. By not creating complexity, as Gass complains, minimalists invite it by deferring gestures like grounding to the reader.

Gass is also correct to note that the minimalist style avoids subordination. Instead, its predominant syntactical formula is parataxis, the juxtaposing of phrases and clauses without those coordinating conjunctions (*and, but*) whose rhetorical function—the arrangement of discourse into logical sequences—Gilman parodies in "The Yellow Wallpaper." In minimalism, as Philip E. Simmons suggests, parataxis "establishes the primacy of sequence [in the "flowing" sense] over consequence" (48). In "Shiloh," for example, the randomness of parataxis dramatizes the pathos of Leroy Moffitt's search for a sense of purpose in the hobbies he momentarily takes up: "He makes things from craft kits. He started by building a miniature log cabin from notched Popsicle sticks. He varnished it and placed it on the TV set, where it remains. It reminds him of a rustic Nativity scene. Then he tried string art (sailing ships on black velvet), a macramé owl kit, a snap-together B-17 Flying Fortress, and a lamp made out of a model truck, with a light fixture screwed in the top of the cab" (1–2). According to Bob Perelman, such passages reveal how a new type of sentence solicits interpretative authority from readers who must account for connections between verbal elements. "The internal, autonomous meaning of a new sentence," with the content seemingly locked within syntactic structures, "is heightened, questioned, and changed by the degree of separation or connection that the reader perceives with regard to the surrounding sentences." Thus, even if parataxis is "the dominant mode of postindustrial experience," it need not reflect only alienation and fragmentation. By "making the reader renarrativize" sentences to discover a larger "narrative whole" that traditional syntactic structures like subordination dictate, parataxis provides the opportunity for that "contributory feedback" that, according to Karl Kroeber, is the central function of the narrative exchange.[17]

Jameson and Perelman both treat parataxis exclusively as a postmodern phenomenon, yet its peculiar structural organization is characteristic of oral storytelling traditions, including the Greek epic. Similarly, if the present tense seems fairly exotic in written narratives, it is the predominant tense in oral storytelling where it serves the vital interpersonal function of emphasizing the performative act by functioning as a form of direct address. It is not, however, an address that formally invites reader participation, as the pronouns *you* and *one* in "Life in the Iron Mills" do; it provides instead a metalinguistic reminder of the storyteller's presence. This oral strand marks the second revisionary aspect of the present tense, the rhetorical transformation of minimalism's addressivity. Irving embeds the oral roots of "The Legend of Sleepy Hollow" within multiple acts of rewriting (Knickerbocker's transcription of the story, Crayon's inclusion of it in his sketch book). Mason and Carver go to the opposite extreme, however, for through the present tense they hide signs of writing in favor of conversational spontaneity to create a storytelling environment that emphasizes the community and commonality of contact.

This oral strand is not an evocation of the immediacy that, as I suggested in the first chapter, Romanticists employed to undermine the authority of the written word. Instead, it is a technologized style of address; for much as television broadcasts picture and sound, minimalism appeals to the visual and aural faculties. Its "televisual" quality might be properly described as "to tell a visual," for the narration unfolds simultaneously with the events that it narrates, creating an uncertain perspectival relationship between the audience and the drama. On the one hand, as Jameson suggests, the lack of "temporal continuity" in paratactic styles breaks down the connections between words; experienced in isolation, outside its sequential ordering, language becomes more "material" or "literal . . . ever more vivid in sensory ways" so that "the world comes before [us] with heightened intensity, bearing a mysterious and oppressive charge of affect, glowing with hallucinatory energy . . . reorient[ing] the subject or speaker to a more literalizing attention toward those words" (120). Yet the metalinguistic emphasis on the storyteller's presence reminds us that these images are indeed narrated, thus encouraging, as Perelman suggests, "attention to the act of [narration] and to the [storyteller's] particular position within larger social frames" (316). The effect here is analogous to a cinematic voice over in which a visual event is simultaneously narrated, or a first-person narrator (a "talking head"), who announces actions while performing them. As readers, we experience the drama secondhand, aware that the actions that seem utterly immediate and vivid are indeed filtering through a narrative perception.

Mason's "Shiloh" and Carver's "Where I'm Calling From" foreground their narrativity through the present tense as they dramatize the temporal dislocation of the postmodern age. "Shiloh" explores the relationship between public and private history, dramatizing how life loses its sense of meaningful progression as its characters become disengaged from the realm of linear time and find themselves subjected instead to an anxious sense of stasis and immobility. In several of Carver's present-tense narratives, including, most prominently, "Where I'm Calling From," storytelling is a central dramatic motif. As his narrators search for the significance of events in their life, the act of sharing becomes a therapeutic exercise for reconciling past failures with the sobering fact of change. For both writers, the audience's temporal investment in these texts—the pace and rhythm of individual reading styles—significantly determines perceptions of the unfolding drama as the authors create opportunities for collaborative storytelling.

11

Bobbie Ann Mason: "Shiloh" and the Insides of History

The structural flow and conversational spontaneity created by the present tense allow Mason to locate "Shiloh" in a narrative "meantime," a realm in which conventional time is no longer the ultimate authority for explaining the progression of events. The style is particularly relevant to the story's theme, for in the final scene, Leroy Moffitt recognizes that he has ignored the "insides of history," those private pulses of relevance that, in the context of linear time, seem insignificant and meaningless. Leroy makes this recognition only when his marriage falls apart, only after he comes to fear the force of change that his wife Norma Jean represents when their history as a couple no longer matters to her. The temporal displacement that the present tense acts on the reader has a gender-linked corollary: Linear time, as numerous feminist studies argue, is governed by patriarchal values that can exclude women from history by devaluing private temporal modalities.[18] The televisual nature of minimalism is central to conveying this theme. By assuming Leroy's perspective, Mason's storyteller holds Norma Jean in a gaze. She is the object of the narrative eye, and to make sense of her marital dissatisfaction in the absence of more pronounced authorial clues, one must avoid relying on cause-and-effect sequentiality. This interpretive struggle thus parallels Norma Jean's drama, for the audience must free itself from the same linear time scheme that binds her.

This tension between time and its *insides* in "Shiloh" can best be traced by following how the style realizes the theme. On the one hand, Mason supplies enough clues (the characters' ages, references to *Dr. Strangelove* and *Star Trek*) so one may identify a specific historical frame for the story—roughly 1980. Yet within this frame, moments are connected by adverbs of ambiguous temporal value, including *always, sometimes, for a long time, today, in the morning, the next day, four months ago, now, for three months, years ago, all the time, for the past few years, at the moment*. Obviously, any story will contain similar references to time, but Mason employs them so frequently, often bunching them two and three in a single sentence, that they lose their specific reference, creating instead a frustrating sense of "in-betweenness" or alienation from the security of conventional temporality.

Significantly, this alienation is the source of Leroy's own frustration when a trucking accident suddenly makes him homebound: "He has begun to realize that in all the years he was on the road he never took time to examine anything. He was always flying past scenery." For Leroy, time is a "departure, progression and arrival—in other words, time as history," as Julia Kristeva describes linear temporality. As long as highway miles provide the satisfying illusion of "flying" toward a particular destination, Leroy feels both movement and, paradoxically, stability. Progressive temporality feeds what Kristeva calls "monumental time," a register that "has so little to do with linear time (which passes) that the very word 'temporality' hardly fits" (191). Monumental time is infinite like space; within this realm, Leroy's flight finds its structure. The repetition of the intransitive verb *to be* ("Leroy is a truck driver") reveals a durative, fixed concept of identity shoring the ruin of his punctual-present reality. But with his rig now abandoned in the backyard "like a gigantic bird that has flown home to roost," monumental time becomes arrested motion, and he must find "something to kill time" to free him from this uncomfortably static existence. He toys with various craft kits, but his master plan is to build a log cabin, "soon as I get time." With his fall from the masculine realm of linear time, Leroy's homebound life assumes feminine characteristics. As his mother-in-law says when she discovers his needlework, "That's what a woman would do. . . . Great day in the morning!" (6).

Leroy recognizes another temporal register associated with female subjectivity—Kristeva calls it cyclical time—which measures not progression but return and repetition. On the road, Leroy often recounted his life story to hitchhikers: "He would end with a question: 'Well, what do you think?' It was just a rhetorical question. In time, he had the feeling that he'd been telling the same story over and over to the same hitchhikers" (9). At home, the disturbing sense of repetition without progress grows more persistent as Norma Jean's unhappiness becomes increasingly obvious. Again and again, she stares toward the kitchen corner while cooking, "as if she can't bear to look," and she feeds the goldfinches that repeatedly swoop past the window. For Leroy, the repetition of the birds is empty motion because they never seem to achieve anything or complete a goal. In their circular movement, he sees an image of his own spiraling marriage: "They close their wings, then fall, then spread their wings to catch and lift themselves. [Leroy] wonders if they close their eyes when they fall. Norma Jean closes her eyes when they are in bed. She wants the lights turned out. Even then, he is sure she closes her eyes" (7).

Leroy assumes that they can save the marriage if they simply "start afresh," but his memories perpetuate his immobility. In particular, he remembers the scene from *Dr. Strangelove* playing at the drive-in when his infant son died: "The President was talking in a folksy voice on the hot line to the Soviet premier about the bomber accidentally headed toward Russia. He was in the War Room, and the world map was lit up" (5). The peculiar shift to the past tense (the present tense typically expresses cinematic time) emphasizes the lack of motion, for Leroy's memories have become arrested images, frozen in time. Aware that he merely counts passing hours, waiting for some reassurance from his wife, his alienation erupts into a distinctly masculine anxiety: "Am I still king around here?" he asks, fearful that Norma Jean is having an affair (13).

Leroy believes that history is cruise control motion in which present and past are regulated by the consistent rhythm of monumental time. He judges his wife against this linear model of progress. In his eyes, her self-improvement projects are ill-planned and perfunctorily executed, for she has no log cabin, no final goal, no arrival point. She graduates from a body-building class and enrolls in an adult-education composition course, then toys with an organ that Leroy purchases for Christmas only to abandon it to cook ethnic dishes like Bombay chicken. For Norma Jean, however, the present is an isolated spot of time without connection to history. More than self-improvement, her spontaneity is a form of improvisation, as when she augments "Sunshine Superman" on the organ with Latin rhythms. She recognizes that the past can never be recouped into the present, for a second honeymoon would only perpetuate her entrapment in cyclical time. "You and me could start all over again. Right back at the beginning," Leroy says when she announces that she wants to leave him. "We *have* started all over again," she responds. "And this is how it turned out" (15).

What prompts Norma Jean's "improvised" identity is Leroy's need to idolize her as a symbol of cyclical and monumental time, thereby confining her to a fixed identity that is "small and helpless." As Kristeva argues, the "cycles, gestation, [and] eternal recurrence of a biological rhythm" that engender cyclical time can stereotype women into a single sex role: motherhood (191). Leroy still views her this way, though their child died fifteen years earlier. Her identity is as static as his memories: "She is still pretty," he decides, as if time had not touched her. Both her husband and her mother treat her as a teenager: "She won't leave me alone—*you* won't leave me alone," Norma Jean complains, "I feel eighteen again" (15). As this passage suggests, Leroy's attitude is only half of Norma Jean's dilemma. Her mother, Mabel, is equally intent on restricting her to the past. Mabel wants the Moffitts to visit Shiloh because she honeymooned there years earlier, "the only real trip she ever took." She says, "I always thought Shiloh was the prettiest place, so full of history." History offers a secure retreat from the anxieties of the present by projecting the illusion that events can be explained as a progression of causes and effects. Leroy and Mabel share the same passivity. The past is their only hope for the future, and the present is simply time that they must endure. Leroy's identification with his mother-in-law further dramatizes his alienation from linear time and the masculine values associated with it: "Like Mabel, he is just waiting for time to pass" (11).

But unlike Mabel, Leroy does finally recognize that he is a prisoner of history. When the Moffitts visit Shiloh, they discover the battlefield offers no direct statement of its meaning, no direct path to its significance. Instead, monuments are scattered around bluffs and ravines. Norma Jean "drives aimlessly through the park," her lack of direction a vivid counterpoint to the image of Leroy flying through time in his big rig. Realizing that the battleground "looks like a subdivision site," he glimpses the hollowness of linear time:

> General Grant, drunk and furious, shoved the Southerners back to Corinth, where Mabel and Jet Beasley were married years later, when Mabel was still thin and good looking. The next day, Mabel and Jet visited the battleground, and then Norma Jean was born, and then she married Leroy and they had a baby, which they lost, and now Leroy and Norma Jean are here at the same battleground. Leroy knows he is leaving out a lot. He is leaving out the insides of history. History was always just names and dates to him. It occurs to him that building a house of logs is similarly empty—too simple. And the real inner workings of a marriage, like most of history, have escaped him. (15–16)

History in Leroy's mind is a cumulative progression of events, yet his life is complicated by moments that cannot be explained in a sequence. Ignoring the insides of history, he overlooks the most vital part of human interaction, the moment of experience itself. As he thinks, he watches Norma Jean walk through the cemetery on "a serpentine brick path." She moves away, but not *straight* away, and the story ends inconclusively with this ambiguous image, a symbol both of Leroy's newfound awareness and Norma Jean's independence and assertiveness.[19]

The indirection of the walkway provides a fitting metaphor for the temporal development of the story. The influence of the present tense on this ambiguous movement permeates three planes of narrative time: chronology (the temporal unfolding of events), duration (the length of time that dramatic events occupy), and pace (the tempo or speed at which the narration—as opposed to the action—takes place). The effects of the text's shifts in and out of the punctual present are numerous. First, if tense variations typically segment a narrative into episodes with specific temporal references that allow one to collate a time scheme from a non-sequential arrangement, Mason's shifts fail to establish clear boundaries between scenes. Nor do these changes return to the moment previously suspended in story time. As a result, the audience not only constructs the chronology by deciding where these pieces fit but must decide as well whether these scenes mark singular events or whether they are composites of recurring actions. Finally, Mason's tense play often prevents us from deciding the simple issue of who—the storyteller or the character—is speaking. Again, these various effects challenge readers to judge the structural function of sentences in a way that will significantly shape their perception of the drama.

One sign of temporal ambiguity in the opening of "Shiloh" (quoted previously), in which Leroy watches Norman Jean lift weights, is the past perfect tense. The first scene dissolves after a few lines of dialogue into expository material that tells of Leroy's accident, narrated in the past perfect ("Leroy *has been collecting* temporary disability"). Though classified as a past tense, the perfect expresses ongoing conditions and incomplete processes, and precisely because it is not conducive to representing sequences, it rarely appears in narratives.[20] When the storyteller says that "Leroy has begun to realize" his insensitivity toward time, the audience cannot fix that realization to a specific moment in the chronology. Its dramatic potential is muted because nothing in the context suggests a progression toward that recognition.

Temporal ambiguity becomes even more disconcerting when entire scenes take place in this "meantime." When the description of Leroy's accident concludes, nothing in the subsequent scene between him and Norma Jean connects it to the opening passage. There is no mention of weight lifting, nor does the dialogue continue where their conversation was interrupted. Instead, Norma Jean tells Leroy that his log cabin will be out of place in the subdivision, though the log cabin is first mentioned in the narrative summary and not in the dialogue. In fact, another descriptive block cast in the perfect tense commences, modulating ambiguously between the past and present: Leroy has been promising his wife "ever since they were married" that "one day" they would buy their own home instead of renting, as they have "always" done. The small section ends with one final adverb: "It does not even feel like a home, Leroy realizes now." Again, if this exchange continues the first scene that introduced Leroy and Norma Jean, that *now* refers to a specific moment, and Leroy's realization becomes an event with dramatic weight by marking a sudden awareness of the distance separating him from Norma Jean. But if the scene is a composite representation or summary, that *now* refers to a broader time frame, and the drama loses its punctual force, for Leroy has known for "some time" that the marriage is not healthy. By deciding the value of *now*—a responsibility that Elizabeth Deeds Ermath describes as the "new acts of attention" that postmodern writing necessitates (33)—the audience determines the function of each sentence, thus ascribing to the narration a texture that stylistic brevity precludes from being formally represented.

The thematic tension between temporal registers enhances the interpretive dilemmas that the audience faces. After Leroy and Norma Jean stare at the goldfinches for an unspecified "long time," the storyteller introduces a scene with a hint of impending action: "Something is happening." But instead of a dramatic event, the storyteller provides exposition: "Norma Jean is going to night school. She has graduated from her six-week body-building course and now she is taking an adult-education course in composition at Paducah Community College. She spends her evenings outlining paragraphs" (11). Because nothing ties this *now* to the previous scene, exactly how many evenings Norma Jean has spent outlining paragraphs is unclear. That information may not seem vital for understanding the conflict, yet its absence points to the reader's displacement from time. Mason herself has suggested that the present tense by necessity makes impossible this type of temporal hopscotch: "You can't say [a character] answers the phone today and then say it is three weeks later. How did that consciousness skip all that time? Who's doing the plotting? Who's behind the camera?" (460). Yet, as "Shiloh" demonstrates, the storyteller does skip time, moving from *now* to *now* without regard for the distance separating them. As a result, the expectation that time, by structuring cause and effect explains psychological motivation, is disappointed.

In this scene, Leroy's anxiety arises precisely from the loss of causation, for he is struggling to understand why Norma Jean changes her hobbies: "What are you doing this for anyhow?" he asks. Her response is ambivalent, however, and the drama erodes into still more exposition: "Norma Jean used to say, 'If I lose ten minutes' sleep, I just drag all day.' Now she stays up late, writing compositions. She got a B on her first paper—a how-to theme on soup-based casseroles. Recently Norma Jean has been cooking unusual foods—tacos, lasagna, Bombay chicken. She doesn't play the organ anymore, though her second paper was called 'Why Music Is

Important to Me.'" Just how *recently* relates to this unspecified *now* is unclear, and a cause/effect relation between her composition writing and experimental cooking is impossible to determine, either for Leroy or for the reader. This ambiguity further obscures *anymore*, a dependent adverb that typically references cause/effect relationships, and it remains unclear whether the writing or the cooking or both interests have caused her to stop playing the organ. Norma Jean's motivations cannot be reconstructed in sequence; self-improvement for her is self-improvisation in which the process of experimentation is more important than its final product.

The contrast between her indifference to sequence and Leroy's obsession with it is nicely highlighted, for while she writes, he spends night after night constructing a model cabin out of Lincoln Logs because "the thought of getting a truckload of notched, numbered logs scares him," and he wants to be sure that he can put it together in order. The log cabin is an image of the postmodernist house of fiction that dramatizes the audience's struggle to construct the text within a linear temporal frame. Yet just as Norma Jean's actions elude chronology, the significance that a reader seeks lies outside the concatenation of narrative events.

Mason's storyteller also renders time ambiguous by manipulating frequency, the ratio between the narrating act and the events narrated, through the use of what Gérard Genette calls "iterative" commentary or summary, in which events that occur repeatedly are narrated once.[21] Traditionally, such summary provides background. Rather than advance the plot, it enhances the consistency of the fictional world, repetition and routine fleshing out the structural skeleton of dramatic events that happen once. Summary can be distinguished by verb type (in present tense, the progressive present, and the past perfect being the most common) and adverbs that signify spans of time rather than specific moments (*for a while* and *sometimes* as opposed to *suddenly*). Again, the traditional difference in aesthetic value that distinguishes one-time events and those that occur repeatedly is founded on an assumption that actions are more important than commentary. But Mason's storyteller confounds these distinctions, exploiting frequency to dramatize the Moffitts' entrapment in cyclical time.

The image of the goldfinches, for example, first appears in a block of summary. Adverbs signify the repetition of action: "*In the mornings*, Norma Jean disappears . . . *When* she chops onions. . . . She puts on her house slippers almost precisely at nine o'clock *every evening*." As the focus shifts from Norma Jean to Leroy, however, the adverbs disappear, and the scene shifts to that ambiguous "meantime" that might signify either punctual or cyclical temporality: "Norma Jean closes her eyes when they are in bed. She wants the lights turned out. Even then, he is sure she closes her eyes" (7). Does Leroy make this association each time he watches the birds or only once? The audience must decide whether the symbol is background information or an event that signifies his growing awareness. The storyteller thus de-emphasizes action in favor of description, often using narrative summary to supply the drama that the order of events fails to produce.

If the present tense clouds perception of order and frequency so that time is an unreliable interpretive frame, tense switches have the even more basic effect of impeding the reader's ability to determine exactly who speaks. During the course of the story, one faces sentences that can be attributed to either the storyteller (as interpolated commentary) or to the character (as free indirect discourse), resulting in a near fusion of narrative voices that creates the "tell-a-visual" nature of the style. Even in blocks of summary, evaluative speech acts convey the simultaneous perception of narrator and character: "Norma Jean works at the Rexall drugstore, and she has acquired an amazing amount of information about cosmetics. When she explains the stages of complexion care, involving creams, toners, and moisturizers, he thinks happily of other petroleum products—axle grease, diesel fuel. This is a connection between him and Norma Jean" (2). Does this final sentence represent Leroy's thought or is it the storyteller's commentary? The decision is ours, and, once more, any answer adds texture to the story. If one assumes that the narrator comments directly to the audience, the sentence becomes a description that orients us to Leroy's state of mind. But if it is interpreted as free indirect discourse, the sentence implies that Leroy *suddenly* recognizes his need to connect with his wife, and the punctuality of the act gives it dramatic weight. In such examples, the present tense closes the gap between the narrator and the characters, obliterating one device for distinguishing narrative description from action.

This televisual effect arises most forcefully, however, from the third temporal register, the pace of the narrating. Rhythm is the most subjective form of temporal play because its perception is a function of reading time, which, obviously, will vary throughout an audience. Still, as Genette argues, tempo can illuminate the relationship between the narration and the story at two levels: first, in terms of *movement*, which refers to the quantity of text that represents blocks of story time, and second, as the *duration* of motion that various verb types and tense forms convey (93–94). Tempo is important in present-tense narratives because, ideally, rhythm must mimic the flow of the story. If a narrator synchronizes the two temporal planes, the story will contain no ellipses between scenes and no evaluative interpolations that would arrest forward motion so that story time equals narration time. The *noveau roman* popularized by Alain Robbe-Grillet exploits this effect as details pass indiscriminately before the narrative eye; without a retrospective consciousness sifting and arranging materials, the pace of individual reading acts supplies the tempo or momentum that pushes the story forward. Temporal play in "Shiloh" is less extreme but in many ways more exciting than the avant-garde novel. Rather than synchronize the two temporal planes, the narrator exploits a drag between them that signals the storytelling presence as an evaluative filter.

This drag is most detectable in descriptive passages that syncopate the drama. As Genette suggests, the tempo of a scene is modeled on exchanges of dialogue in which call and response evokes the flow of oral conversation. But in "Shiloh" dialogue rarely runs uninterrupted by exposition. Indeed, conversational exchanges are themselves undramatic and tend to begin and end with indifferent abruptness. The burden of drama falls upon description, which slows the tempo of the exchanges. When Leroy meets Stevie Hamilton, his marijuana dealer, at the local supermarket for a buy, the scene, at first glance, seems to have minimal relevance:

> "Where do you get this stuff?" asks Leroy. "From your pappy?"
>
> "That's for me to know and you to find out," Stevie says. He is slit-eyed and skinny.
>
> "What else you got?"
>
> "What else you interested in?"
>
> "Nothing special. Just wondered." (4)

Leroy recognizes in Stevie the ghost of his own dead son Randy, but we infer this connection only because of the abundant descriptive detail that suggests how intensely he stares at the boy. The narrator notes the color of Stevie's shoes, the logo on his T-shirt, remarks on his father's occupation, and even comments on the fact that, in the local phone book, the Hamiltons have a second number listed under "Teenagers." These details may seem gratuitous for a character who says exactly three sentences and disappears, yet their value rests in the fact of their perception, for passages of description imply the act of observation. In reporting details, the storyteller transforms narrative commentary into a story about the activity of perception. In structural terms, the relative absence of dramatic events is deceptive, for the act of orienting oneself to the scene *is* the drama, both for the characters and the readers. Just as Leroy attempts to register what passes before him, so, too, the storyteller acts less as an organizing force than a screen whose background and foreground can be distinguished only by readers.

The point becomes clearer if we examine the function of the scene in storytelling. In granting the illusion of unmediated access to events, the scene marks the highest degree of mimetic fidelity possible. The source of that fidelity rests in the reader's ability to imagine him or herself present, to be invisible amid the action. Like theater patrons, we witness a staged spectacle, but unlike a literal audience, we view this action in the imagination. The scene thus presupposes what Alexander Gelley calls a "specular investment" by requiring us to transfer language into image, to fantasize within the limitations of the frames that the description imposes. As a result, "the reader becomes an unstable subject, seeking to survey and master what is being shown, but continually thwarted by the frame or 'spectacle' that provides [the] means of access."[22] Scenes in "Shiloh" implicate readers in this act of visualization at a metarhetorical level. Rather than directly reveal him or herself, Mason's storyteller relocates the drama outside the scenic frame into the activity of narration itself. One clue to the spectacle of visualization is the abundance of perceptual verbs: Leroy *notices* how the town has changed; Mabel *notices* the dirty laundry; Leroy *watches* the birds and *looks* at his rig in the backyard; he *sees* traces of Norma Jean's features in Mabel. Even the most dramatic scene, what seems to be the couple's break-up, is a drama of observation, not action. Norma Jean, herself looking at the Tennessee River, waves her arms at Leroy: "Is she beckoning to him? She seems to be doing an exercise for her chest muscles" (16). The interrogative and the modal dramatize not only Leroy's inability to make sense of Norma Jean's actions, but the storyteller's commitment to dramatizing the subjectivity of all specular investments. Actions and events thus always orient the audience back to the source of their perception.

Pace is not merely a matter of rhythm, however, for a sense of movement also depends on the duration or length of activity that verbs convey. Not surprisingly, duration plays a part in the visualization of events in "Shiloh"; in particular, Mason's use of the progressive present enhances the lag between story and narration. This verb form typically complements ongoing processes of some length, as in a description like "Rain is falling." Yet the temporal distinction between the progressive and punctual present is rarely maintained in storytelling because the duration that the former conveys is antagonistic to the spontaneous drama that moves the story forward. As a result, according to Suzanne Fleischman, events are frequently cast into the punctual present "to override the inherent duration of these situations, giving them the appearance of instantaneous achievements." Thus, instead of saying "Rain is falling," narrators will say "Rain falls." Tense type thus offers another criterion for texturing the narration as the punctual present conveys dramatic actions while the progressive present typically marks background commentary (30).

Yet Mason often uses the progressive tense in sentences that would ordinarily be classified as actions: "At that moment Norma Jean *is holding* on to the kitchen counter, *raising* her knees one at a time as she talks. She *is wearing* two-pound ankle weights . . . under her breath, she *is counting*. Now she *is marching* through the kitchen. She *is doing* goose steps" (7; emphasis added). Maintaining the duration of Norma Jean's activity has two effects: first, it creates the drag of narrative rhythm. Because the moment that Norma Jean holds the counter has no fixed conclusion, the audience inevitably ascribes an experiential value to the temporal adverb (*moment*) according to the pace of its own reading. Second, the progressive present marks the visualization rather than dramatization of scenes. According to Fleischman, one of the few modes of discourse in which the progressive present is consistently employed is the "current report," as when sportscasters broadcast a game. In a sentence like "the runner is rounding third," the speaker narrates an event while she/he observes it take place (38). Likewise, events in "Shiloh" do not seem to happen without mediation; rather, they are observed and reported at the same time. This point is important because the progressive present is used most frequently to describe Norma Jean's actions. She is the object of a narrative gaze, and the duration conveyed by the progressive present emphasizes Leroy's need to keep her out of linear time. For the audience, however, that tense form slows the forward motion of the narrative sequence, ideally reorienting us away from the drama of actions to the drama of visualizing them.

"Shiloh" is only one of the many stories by Mason in which tense play resists what Kristeva calls "the inherent linearity of language" (192). Significantly, when Mason does write in the present tense, she consistently employs a third-person perspective; only one story in *Shiloh*, "Residents and Transients," is narrated from a first-person perspective. In "Shiloh" itself, the drama of the gap that unfolds between Leroy's need to discover a cause of Norma Jean's unhappiness (one that can be explained in terms of cause and effect) and the audience's effort to interpret and account for this conflict results from the peculiar temporal drag in the representation. Again, the storyteller functions here not as an organizing presence but as a reflective surface, always amorphous but always perceptible. The translucence of such a narrative stance is particular to the undramatized narrator, however. New and different ambiguities develop when the storyteller is a character in the narrative, as is more frequently the case in Carver's stories.

12

Raymond Carver: Tense, Telling, Memory

At first glance, the punctual present tense in the Carver brand of minimalism seems crafted to evoke the tough-guy reticence of Hemingway: "That morning she pours Teacher's over my belly and licks it off. That afternoon she tries to jump out the window." Or "My husband eats with a good appetite but he seems tired, edgy. He chews slowly, arms on the table, and stares at something across the room." Or "We all go into the dining room. Frank Martin cuts the cake. I sit next to J. P. J. P. eats two pieces and drinks a Coke. I eat a piece and wrap another piece in a napkin, thinking of later."[23] In all three excerpts (one could provide countless other examples), the event subsumes the emotion in a way that creates an aura of shunned depth, as though Carver were studiously rejecting both introspection and retrospection in favor of a pure, anecdotal style of observation. So insistent is the surfaceness of this brevity that early critics and reviewers equated the effects of Carver's minimalism with the disaffection and disconnection that plague his characters. From *Will You Please Be Quiet, Please?* (1976) through *What We Talk About When We Talk About Love* (1981) to *Cathedral* (1984), the extreme simplicity of his storytelling was received as a force of pure negativity, an incantatory emptiness that seemed to corroborate what historian Christopher Lasch describes as the "siege mentality" of the "minimal self" seeking refuge from the beleaguering randomness and disorder of the postmodern age. Whether he was dismissed for perpetuating the "barren idiom of our time" or praised for capturing its "stunning inarticulateness," Carver earned an unwarranted reputation as an evangelist of ennui whose rigorous economy of address resulted in short stories that readers found "more transcribed than told."[24]

Yet the relationship between brevity and storytelling in Carver's work is deceptive if not plain misleading. While he, like Hemingway, learned the value of staccato sentences and strategic repetition, his reticence implies something more intimate and involved than the "masculine nudity of the starkest sort" that reviewers in 1927 perceived in *Men Without Women*. For one thing, the two writers differ in the type of utterance that they omit to foreshorten their fiction. As we have seen, Hemingway at his most economical elides all but the most embedded signals of narratorial presence in "Hills Like White Elephants," leaving only stylistic mannerisms like repetition as a clue to his agency. By contrast, Carver, especially in later work like *Cathedral* and the final seven stories of *Where I'm Calling From* (1988), foregrounds narration to the point that the story and its telling interfold and prove indistinguishable. Through this strategy, he demonstrates what he meant when he told an interviewer that "art is not self-expression, it is communication, and I am interested in communication,"[25] for his narrators openly struggle with this end of narration as they attempt to involve their addressees in their tales. These fumbling attempts to make contact expose a humanistic countercurrent to the mute, existential bleakness that for too long stereotyped their author. Instead of passively documenting the indecision and despair ailing the modern world, many of his stories testify to the redemptive power of narration, revealing how "through our stories and storytelling . . . we find in even the most dire times freedom."[26]

This desire for contact with the reader manifests itself most visibly in rhetorical gestures that Roland Barthes describes as the "scraps of language," those "appeals [and] modulations . . . through which a body seeks another body."[27] As the following passage from "Where I'm Calling From" suggests, scraps reveal a self-conscious shaping of the unfolding story, a willingness to comment upon the narrative as it takes shape: "It's eleven o'clock in the morning—an hour and a half until lunch. Neither one of us is hungry. But just the same we look forward to going inside and sitting down at the table. . . . What's J. P. talking about, anyway? He's saying how when he was twelve years old he fell into a well in the vicinity of the farm he grew up on" (280). The adverb *anyway* and the interrogative effect that a perspectival transition from interior moods and feelings to the surrounding environment momentarily pinpoints the place of storytelling—*not* the physical setting or scene but the perceptual space from which the speaker observes and listens while he narrates. If Hemingway would pencil through such subjective signs without blinking, Carver frequently employs questions ("What's to say?" "But so what?"), emphatics ("*Sure*, once in a while he drank the hard stuff") and self-repairs ("*I mean*, he's hardly breathing") to dramatize the struggle of storytellers to make their tales meaningful. However "transcribed" the sparsity of the style may strike us, ample rhetorical clues indicate that the stories are indeed "told."

The confusion over what distinguishes a transcribed story from a told one is indicative of the ambiguous televisual quality that the present tense creates in minimalist fiction. On the one hand, the objective report of external details that Carver achieves in a sentence like "I'm in bed when he calls today to tell me that he's asked his mother to come stay with us for a few days" implies a reportorial narrative stance that records details in stark black and white by filtering out all emotional coloring (from "So Much Water So Close to Home" 237). Although we see the scene from the perspective of this "I," we are alienated from more revelatory feelings and perceptions, those subjective admissions of mood and character that attract our empathy. Given this reticence, it is understandable why critics might equate Carver's brevity with the "camera-eye" style of Hemingway. Yet other passages of the same story can be classified as interior monologue when we recognize that their starkness does give way to a revealing subjectivity, albeit one that fails to burst and explode with the Technicolor exaggeration of Dave's exclamations in "Almos' a Man." Elsewhere the same character from "So Much Water So Close to Home" says, "I must get over it, put it out of sight, out of mind, etc., and 'go on'" (214). At such moments, the focus of the narrative perspective shifts inward, and we are suddenly privy to the anxieties and emotional eruptions that Claire cannot articulate to her unresponsive husband Stuart. In stories like "So Much Water," this interiority of perception marks the frustration of having a story to tell but no audience to hear it, for "something has come between" this couple, "though he would like me to believe otherwise" (213). This "something" is his appalling decision not to interrupt an annual fishing trip when he and his friends discover a female corpse floating in a backwoods river. Claire's need to explain his callousness, to reconcile it with her intuitive identification with the raped and murdered woman, propels the narration, for she must find the "connection to be made of these things, these events, these faces, if [she] can find it" (234). As is typical in Carver's stories, she fails, yet the lack of formal resolution affords readers the latitude to discover their own thematic and symbolic connections. While the immediacy and transitoriness of the tense preclude her from discovering the deeper meaning she desires, they license us to offer it.

Much as Mason's manipulation of chronology, frequency, and pace allows her to recreate the theme of temporal dislocation within the style of "Shiloh," Carver employs the present tense to dramatize a recurring motif: the mutability of memory. Repeatedly, he reveals how the act of remembering is a form of narration by which we seek to understand experience, to resolve the past by reimagining it from the perspective of the present. In "Fat," a waitress recalls serving an obese customer a luxuriant meal during a busy late shift. Enhancing the memory's mood of uncertainty and irresolution is the doubling of the text's structure of address, for the narrator is not telling the story directly to us but instead describes how she tells it to Rita, who occasionally interrupts to question its development: "What else? Rita says. . . . The story's getting interesting now" (68). Rita's responses presumably mirror our readerly desire to know the point, for she encourages the storyteller to explain just why this chance encounter with the fat man lingers in her memory. Yet this encouragement proves destructive, for the waitress does not know why she finds it important. It may well be, as Kirk Nesset argues, that "just as he is at the mercy of his appetite, and whatever lies behind [it] . . . she too is at the mercy of her world, oppressed by a husband and work environment insensitive to her needs" (15). Yet this is a conclusion that the narrator fails to articulate, for in lieu of a sudden epiphany, she remembers thinking of the fat man while she and her husband Rudy made love later that night: "But here is the thing. When he gets on me, I suddenly feel I am fat. I feel I am terrifically fat." When Rita lets it be known that "she doesn't know what to make of" that ending, the narrator brings an abrupt halt to the conversation, declaring that "I won't go into it with her" because "I've already told her too much." Rita's expectation for some clarification, some resolution to the remembrance ultimately annoys the woman: "She sits there waiting, her dainty fingers poking her hair. *Waiting for what?* I'd like to know" (69). With its refusal to name the point, "Fat" implies that memory is too fragile, too unstable a medium to manifest its meaning. Remembering is a *process* of discovery, not a *product*. By analogy, Carver implies, storytelling is also a process. As an evaluative device, the present tense justifies the irresolute flow of this process, cautioning us not to expect it to culminate in a formal resolution. Only by offering our insights—as Rita fails to do—can we begin to make the story meaningful.

The struggle to discover the meaning of a haunting memory appears consistently throughout Carver's first-person, present tense stories. In "Whoever Was Using This Bed," a woman named Iris recalls a dream interrupted by a late-night phone call from a stranger searching for someone named Bud: "I can just about remember it, but I can't remember exactly. Something about, about—no, I don't know what it was about now. . . . God damn that woman and her phone call. '*Bud*'. . . . I'd like to punch her" (427). Over the next half-hour, as her husband Jack unplugs the telephone to avoid the stranger's persistent intrusions, only a few details return to her. Like Rita in "Fat," Jack pressures his wife to get to the point: "Why are you telling me this?" he demands, offended when he fails to appear in her dream. "What happened then, honey?" he asks a moment later, "finish telling the dream, and maybe we can go to sleep then." Iris remembers nothing else, however, and the significance of the event seems lost on both of them—until, after another hour passes, Jack finds himself looking at the tangled bed sheets where they have spent this sleepless night: "It looks like whoever was using this bed left in a hurry. I know I won't ever look at this bed again without remembering it like this. We're into something now, but I don't know what, exactly" (439). His inability to determine the import of this symbol beyond a vague sense of change parallels Iris's uncertainty about the meaning of her fragmented dream. In both cases, reciting the experience is an effort to discover a deeper relevance that is ultimately elusive. Carver implies that even in the absence of a definitive sense of significance, we continue to tell our stories to take shelter in a shared moment of conversation from the storminess of our confusion.

Carver's most complex rendering of this theme takes shape in

"Where I'm Calling From." Here the narrator, an alcoholic on his second trip through a "drying-out facility," meets J. P., a former chimney sweep, and listens to his confession because "it's taking me away from my own situation" (285). Both men resemble Leroy Moffitt in "Shiloh": They do not know how their life got off track, how the happiness of home eroded into discontent. But if Leroy's anxiety drives him to a relatively pathetic form of self-delusion (his desire to build a log cabin in the Kentucky suburbs), these men are far more self-destructive, and much of the pain of their recovery centers not only upon the bad case of the physical "shakes" they suffer, but their need to absolve themselves of the anger and abuse to which drinking has led them. "Who knows why we do what we do?" the narrator asks rhetorically when J. P. wonders aloud how he lost control of his life. Unlike Rita or Jack, the storyteller is an ideal audience, for he allows J. P. to tell his tale without demanding that he get to the point. Whenever his friend hesitates or seems to lose the thread, he encourages him to continue, to "keep talking," not because he is anxious for a conclusion but because he knows J. P. needs to feel that someone is interested in hearing his story.

The narrator willingly assumes this role because he knows that for he and J. P. remembering is an act of acceptance; only by telling their tales can they reconcile themselves to the inevitable loss that they face outside the confines of the clinic. Near the end of the text, during a visit from J. P.'s wife Roxy, the storyteller sits on the clinic steps, trying to escape the desire to drink: "I'm thinking about chimney sweeps—all that stuff I heard from J. P.—when for some reason I start to think about a house my wife and I once lived in. The house didn't have a chimney, so I don't know what makes me remember it now. But I remember the house and how we'd only been in there a few weeks when I heard a noise outside one morning" (294–95). The memory leads to a humorous story: He discovers his landlord peeping into his bedroom window, but he fails to understand why the old man is laughing until he realizes that he is naked. Like similar scenes of remembering in "Fat" and "Whoever Was Using This Bed," this memory offers no clue as to why his marriage failed. In fact, uncertain about what even sparked it, the narrator is content to dismiss the issue with an inconclusive "some reason." Yet the ambiguity of this paratactic connection between his physical space and the memory that it inspires becomes, for the reader, the narrative enigma that the plot would otherwise seem to lack. Such moments invite audience participation by asking us to articulate what the narrator cannot, for what leads to this recollection is a sudden realization of the lost intimacy between him and his now-former wife, a realization made all the more palpable by J. P. and Roxy's tentative attempt at reconciliation. Significantly, the story closes with the narrator thinking of telephoning his ex-wife: "I won't say anything about New Year's resolutions. There's no way to make a joke out of this," he admits. He then resolves "after I talk to her, I'll call my girlfriend. . . . 'Hello, sugar,' I'll say when she answers. 'It's me'" (296). All he wants is to reach someone on the phone, to hear a voice respond, even if he does not know quite what to say.

Carver's use of the present tense allows him to convey the fragile and subjective nature of memory through a variety of means. Most frequently, he appropriates a traditional structural function of tense switching, the dividing of a text into discrete scenes and events, to challenge our tendency to look to the plot to reveal the point while slighting the importance of narration. In "Where I'm Calling From," he experiments with two additional effects. First, he, like Mason, manipulates our sense of pace. But instead of adopting the progressive present ("she is lifting") to slow the flow of events, Carver shifts abruptly from the past to present so that actions pulse and flicker rather than unfold in a causal chain. Even more strikingly, he demonstrates his ear for oral storytelling by disassociating tense from time altogether. At one point, for example, the narrator describes how J. P. remembers courting his wife Roxy: "Roxy *starts* going out with him on dates. And little by little he *talks* her into letting him go along on jobs with her. . . . So she and J. P. *saw* some movies together. But mainly the courtship *revolved* around their cleaning chimneys together" (283; italics added). In such cases, tense switches do not index different temporal registers. Instead, they function as a type of aural italics that emphasize events whose importance readers must determine.

At first glance, his early work seems to employ the punctual present as a narrative frame that, much as in "Bartleby," separates the story from its telling. Narrators will introduce themselves, offer a clue as to why they need to share their tale, then slip into the past tense to recite the chronology of events. These tense switches *should* foreground the plot from surrounding commentary and background detail, yet this framing often proves ironic, for the artificial boundary between present and past grants storytellers an illusory distance from their memories. Ultimately, the reader recognizes that why these narrators need to separate themselves from their stories is more revealing than what they narrate.

"What Do You Do in San Francisco?" begins with a present-tense disclaimer from a postman named Henry Robinson, who assures us that the story he will tell "has nothing to do with me" but focuses instead upon an odd hippie couple, Jerry Marston and his unnamed wife, who briefly lived on his small-town route. His insistence that he is a disinterested observer is naïve, however, for as he observes their disintegrating relationship—she eventually runs off with another man—Henry fails to offer Marston the counsel he so obviously needs. Only when he delivers a letter from the absentee wife does he make an awkward attempt at empathy: "Why don't you go to work and forget her? What have you got against work? It was work, day and night, work that gave me oblivion when I was in your shoes" (62). The confession alludes to a telling detail Henry reveals in introducing this story that is not about him: He suffered a divorce that has kept him separated from his children for nearly twenty years. Yet Henry fails to elaborate on this connection that the two men share, for by telling Marston to bury his grief in work, he is denying the pain of his own loss, much as he has for two decades. The pathos here lies not so much in Marston's shock at his abandonment but in Henry's certainty that "a man who isn't working has got too much time on his hands, too much time to dwell on himself and his problems" (53). Because it conveys the self-deceptive permanence and stability that Henry feels the routine of work affords him, his present-tense narration and not the events he relates provides the textual space in which we discover this muted emotional meaning.

Like Henry, the narrator of "Distance" also seeks to avoid confronting painful memories, only less successfully. In another present-tense narrative frame, a daughter encourages her father to tell stories from her childhood, before her parents divorced. The father hesitates—"What can I tell you?" he asks—but she insists. As if to avoid acknowledging the effect of the divorce upon her, he promises a tale that involves her "but only in a minor way." The text then shifts to the past tense as the father recounts a seemingly insignificant squabble. Once the daughter suffered a small fever on the same day he was scheduled to hunt waterfowl with a friend. His unwillingness to cancel the long-awaited trip forced an ultimatum from the wife: He could choose between his family and his friends. Appropriately, he changed his plans, and the couple reconciled with a promise never to argue again. What is striking about this otherwise commonplace story is the father's inability to identify himself as one of its characters, for he refers to himself as "the boy" and his former wife as "the girl," as though they were entirely different people. Speaking of himself in the third-person, past tense is the only way he can admit the couple's marital naïveté to the person most affected by it. While the title dramatizes the emotional alienation that this family suffers as a result of the divorce (the father and daughter meet only on rare occasions), it also conveys his need to distance himself from his guilt. Only indirectly through occasional interjections can he reassure his daughter that the couple were once happy together: "These two kids, I'm telling you, were very much in love" (187).

Yet the space he seeks to locate between past and present evaporates, for in the concluding frame the daughter wants a more straightforward explanation: that story "was very interesting," she tells him, "but what happened? I mean later." The best answer he can offer is a superficial "things change," at which point the disappointed daughter decides they should stop talking and go for a walk in the newly fallen snow. Unlike Henry, the father recognizes that, much like the ingenuousness that ruined the marriage, his hope to placate the daughter's curiosity without pain is naïve. Standing by a chilled window, he recognizes that while the couple "had leaned on each other and laughed until the tears had come, while everything else—the cold and where he'd go in it—was outside, for a while anyway" (197), his inability to talk about the divorce has precipitated another sort of chill between him and his daughter.

In such stories, tense shifts serve more of a thematic than affective function, for they help underscore the point by encouraging readers to search for significance within the narrative situations that inspire each tale's telling. In his later work, Carver erodes these barriers between past and present, between drama and narration, by employing the present tense more extensively. (Of the seven final stories in *Where I'm Calling From*, the last Carver wrote before his death in 1988, four are cast into the punctual present, while the remaining three contain intriguing passages that shift out of the past tense for no apparent reason.) Tense heightens the uncertainty that the characters suffer; these talking-head narrators comment upon their actions and emotions as they struggle to account for the change threatening their stability. The predominant effect is not unlike the temporal drag between story and narration that Mason exploits in "Shiloh." As the plot advances at a glacial pace, as events are smothered in layers of observances and evaluative asides, readers must recognize that the meaning is experiential and not causal.

In one of his most clever present-tense fictions, "Gazebo," Carver makes this point by clouding the temporal relationship between the story and its telling. The tense seems to set both time frames on the day that Holly and Duane lock themselves in an upstairs suite in the hotel they manage: "We are sitting on a sofa," Duane reports. "We are drinking Teacher's with ice and water." As Holly vents her rage at his adultery, he self-consciously attempts to demonstrate remorse ("Maybe I should be looking at the floor," he tells himself) while plagued by a continuing attraction to his lover ("I am thinking of Juanita. This is awful"). Much like Leroy in "Shiloh" or even the American in "Hills Like White Elephants," Duane survives through denial; he believes that his marriage can survive if both agree not to make an issue of his infidelity. Holly, however, recognizes that the relationship is over. In the story's central exchange, she ridicules her naïveté by dismissing a treasured memory of meeting an aged couple whose backyard gazebo symbolized their weathered but stable relationship: "I thought we'd be like that too when we got old enough," she admits to her husband, "dignified. And in a place." When Duane tries to convince her that they will discover the security that has eluded them, the wife can only sigh with exasperation: "'Duane,' Holly goes. In this too, she was right" (146). This unexpected shift to the past tense is a trick ending that implies that Duane tells his story from a more removed perspective than the present tense would suggest. The tale and its telling do not occur simultaneously; instead, he is narrating this memory at some unspecified time after it occurred. The ending invests a hidden depth and pathos in Duane's storytelling, for his unwillingness to accept Holly's dismissal of the gazebo memory proves ironic. Simply by remembering their break-up, he is silently acknowledging his loss.

"Intimacy" exploits similar temporal ambiguity without resorting to the trick ending. Here a Carveresque writer visits a former wife embittered by his exploitation of their private life in his fiction. "In my opinion," she tells him, "you remember the wrong things. You remember the low, shameful things." Agreeing with her, the narrator allows the woman to insult him and his writing, all while he passively sits in her living room sipping coffee. Although he does not reveal what inspired him to search her out for the first time in four years ("I don't know what I am going to find" is all he says), it soon becomes clear that he has come seeking forgiveness, although he cannot quite admit this to himself. In the story's one moment of dramatic action, he tries to touch her: "And then I do something. I reach over and take the sleeve of her blouse between my thumb and forefinger. That's all. . . . Then here's the thing I do next. I get down on my knees, a big guy like me, and I take the hem of her dress." Again, these events do not simply happen but are narrated as they take place. The storyteller performs these actions as though he were a spectator present at the scene to evaluate them: "What am I doing on the floor? I wish I could say. But I know it's where I ought to be, and I'm there holding on to the hem of her dress" (450). Such passages can be read at least two ways. If the question is a direct address to the reader, it marks a shift to a later moment in time in which he remembers the encounter (the adverb *there*, by inflecting a sudden perspectival distance into the scene, substantiates this possibility). Or it can be read as interior monologue, in which case, he interrogates his own motives at that time. The temporal frame to which we ascribe the passage affects our perception of its function. If a direct address, the narrator comments upon the uncertainty he was *then* suffering; in the second possibility, however, that uncertainty assumes more dramatic importance, for it foregrounds his struggle to account for his actions *at that moment*. By asking us to determine the temporality of textual utterances, the otherwise unidimensional present tense grants us the freedom to invest significance in actions and events of our choosing. We effectively layer a story that, on the surface, denies its own complexity.

Carver's most intriguing temporal play occurs in "Where I'm Calling From," whose present tense alternately refers to not two but *three* different time frames. The New Year's Day in which the story is set often gives way to memories of the previous night when J. P. first tells of his fall into alcoholism. Although he casts these scenes into the present tense, the narrator will shift suddenly to the past tense ("But he *told* me . . ."; "I *was* interested") to reveal that he is remembering the intimacy of their therapeutic storytelling sessions. At other points, the present dramatizes scenes from an even more remote past. Although these flashbacks begin in the preterit ("When he was eighteen or nineteen years old"), the tense shifts in and out of the present: "Then the doorbell *rings*. . . . This young woman chimney sweep is there with her cleaning things. . . . She *was* all-right-looking, too, J. P. *said*" (282; emphasis added). Such switches dissolve the temporal authority by which we might be tempted to reconstruct the story line. Instead of looking to a chronology to explain J. P.'s dissolution, we flow through concentric circles of time as Carver layers retelling upon retelling.

In addition to confounding our ability to mark the boundaries of events, Carver's tense switches also manipulate our sense of the narrative pace. Mason's storyteller impedes the linear movement of "Shiloh" by casting events in the progressive present so that the rhythm of the audience's reading determines their temporal value. Carver, by contrast, clusters his shifts around the temporal conjunctions and adverbs that normally convey sequentiality: "From J. P.'s friend, [Roxy] took a check that had been made out to her by his parents. And then she *asks* the friend if he wants to kiss her . . . " Envious of his friend, J. P. asks Roxy for a kiss. A shift to the past tense follows the conjunction: "'Sure,' Roxy says. 'Why not? I've got some extra kisses.' And she *kissed* him a good one right on the lips and then turned to go" (282). What slows the forward flow here is a contrast between the completion that the past tense implies and the on-goingness the present conveys. That is, the present tense describes scenes in the process of happening; as such, the speed of our reading becomes the most immediate measure of the flow of events. Roxy's actions in the first excerpt are accomplished *before* the sentence concludes, but the act of asking for the kiss is completed only *as* the reader maneuvers through the syntax of the following utterance. Similarly, in the second passage, the pace of

Roxy's speech arises not from its integration in the surrounding drama but from the rhythm of the reading act; the temporal value of the actions represented is congruent to the time it takes readers to navigate the length of the sentence. In the subsequent quotation, however, the action has culminated before the sentence concludes. By switching tenses around coordinating conjunctions, Carver alters the rhythm of the experiences dramatized even though the syntax is relatively similar. Splitting sequences into ambiguous fragments, he toys with our sense of what a narrative event is as chains of actions are represented as separate and unconnected, their intensity pulsing rather than progressing.

Carver's tense switches also invite audience participation by having nothing whatsoever to do with marking time. In print, the seemingly arbitrary shifts in "Where I'm Calling From" are visually striking because the conceptual subordination by which written narratives are organized necessitates a logic of tense usage, which is typically grounded in the authority of linear time. In oral storytelling, however, tense may not serve as a temporal frame but as an internal evaluation device, a type of aural italics that emphasizes certain events or actions, thus highlighting their importance for the reader. It is a sign of Carver's ear for oral conversation, in fact, that he employs changes in tense rather than a written convention like italics. The effect is again particular to the televisual nature of minimalist storytelling in which the action is always the subject of an implicit running commentary. Rick Altman describes the aural appeal of a predominantly visual medium like television as a "sound hermeneutic" that draws a non-attentive viewer to the screen: "the sound asks the question 'Where?' to which the image, upon identifying the source, eventually responds 'Here!'"[28] Similarly, Carver's tense shifts may "initiate [our] involvement" by sparking curiosity and challenging us to account for their purpose.

Commenting on the aridity and bleakness of the minimalist style, John W. Aldridge suggests that Carver is both "product and victim of a social situation that is extremely limited in dramatic potential and in which the resources for the display of depth and complexity, whether of character or relationship, are greatly diminished" (56). Again, the assumption here is that readers locate drama within the story rather than within their own interaction with the text. One can suggest, however, that a good deal of dramatic potential rests in the spaces between sentences that readers must collapse and congeal to create a sense of a narrative whole. In the final paragraph of "Where I'm Calling From," one witnesses the narrator review his options as he prepares to phone his estranged wife: "If she answers, I'll wish her a Happy New Year. But that's it. I won't bring up business. I won't raise my voice. Not even if she starts something" (296). While an obvious sequence of intent accrues here as the speaker tries to commit himself to a plan of action, the linearity is fraught with an unspoken tension resulting from the revisionary impulse to refine and reduce the implications of the preceding utterance. What sanctions the interpretive freedom to explore this tension is the lack of temporal rigor in both the present tense and the paratactic arrangements. If the logic of sequence governs response by foregrounding the linkage of dramatic events to the detriment of narrative description, Carver's minimalism invites readers to create the plenitude of a story through their own evaluative responses.

Epilogue

By foregrounding the immediacy of perception in narrative performance, Mason and Carver heighten the experiential at the expense of the sequential, subordinating content to contact. In doing so, they expose the high stakes of confessional intimacy by dramatizing the verbal stutters and stammers that mark language as a production and meaning as improvisation. Of course, the present tense is but one device of economy in the mode. Mason regularly uses the form in *Shiloh*, but in *Love Life* (1989), she experiments with the traditional retrospective stance, claiming that she wrote in the present tense "because it seemed right at the time. . . . But I got bored with it. I started seeing it everywhere and it just made me feel like doing something different" (qtd. in Lyons and Oliver 459). In Carver's collected stories, the present tense is an exception rather than a routine habit. Yet even when employing the standard past tense, these storytellers avoid capitulating to the illusion that time explains all secrets, as though causation were its own breed of fiction. The emphasis on mood and feeling in minimalism, sometimes understated, sometimes disarmingly blunt, conveys the spectrum of emotions that occurs when linear time's limitations are too obvious to trust or ignore. Freedom from the rigors of linearity may be terrifying, but storytelling offers a way of understanding those pivotal moments to which we compulsively return when their significance proves elusive.

In a 1987 *New Yorker* story, John Updike's sometime alter-ego Henry Bech crosses the Iron Curtain to meet a seminar of Czechoslovakian students eager to hear of the latest American literary fads. A befuddled Bech professes little interest in the "new wave," which strikes him as "just more and more backwash": "After the minimalists, what can there be but blank paper? It'll be a relief in a way."[29] The remark is only a partial put down, for Bech imagines within literature's evaporating expression sweet release from the curse of his habitual writer's block. Nevertheless, the comment is indicative of the way in which traditionalists like Updike have mistaken the brevity of the mode for internal emptiness. Because minimalism, unlike modernism, was never a movement in the sense that its artists shared a general aesthetic agenda, it has been defined more by its detractors than its practitioners. Yet rather than indulge in anomie, much of its fiction concerns a basic theme: the failure of the spoken word. "It's hard for people to talk and say what they really mean," Carver told one interviewer. "But there are other ways of communicating. Things do happen, things do get done and said in the stories, even though sometimes people may be talking at cross-purposes at times, or seemingly to no good purpose" (qtd. in Gentry and Stull 200). As we gain distance from minimalism, this preoccupation with communication, not nihilism or stark simplicity, will offer a way to understand what writers like Carver and Mason strive for in their style. Like the oral storyteller for whom the text is both the story and its telling, their narrators rely on the ambiguous "other ways of communicating" that give the work a performative richness only implied on the printed page.

Postscript: Whither Brevity?

In the conclusion to his *Maupassant and the American Short Story* (1994), Richard Fusco notes how one early critic expressed concern over "a competing duality in [his] thesis," which, by his own account, strives to interweave a "theoretical approach to fictive structure with historical trends in the history of a genre." Without apology, Fusco corrects his reader by noting several other argumentative threads and fibers, all of which "became inextricably twisted in my vision of short-story history" and were thus integral to girding together his book. A plethora of issues and themes apropos of literary influence had to be addressed, he insists, were he to analyze successfully the proliferation of the Maupassantian trick ending in late nineteenth-century short fiction: "I could not divorce literary history from fictional form," he concludes. "To pluck one thread was to risk unraveling the entire fabric."[1]

The fabric I weave in the preceding pages takes shape in response to an equally emphatic belief that today's short-story critic must integrate the synchronic within the diachronic. As the most diverse and thus most elusive of popular American literary forms, the short story deserves critical approaches that both historicize the many definitions it has inspired while theorizing the history that made them possible. Unlike a majority of story critics, including Fusco, I argue this prerogative can best be achieved by turning away from form and structure toward rhetoric. Doing so allows us to avoid the reductivity that ails many efforts to account for the short story's most obvious generic trait, its brevity. By approaching this feature with the tools of narrative theory, we define it as a process (and not a spatial product) that determines the relative visibility of a text's structure of address. From a historical perspective, the method offers a corrective to extant surveys that tend to privilege one type of brevity (presentational immediacy) while constructing the development or evolution of the short story. From a theoretical perspective, it allows us to transcend the oversimplification of classifying the form as a dual-tradition genre. As I previously stated, the specific devices of addressivity I analyze (storytelling frames, direct addresses, attributional forms, and tense) are not the only possible foci of economy. Rather, these features allow me to explore in specific terms the interpretive work that stories demand within their historical setting. A similar project could be undertaken that would focus on a different set of stylistic conventions in a different sampling of stories and would prove, I have faith, much the same argument. But my central assertion that rhetorical economy and storytelling work at cross-purposes throughout the history of American short stories begs finally the same question that Updike's befuddled Bech tries to answer: Wither brevity in the near-decade aftermath of minimalism?

Even before Carver's premature death in August 1988, Dan Pope imagined the emergence of a "post-minimalist short story" that would restore the formalist plenitude that Carver and Mason had weaned from their work. "Perhaps in reaction against the minimalists' colorless, sparse style," storytellers would turn toward "haphazard, adjective-heavy, euphoric narration." Instead of ennui and apathy, its emotional palette would prove "super-charged" and "poetic." Rather than convey the evaporation of time, it would commit itself to "investigating the past as the unignorable, guiding force which shapes their characters' existence—a force which is never brushed aside by use of an indefinite present tense." One of minimalism's crankier critics, Sven Birkerts, hoped he detected a similar trend in story collections like David Foster Wallace's remarkable *Girl with Curious Hair* (1990). While minimalists do acknowledge that "larger and larger portions of what our lives are made up of cannot be encompassed in coherent narrative form," their extreme inward economy is "ultimately a cul-de-sac, leaving the larger part of life untouched." Wallace's outward-bound method, by contrast, can address the titanic banalities of modern existence "not [by] announcing as news the irreparable fragmentation of our cultural life . . . [but by] com[ing] toward us as a citizen of that new place, the place that minimalists have only been able to point toward." If Carver's and Mason's confessional stutters and stammers imply a wary desire to cut through the void of ennui and despair to make redemptive contact through stories, Wallace dramatizes the promiscuity of talk in the information age. With "a calculated pastiche of the prose [of] TV, ad brochures, and commercial newspeak," he cobbles "his expression together from everywhere," and, as a result, reveals how we are "frighteningly, *awesomely*, nowhere." In this style of "*post*-postmodernism," Birkerts argues, story writers will discover a better currency for capturing the vacuity of the 1990s than minimalism's verbal stinginess can afford.[2]

But while critics like Pope and Birkerts imagined a more expansive *fin-de-siécle* short story, others foresaw its future as the literary equivalent of nuclear fission, for an "explosive new literary form" was emerging: the *short* short story. According to Robert Shapard, the continuing diminution of the genre owed to a renewed interest in miniature storytelling forms, whether "sonnets, ghazals, folk tales, koans." Writers turned toward these more compact styles and structures as "a reaction to the overabundance of information in our time." The literariness of the "requisite descriptive exposition and character development" of the modern short story was losing its distinctiveness in a world bloated with factoids and infotainment; only by contracting its scope to "confer form on small corners of chaos" could the genre stand out against the ever irrelevant chatter of contemporary discourse.[3]

In introducing another anthology of these "sudden fictions," Charles Baxter explained the (putative) popularity of this ultra-abbreviated style of storytelling through the spatial metaphor of "reduced geographies." Unlike the novel, which is an "estate," the short story "is like an efficiency on the twenty-third floor. As it happens, more people these days live in efficiencies than on estates. The result may be that we will start to see a shift in the imperial self of the traditional novel to the *we* and *they* of communal stories."[4] The claim nicely conflates many of the commonplaces that traditionally define the short story. The evocation of *we* recalls the community-building that Benjamin claims is the central cultural function of storytelling, while the plurality of the pronoun also marks the genre as more democratic than the "imperialistic" novel, not unlike Bret

Harte's early celebration of the oral roots of the tale. Baxter's metaphor of "efficiency" as a sort of humble Spartan utility even counteracts Henry Seidel Canby's pejorative use of that word to dismiss the short story as a disposable consumer item. Finally, the description complements John Barth's argument in "It's a Long Story" (the source of my introductory image of readers "feed[ing] on short stories like living ducks") that the speed of contemporary history has rendered the big novel, that totem of "ampler times," a virtual museum piece. In a quick-cut, sound-bite culture, the promoters of the short-short claim, the short story is one traditional literary genre capable of accommodating the hyperaccelerated pace of life.

It should not surprise those who believe in the cyclical nature of literary history that neither prophecy was particularly original. In the early twentieth century, when aesthetes mourned the proliferation of "buttonholing" prose styles associated with the rise of the mass-market short story, one *Atlantic Monthly* contributor imagined a veritable palace coup by its practitioners: "If we must write our stories . . . in the flat prose of the newspaper column . . . sooner or later the spirit of style will ferment, will work, will grow violent under restraint. There will be reaction, explosion, revolution." At the very same time, as Andrew Levy has noted, the publishing industry was promoting the emergence of a "new" genre—*the short-short story!*[5]

Nor may it surprise readers that the short story of the 1990s has managed to fulfill both predictions. If one can take the most critically and commercially successful story collections of the past five years as representative, works as diverse as Wallace's *Girl*, Tim O'Brien's *The Things They Carried* (1990), Sandra Cisneros' *Woman Hollering Creek* (1992), Robert Olen Butler's *A Good Scent from a Strange Mountain* (1992), and Pam Houston's *Cowboys are My Weakness* (1993) are at once more "full-blooded" than Carver's and Mason's tales while retaining their anecdotal structures. What remains consistent in this body of short fiction is the foregrounded narrative context. As if recognizing the importance of encouraging the reader's response, these writers experiment with a variety of those "scraps of language" that intrigued Carver. I offer random excerpts:

- The narrator of Wallace's "Westward the Course of Empire Takes its Way" critiques his own performance: "That was all both too quick and too slow, for background—both intrusive and sketchy. But please, whether your imagination's engaged or not, please just acknowledge the propositions, is all. Because time is *severely limited, and whatever might be important lies ahead.*"

- Echoing "Dulce et Decorum Est," the storyteller of O'Brien's "How to Tell a True War Story" warns the reader that "if at the end of a war story you feel uplifted, or if you feel that some small bit of rectitude has been salvaged from the larger waste, then you have been made the victim of a very old and terrible lie."
- The Chicana voice of Cisneros' "Anguiano Religious Articles . . ." asks her audience, "You know that religious store on Soledad across from Sanitary Tortillas? Next to El Divorcio Lounge. Don't go in there. The man who owns it is a crab ass."
- A Vietnamese immigrant in Butler's "A Ghost Story" offers this proposition: "Let's say I got onto a bus, a Greyhound bus, and you saw me coming down the aisle. . . . if you would keep your eyes on me to let me know it's okay for me to sit next to you, I would tell you a true story about Vietnam."
- Finally, Houston's "How to Talk to a Hunter" begins with this prediction: "When he says 'Skins or blankets?' it will take you a moment to realize that he's asking which you want to sleep under. And in your hesitation he'll decide that he wants to see your skin wrapped in the big black moose hide."[6]

If Wallace imagines an audience growing impatient with his long-winded digressions, O'Brien gives us the essential criteria for evaluating the veracity of his story. While Butler emphasizes the necessity of hearing what his narrator has to say by incorporating the reader into his narrative frame, both Cisneros and Houston inscribe us into the action by making "you" their central character. To whatever degree they dramatize our participation, these storytellers involve us in their fiction; their addressivity seeks to engage us not through obstructionist devices that force us to infer details but by challenging us to account for their effect. In telling a story, they openly acknowledge our desire to identify and connect with the events they recount, to co-create them through our emotional and evaluative responses.

If measured for their ratio of stylistic brevity to storytelling then, many contemporary stories decidedly favor the latter. They offer themselves as aesthetic and cultural events and seek to achieve what all good stories aspire to: retaining a place in our memory by encouraging us to take of their body and blood and make something of them.

Notes to Introduction

1. John Barth, "It's a Long Story," *Harper's* (June 1990): 72.
2. Clare Hanson, "'Things out of Words': Towards a Poetics of Short Fiction," in Re-reading the Short Story, ed. Clare Hanson (London: Methuen, 1990), 28. See also Mary Rohrberger and Dan E. Burns, "Short Fiction and the Numinous Realm: Another Attempt at Definition," Modern Fiction Studies 28 (spring 1982): 5–12. Rohrberger and Burns, like many formalist critics, imply that authorial presence passifies readers by excusing them from the burden of interpretation. "As the form evolves from Hawthorne to Barthleme," they argue, "the reader is increasingly called upon to supply the temporal, causal, and overt thematic links formerly supplied by the author. Thus, the contemporary reader is required to participate in a kinship relation with the author that is even more active than the one Poe suggests" (6; emphasis added). The reader in such examples is portrayed as responding exclusively in aesthetic terms; this presumption will be questioned in the prologue to Part 2 and in Chapters 4, 5, and 6, which explore how direct addresses negotiate the non-artistic, socially oriented goals of the narrative exchange.
3. Ross Chambers, *Story and Situation: Narrative Seduction and the Power of Fiction*, 28. One drawback to defining the short story as an extension of oral storytelling traditions is that its persuasiveness depends in part on ignoring the genre's material dependence upon the periodical industry; nevertheless, the claim is pervasive in short-story criticism. See Bliss Perry, *A Study of Prose Fiction*, 304; James Cooper Lawrence, "A Theory of the Short Story," in *Short Story Theories*, ed. Charles E. May (Athens: Ohio University Press, 1976), 60–71; Warren S. Walker, "From Raconteur to Writer: Oral Roots and Printed Leaves of Short Fiction," in *The Teller and the Tale: Aspects of the Short Story*, ed. Wendell M. Aycock (Lubbock: Texas Tech Press, 1982), 13–26, to cite a small sample.
4. G. R. Thompson, "Literary Politics and the 'Legitimate Sphere':

Poe, Hawthorne, and the 'Tale Proper,'" *Nineteenth-Century Fiction* 49 (fall 1994): 195. See also Eileen Baldeshwiler, "The Lyric Short Story: The Sketch of a History," in *The New Short Story Theories*, 231–41; Walter Evans, "Nineteenth-Century American Theory of the Short Story: The Dual Tradition," *Orbis Litterarum* 34 (1979): 314–30; Clare Hanson, *Short Stories and Short Fictions, 1880–1980*, 4–9.

5. For many critics, genre definition remains the primary imperative of short-story study. According to Allan H. Pasco, "The short story genre has a central, identifiable set of characteristics which each age and each author deploys in different ways and with different variables. The result is generically recognizable, allowing for parallel and oppositional play, but specific to the author, age, and culture." Pasco rejects the idea that genre definition is an exclusionary practice resulting in prejudiced versions of literary history. As he argues, critics should acknowledge the practical benefits of definition: "It may be impossible to define a genre, but readers do it all the time, and they use their definitions as guides." He claims that "the work of defining a genre succeeds when the definition corresponds to general practice and understanding, when it includes the samples generally included, and excludes those normally left out, when its categories do not erroneously focus on elements which cause misapprehensions." See Allan H. Pasco, "On Defining Short Stories," *New Literary History* 22 (spring 1991): 410–11; repr. in *The New Short Story Theories*, 114–30. See also his "The Short Story: The Short of It," *Style* 27 (fall 1993): 442–63.
6. For a sampling of historical criticism, see Fred Lewis Pattee, *The Development of the American Short Story: An Historical Sketch*, with subsequent references cited parenthetically; Edward J. O'Brien, *The Advance of the American Short Story;* William Peden, *The American Short Story: Front Line in the National Defense of Literature*; Arthur Voss, *The American Short Story: A Critical Survey*. Four of the eight Twayne volumes on short fiction deal with the American short story: Eugene Current-Garcia, ed., *The American Short Story, Before 1850*, vol. 1; J. Donald Crowley, ed., *The American Short Story, 1850–1900*, vol. 2; Philip Stevick, ed., *The American Short Story, 1900–1945*,

vol. 3; Gordon Weaver, ed., *The American Short Story, 1945–1980*, vol. 4.

For theoretical analyses not discussed in this introduction, see Mary Rohrberger, *Hawthorne and the Modern Short Story: A Study in Genre*; Helmut Bonheim, *The Narrative Modes: Techniques of the Short Story*; Valerie Shaw, *The Short Story: A Critical Introduction*. The two most recent collections of genre criticism are *Short Story Theory at a Crossroads*, ed. Susan Lohafer and Jo Ellyn Clarey, and *The New Short Story Theories*, ed. Charles E. May, a significant update of May's influential 1976 sourcebook.

At least three recent works on the short story also address the need to move beyond generic taxonomies to merge theory and history. In *The Culture and Commerce of the American Short Story*, Andrew Levy offers a historical analysis of the "cultural capital," both aesthetic and economic, that has been invested in the form. His chapters on the various institutions that have sought to consecrate the short story as "America's workshop" are particularly intriguing: surveying the magazine industry, the textbook business, even creative-writing programs (in which the author was once enrolled), Levy explores how the categorical defiance of the genre—its ability to be at once "indirectly or directly profitable, while preserving a partial foothold in the high culture"—contributes to its historical identity crisis. While the author-centered chapters on Edgar Allan Poe, Edith Wharton, and Bobbie Ann Mason are too sketchy to be entirely persuasive, the study makes the valid point that there is much to be said about the cultural formations regulating perceptions of the short story that extant criticism, with its emphasis on the close readings of canonical texts, routinely ignores.

In *The Nineteenth-Century American Short Story: Language, Form, and Ideology*, Douglas Tallack applies poststructuralist theory to the history of the genre to undermine critical orthodoxies about brevity as a formal or structural device. Defining shortness in Derridean terms as a "restricted economy," Tallack focuses on what "has been eclipsed," marginalized, and even suppressed in extant short-story theories, exploring "what can be recovered by reading against the grain"—namely, the antigeneric phenomena that undermine notions of formal continuity and "development." By the author's own admission, this work is meta-critical in its interrogation of the sacred concepts of Romanticism and modernism that lend their authority to definitions of the short-story form; especially in the chapters on Poe, Tallack reinvigorates poststructuralism's own aging orthodoxies—polysemy, *différance*, dissemination—generally thought to be losing their currency in literary studies in favor of the materialist orientation of New Historicism. The terminology of deconstruction may be off-putting for non-specialists, but for those with even an introductory appreciation of the aims of poststructuralism, this study can be thought of as a more extended challenge to critical practice in the spirit of Friedman's "Recent Short Story Theories" (see note 7); that is, it demands that impressionistic critics examine their assumptions before defining the short story.

My own approach is probably most analogous to Dominic Head's *The Modernist Short Story: A Study in Theory and Practice*, which takes aim at the notion that brevity affords formal unity by tracing the *discontinuity* of presentation in the stories of British modernists, including Joyce, Woolf, Mansfield, and Lowry. While Head's introduction offers yet another important survey of the truisms of form and structure that have dominated short-story theory, it is his exploration of the relationship between literary technique and narrative authority that I find most intriguing. Indeed, no discussion of the Joycean epiphany as a device for narrative closure will ever seem as convincing as it traditionally has after reading Head's exploration of its disruptive effects on structural development. Because the focus is on modernist writers, however, Head tends to accept and even perpetuate the critical tendency to define brevity in spatial terms.

7. Norman Friedman, "Recent Short Story Theories: Problems in Definition," in *Short Story Theory at a Crossroads*, 16. Subsequent references will be cited parenthetically.
8. Edgar Allan Poe, Review of *Twice-Told Tales*, in *Edgar Allan Poe: Essays and Reviews*, ed. G. R. Thompson, 570–71. This May 1842 review from *Graham's Magazine* is the second of three essays in which Poe defined the short story in response to Hawthorne's tales. He had touched upon the subject in the

April 1842 issue of *Graham's* and would expand it yet again in *Godey's Lady's Book* in November 1847.

9. Of the various spatial measures of brevity, length has been most discredited. As Mary Louise Pratt notes, size is "altogether too quantitative, too material a feature" upon which to hinge a definition, for analyzing the amount of space that a story occupies affords little exploration of drama or texture. Pratt notes another handicap: *short* implies diminution, as in *shorter than the novel.* That pejorative connotation, Pratt argues, perpetuates a "hierarchical [relation] with the novel on top and the short story dependent" because *short* fails to measure up to *big* in terms of aesthetic achievement. Simply stated, if the measure of brevity is calibrated according to the length of the novel, short-story criticism risks suffering a perpetual Napoleon complex. See Mary Louise Pratt, "The Short Story: The Long and Short of It," *Poetics* 10 (1981): 179–80; repr. in *The New Short Story Theories*, 91–113.

The limitations of formalist and structuralist genre criticism are more complex, for these approaches are more apt to attribute brevity to one trait or characteristic. Consider three well-known examples of formalist criticism: In an influential study, Frank O'Connor argues that brevity necessitates an isolated narrative perspective, which allows the short story to dramatize alienation, the prevailing condition of modern life. Charles E. May claims that short stories by necessity deal with a brief experience whose manifold implications can only be alluded to vis-à-vis the epiphany, which forces readers to resort to a mythic mode of perception. Meanwhile, Clare Hanson suggests that brevity forces writers to foreground details and images that resist translation into more symbolic language, thus prompting a style of reading akin to dreaming. See Frank O'Connor, *The Lonely Voice: A Sketch of the Short Story*; Charles E. May, "The Unique Effect of the Short Story: A Reconsideration and an Example," *Studies in Short Fiction* 13 (summer 1976): 289–97; and "The Nature of Knowledge in Short Fiction," *Studies in Short Fiction* 21 (1984), 327–38, repr. in *The New Short Story Theories*, 131–46; Clare Hanson, "'Things out of Words': Towards a Poetics of Short Fiction," 22–33. Because these definitions claim to isolate qualitative differences between the short story and the novel, their limitations are painfully obvious: One can name alienated novel narrators, locate the epiphany in novel chapters, and identify short stories that do not foreground imagistic details. The point is that searching for a single, intrinsic trait can place us in the position of accounting for the exceptions to our rule as much as the examples illustrating it.

Structuralist approaches afford more flexibility because they present themselves as methodologies (rather than definitions) and offer a set of procedures that subsequent critics can modify and adapt. But flexibility only partly accounts for their broader applicability. Some of the credit must go as well to their expanded purview, for structuralist critics are typically interested in describing readers' responses to brevity. The two best-known structuralist studies are Susan Lohafer's *Coming to Terms with the Short Story* and John Gerlach's *Toward the End: Closure and Structure in the American Short Story*, which are often invoked in the same breath, despite their considerable differences. Lohafer contends that short stories speak a "contracted language" that heightens the reader's awareness of sequentiality. Experiencing an "impetus toward closure," we encounter "interferences" like the density of style or connotative ambiguity that inhibit our reading (34). Gerlach, meanwhile, argues that endings serve different functions in different historical periods and offer a taxonomy of signals of closure that distinguishes the nineteenth-century tale from the modern short story. These signals either satisfy or disappoint the reader's expectations for plot resolutions because "endings are in one sense in the reader's head; the reader feels them, creates them" (16). In "Recent Short Story Theories," Friedman notes a common drawback to these arguments: Both Lohafer and Gerlach accept Poe's blanket statement that brevity offers a greater "totality" of effect, leaving "the soul of the reader . . . at the writer's control." By assuming that shortness is *inevitably* more intense than longer forms, structuralist critics fail to entertain the possibility "that because a short story takes less time to read, even though we may remember its details for a while, it may make *less* of an impression on us in the long run than a novel, simply because we spend less time with it" (26).

I would call attention to a related handicap: Not only is brevity said to create an intensity of effect, but it is presumed to affect all readers in the same way. When Lohafer, for example, writes that "readers of short fiction are the most end-conscious of readers" (94) or when Gerlach describes the short story as "that genre in which anticipation of the ending is always present" (17), one wishes to ask just who these readers are. They come to the text with a single set of expectations, motives, and responses, which Gerlach goes so far as to claim constructs "an underlying narrative grid that . . . each reader applies to any story and that every writer depends on the reader knowing." But what of readers who lack this competence? Do they experience brevity differently, or at all? Such questions dramatize the fact that studies like *Coming to Terms* and *Toward the End* locate effects within narrative devices so that structure determines our reaction. Our temperament is not important here; we merely enact the response dictated by the text.

Because both Lohafer and Gerlach admit that they are more interested in the poetics of brevity rather than its history, it may seem unfair to criticize them for not addressing the historical relevance of the effects they outline. My point is that they were written at a certain moment in the development of reception theory and that audience-oriented approaches now attempt to delineate textual effects in a way that should alleviate Friedman's wariness of short-story theory relying too heavily upon "present-day reader response terms" (25). Indeed, I would replace the phrase *present day* with *first generation*, for these works are indebted to Wolfgang Iser's *The Implied Reader: Patterns of Communication in Prose Fiction from Bunyan to Beckett* and Stanley Fish's *Surprised by Sin: The Reader in "Paradise Lost"* and *Self-Consuming Artifacts: The Experience of Seventeenth-Century Literature*. These founding texts of reception theory were the first to explore the reader's power to make meaning and inspired a range of applications illustrated in collections like Susan R. Suleiman and Inge Crosman's *The Reader in the Text* and Jane P. Tompkins' *Reader-Response Criticism*. But critics now recognize that Iser's and Fish's interpretive models idealized reception by not accounting for the cultural conditions that shape a particular audience's interpretive habits. In light of the current emphasis on the historicity of response in second-generation reception theory like James L. Machor's *Readers in History: Nineteenth-Century American Lit-*

erature and the Contexts of Response, it seems appropriate to suggest that we can surefootedly describe the consequences of brevity—so long as we strike a balance between the powers of texts and readers alike. Since *Coming to Terms*, in fact, Lohafer has moved in this direction. Her current work, modeled upon cognitive analysis, draws from data such as student journals to analyze different ways narrative structures can be experienced. The approach is reminiscent of the subjective criticism of David Bleich and Norman Holland, for rather than suggesting how the closure of a story dictates audience response, she now examines how a variety of respondents single out moments in the text that, for them, "preclose" the structure and shape their experience of suspense and drama. See Lohafer, "Preclosure and Story Processing," in *Short Story Theory at a Crossroads*, 249–75; and her "A Cognitive Approach to Storyness," in *The New Short Story Theories*, 301–11.

Whether structuralism and reception theory can properly acknowledge cultural conditioning remains an issue of debate among short-story critics. In "Recent Short Story Theories," Friedman insists that form and structure should only be regarded as the symptoms, not the sources of brevity. "We can only begin with the fact of brevity and explore its possible causes," he argues (28). Rather than explore questions of effect that are generalizations, he recommends a methodology first suggested in his influential 1958 essay "What Makes a Short Story Short?," repr. in *Essentials of the Theory of Fiction*, edited by Michael J. Hoffman and Patrick D. Murphy. The approach seeks to overcome the reductiveness of formalist theories by defining brevity as a function of dramatic scope, not size, that measures the dimension of a particular plot rather than its length. A story's abbreviated breadth might contain an "inherently small" single "action," ranging from a single speech (Dorothy Parker's "A Telephone Call") to a scene (Ernest Hemingway's "Hills Like White Elephants") to an episode (Hemingway's "Ten Indians"), or it may encompass a number of episodes that must be cut down to size (Tolstoy's "The Death of Ivan Ilyich").

The method *should* allow one to explore what makes a story "short in the telling," but Friedman's focus does not shift far enough from form to expression and thus limits its own applicability by restricting attention to spatial issues. Accounting for "how and why a story gets to be short" proves a speculative enterprise: "Why an author makes a certain initial choice regarding size we can only guess, except that he probably senses that he has a whole and complete action in itself and that this will suffice as a basis for separate treatment. This is a matter, then, of the original conception, and all that we can say is that a writer chooses to treat actions of different sizes because he feels, whether by habit or deliberate choice or intuition or some combination, that any given one embodies all that is relevant to his purpose." If brevity is solely a function of an author's purpose, Friedman's approach is at best the study of composition history. At worst, it invokes the intentional fallacy, as when he accounts for the episodic construction of John Steinbeck's "Flight": "We may infer that Steinbeck intended to leave us with feelings of mingled pity and admiration for this boy as his story unfolds" (164). In either case, brevity is fixed neatly within the text as a structural constituent, and broader contextual inquiries about why episodes might be a more common feature of short stories than scenes (or vice versa) go unaddressed.

10. Henry T. Tuckerman, "Nathaniel Hawthorne," repr. in *The Recognition of Nathaniel Hawthorne: Selected Criticism Since 1828*, ed. B. Bernard Cohen (Ann Arbor: University of Michigan Press, 1969), 55–63.
11. Henry James, *The Art of the Novel*, ed. Richard P. Blackmur (New York: Scribner's, 1932), 219–20. Subsequent references to this edition will be cited parenthetically. James's comments on American definitions of brevity in the short story are foreshadowed in a more obscure essay, Henry James, "The Storyteller at Large: Mr. Henry Harland," in *The American Essays of Henry James*, ed. Leon Edel (Princeton: Princeton University Press, 1989), 186–93, first published in 1898 and uncollected in James's lifetime. For a fuller examination of James's attitude toward short-story brevity, see Richard A. Hocks, *Henry James: A Study of the Short Fiction*.
12. Ernest Hemingway, "The Art of the Short Story," in *New Essays on the Short Stories of Ernest Hemingway*, ed. Jackson J. Benson (Durham: Duke University Press, 1991), 5. Subsequent ref-

erences will be cited parenthetically. For other allusions to the "thing left out," see Hemingway, *Ernest Hemingway: Selected Letters, 1917–1961*, ed. Carlos Baker (New York: Scribner's, 1981), 176, 180; *Death in the Afternoon*, 132; George Plimpton, ed. *Writers at Work: The Paris Review Interviews* (New York: Penguin, 1977), 229*ff*; *A Moveable Feast* (New York: Scribner's, 1964), 211.

13. Paul Smith, "Hemingway's Early Manuscripts: The Theory and Practice of Omission," in *The Journal of Modern Literature* 10 (June 1983): 268–88. For another study of Hemingway's composition process, see Susan F. Beegel, *Hemingway's Craft of Omission: Four Manuscript Examples*.
14. Flannery O'Connor, "Writing Short Stories," in *Mysteries and Manners: Occasional Prose*, ed. Sally and Robert Fitzgerald (New York: Farrar Straus Giroux, 1969), 93. Subsequent references will be cited parenthetically.
15. Raymond Carver, "On Writing," in *Fires: Essays, Poems, Stories* (Santa Barbara: Capra Press, 1983), 16–18.
16. Eudora Welty, "Looking at Short Stories," in *The Eye of the Story: Selected Essays and Reviews* (New York: Random House, 1978), 97–118. This essay revises a 1949 *Atlantic Monthly* article by Welty entitled "The Writing and Reading of Short Stories," which is reprinted in *Short Story Theories*, 159–77. For an introduction to the origins of the showing vs. telling debate, see Wayne C. Booth's *The Rhetoric of Fiction*, whose first three chapters detail the standard arguments for eliminating the narrative context. Indeed, Booth's exacting critique of the inconsistencies of this dogma is still valid despite its formalist orientation: "Everything [that] shows will serve to tell; the line between showing [*mimesis*] and telling [*diegesis*] is always to some degree an arbitrary one [because] the author's judgment is always present, always evident to anyone who knows how to look for it" (20).
17. T. Alan Broughton, "How Short is Short?" *The Writer* 106 (July 1993): 15. See also Rust Hills, *Writing in General and the Short Story in Particular: An Informal Textbook*, who claims that "the need for exposition is seldom sufficient to make up for the sense of consequencelessness that often results from uninvolved narration" (128). *Uninvolved* refers to the storyteller's

relationship with the text, not the audience's; for Hills at least, the two are mutually exclusive.

18. Bret Harte, "The Rise of the 'Short Story,'" in *Discussions of the Short Story*, ed. Hollis Summers (Boston: D. C. Heath, 1963), 6. First published in 1899. For Brander Matthews's comment, see "The Philosophy of the Short-Story," in *The New Short Story Theories*, 79–80, footnote 6. To recognize more fully how orality for Harte is a folk culture tradition rather than a literary one, I recommend that readers contrast this essay to William O'Rourke's "Morphological Metaphors for the Short Story: Matters of Production, Reproduction, and Consumption," in *Short Story Theory at a Crossroads*, 193–208, which attempts to redefine the short story as a "written" genre. Like the sermon, which is the tale's "least discussed progenitor," the short story "asks readers to contemplate what they experience while experiencing it," provoking them "to be reflective, self-examining, conscious of their apprehension of the story." Not coincidentally, these interpretive demands are "the hallmark of the written form," and—in a revealing word choice—they are said to "compensate for the major fact of its oral form: the relationship of the spectator to the teller, just the oral element that the modern short story retains" (201).

    O'Rourke's strategy here is to shift from writing to orality the burden of a certain supposed drawback—its "audience directed" quality, the author-audience relationship—in order to emphasize the interaction of reader and text. By claiming that the short story forces readers to pay more attention to content than context, he projects onto the genre the very features that make it recoverable as a literary or "written" form—exactly the opposite approach that Harte takes. To make it clear that the interpretive demands of the genre complement writing more than orality, O'Rourke even adds a gratuitous slur: "the oral traditions of the tale (which were found abundantly in the popular short story of the twenties and thirties) now find themselves cozily at home in the empty mansions of the best-selling romance novel." He cleverly implies, in other words, that "oral traditions"—which, it should be noted, are never specifically defined—account for the supposedly baleful popularity of romance fiction.

19. "The Art of Story-Telling," in *The American Magazine and Historical Chronicle* (1744): 470; John Neal, "Story-Telling," in *New-England Magazine* (January 1835): 1–8; Mark Twain, "How to Tell a Story," in *The Complete Essays of Mark Twain*, ed. Charles Neider (Garden City: Hanover, 1956), 156. Several excellent histories of the influence of American vernacular on literary styles are available. See, for example, Leo Marx's well-known essays "The Vernacular Tradition in American Writing" and "'Noble Shit': The Uncivil Response of American Writers to Civil Religion," in *The Pilot and the Passenger: Essays on Literature, Technology, and Culture in the United States* (New York: Oxford University Press, 1988), 3–17 and 261–90 respectively; Richard Bridgman, *The Colloquial Style in America*; and Cecelia Tichi, *Shifting Gears: Technology, Literature, Culture in Modernist America*, which offers an informative contextual analysis of the cultural influences of rhetorical economy on modernism.
20. Walter Benjamin, "The Storyteller," in *Illuminations*, trans. Harry Zohn, ed. Hannah Arendt (New York: Schocken, 1969), 87. Subsequent references will be cited parenthetically.
21. Susan Snaider Lanser, *The Narrative Act: Point of View in Prose Fiction* (Princeton: Princeton University Press, 1981), 269.

Notes to Part 1

1. Edgar Allan Poe, Review of *Twice-Told Tales* and *Mosses from an Old Manse*, in *Edgar Allan Poe: Essays and Reviews* ed., G. R. Thompson (New York: Library of America, 1984), 583–84. This essay—the last of Poe's three reviews of Hawthorne's short fiction—is better known by the title "Tale Writing—Nathaniel Hawthorne."
2. Quoted in Fred Lewis Pattee, *The Development of the American Short Story*, 146 and 31–32, respectively.
3. Rufus Griswold, *The Prose Writers of America*, 275. For representative adaptations of Poe's short-story theory, see Champion Bissell, "Serials and Continuations," *Sartain's Union Magazine* 8 (1851): 273; and "Review of New Books," *Graham's Magazine* 40 (1852): 443. See also Robert F. Marler,

"From Tale to Short Story: The Emergence of a New Genre in the 1850s," in *The New Short Story Theories*, 171–72.

4. "The New Copyright Law," in *American Monthly Magazine* 11 (February 1838): 109.
5. Kristie Hamilton, "Toward a Cultural Theory of the Antebellum Literary Sketch," *Genre* 23 (winter 1990): 305. Subsequent references will be cited parenthetically.
6. W. S. Penn, "The Tale as Genre in Short Fiction," *Southern Humanities Review* 15 (1981): 234–35; repr. in *The New Short Story Theories*, 44–55.
7. Ann Douglas, *The Feminization of American Culture*, 287; Sandra A. Zagarell, "Narrative of Community: The Identification of a Genre," *Signs* 13 (spring 1988): 498–527.
8. Ross Chambers, *Story and Situation*, 25–26.
9. Alessandro Portelli, *The Text and the Voice: Writing, Speech, and Democracy in American Literature*, 188, 196.
10. Washington Irving, "The Art of Book Making," in *The Sketch Book of Geoffrey Crayon, Gent.*, ed. Haskell Springer (Boston: Twayne Publishers, 1978), 65–66, vol. 8 of *The Complete Writings of Washington Irving*. Subsequent references will be cited parenthetically; references to Irving's correspondence and journals will be cited in the text by volume.
11. Irving's indifference to Americanisms is nicely captured in an 1817 journal entry: "There is an . . . endeavour among some of the writers of the day (who fortunately have not any great weight) to introduce into poetry all the common colloquial phrases and idioms. . . . In their rage for Simplicity they would be coarse and commonplace. Now the Language of poetry cannot be too pure and choice" (2: 104).
12. Ian Reid, "Destabilizing Frames for Story," in *Short Story Theory at a Crossroads*, 304. Subsequent references will be cited parenthetically.
13. Review of *The Sketch Book of Geoffrey Crayon, Gent.* by Washington Irving, *Western Review and Literary Magazine* 2 (May 1820): 248. Subsequent references will be cited parenthetically. At least one other reader challenged the "reasonableness" of Irving's tales: Editor William Coleman, attaching a brief qualification to a *Sketch Book* review in the *New York Post*, suggested that the "probability" of fiction "should not be

overlooked" when evaluating literature. See the *New York Post* 26 June 1819: 1. According to Haskell Springer, Irving may have modeled the resisting reader in the postscript of "Sleepy Hollow" upon Coleman (8: xxvi).

14. William H. Prescott, "Essay Writing," *The North American Review* 14 (April 1822): 333; William Landor [pen name of Horace Binney Wallace], "Washington Irving: His Works, Genius, and Character," *Sartain's Union Magazine* 7 (1850): 289. Wallace later republished this essay under his own name, see *Literary Criticisms and Other Papers* (Philadelphia: Parry and McMillan, 1856), 67–91.
15. R. Jackson Wilson, *Figures of Speech: American Writers and the Literary Marketplace, from Benjamin Franklin to Emily Dickinson*, 104–5. Subsequent references will be cited parenthetically. For an introduction to biographical readings of the tales, see Parts III and IV of Andrew B. Myers, ed., *A Century of Commentary on the Works of Washington Irving* (Tarrytown: Sleepy Hollow, 1976).
16. Jeffrey Rubin-Dorsky, *Adrift in the Old World: The Psychological Pilgrimage of Washington Irving*, 113.
17. Knickerbocker's transitory social authority is established by Irving in a notebook entry written in 1810, one year after his *History of New York* was published: "Diedrich . . . great block[hea]d. at school . . . only signs of mind were a great turn for reading . . . his historic turn may have arisen from his early reading[,] for the first books he read was the history of Giles Gingerbread. . . . Diedrich seized with an unconquerable ambition of being renowned—cut his name on every fence & even in the village steeple" (2: 20).
18. That is, a community of accepting readers who are most likely men. Judith Fetterley has argued that the story excludes women readers from identifying with it; the stereotype of the "termagant wife" establishes woman as the oppositional authority against which the character rebels. As a result, a woman reader "is no part of the act of resistance, nor does she recognize herself in that which is being resisted." See Judith Fetterley, *The Resisting Reader: A Feminist Approach to American Fiction*, 10. As James L. Machor has suggested, however, an antebellum woman reader might not have experienced the

story as a misogynist work but "a cautionary tale about marriage and wifehood": "Reading within a cultural ideology that expected her to attract a man and then nurture his devotion to family life, [she] could respond to Dame Van Winkle not as an embodiment of womanhood but as a wife whose shrewishness prevents her from being a good spouse. . . . Dame Van Winkle could become [for her] a warning about traits to avoid for a sound domestic relationship." See James L. Machor, "Historical Hermeneutics and Antebellum Fiction," in *Readers in History: Nineteenth-Century American Literature and the Contexts of Response*, 57–58.

19. Terence Martin, "Rip, Ichabod, and the American Imagination," *American Literature* 31 (May 1959): 144–45.
20. Joshua Leavitt, *Easy Lessons in Reading for the Use of the Younger Classes in Common Schools*, qtd. in Nina Banton Smith, *American Reading Instruction: Its development and significance in gaining a perspective on current practices in reading* (Newark: International Reading Association, 1965), 41. See Smith's entire chapter, 36–73, for insight into the pedagogy of "oral reading." See also David D. Hall, "The Uses of Literacy in New England, 1600–1850," in *Printing and Society in Early America*, ed. William L. Joyce, et. al., 1–47; E. Jennifer Monagham and E. Wendy Saal, "The Reader, the Scribe, the Thinker," in *Formation of School Subjects: The Struggle for Creating an American Institution*, ed. Thomas S. Popkewitz (New York: Falmer, 1987), 85–89.
21. For a survey of the "reading-as-eating" trope in Romantic criticism, see Nina Baym, *Novels, Readers, and Reviewers: Responses to Fiction in Antebellum America*, 54–58.
22. As Jeffrey Rubin-Dorsky suggests, "Having turned into a curmudgeon, and disturbed to learn both the real events of that fateful night and that he has now become a figure of comic derision, he insists that the portrait of himself must be a fiction. Ironically, having once believed in magic and the imagination, he now insists on law and logic. Yet he is still the victim of a joke." Though no textual evidence substantiates the claim, Rubin-Dorsky makes an imaginative connection that Irving would appreciate. See Rubin-Dorsky, *Adrift in the Old World*, 119.
23. See *Salmagundi No. 12*, vol. 3 of *The Complete Writings of*

Washington Irving, in which Jeremy Cockloft wonders aloud whether "it takes greater ability to mend a law than a kettle . . . [especially] laws that are broken a hundred times a day with impunity" (229). For background on New York's municipal government during the Irving era, see Graham Hodges, *New York City Cartmen, 1667–1850*, especially Chapter 9, "Creating Security within the Municipal Government, 1801–1818" (108–28).

24. Hedges complains of this "technical inconsistency" that nevertheless does not break the "unity of interest and feeling" in *The Sketch Book* so the audience "finally wants to read 'Rip Van Winkle' and 'The Legend of Sleepy Hollow,' if not as stories told by Crayon instead of Knickerbocker, then at least as stories that have touched Crayon almost personally." See William Hedges, *Washington Irving: An American Study, 1802–1832*, 60. For Rubin-Dorsky, Knickerbocker reflects different aspects of Crayon's persona: "Like so many of Crayon's views and notions, the tales have been picked up along the route of his incessant travels. . . . [T]hey assume importance in *The Sketch Book* because they are fundamentally expressive of Crayon's concerns. Above all, they address the question of what role the imagination is to play in the life of an early-nineteenth-century American author" (101). Neither critic takes into account the third voice, the original storyteller.
25. Thomas M. Leitch, *What Stories Are: Narrative Theory and Interpretation*, 22. For Jefferson's comments on "Rip," see Pattee's *Development of the American Short Story*, 38–39.
26. G. R. Thompson, *The Art of Authorial Presence: Hawthorne's Provincial Tales*, 38. Subsequent references will be cited parenthetically.
27. Quoted in Hawthorne's *The Centenary Edition of the Works of Nathaniel Hawthorne, Volume XIV:* Twice-told Tales, ed. William Charvat (Columbus: Ohio University Press, 1968), 513. All references to Hawthorne's work are drawn from this edition; individual volumes will be cited parenthetically in the text.
28. Jorge Luis Borges, "Nathaniel Hawthorne," in *Borges: A Reader*, ed. Emir Rodriguez Monegal and Alastair Reid (New York: E. P. Dutton, 1981), 226. Subsequent references will be cited parenthetically. For an example of how formalist criticism

dismisses "Wakefield," see Hyatt Waggoner, *Hawthorne: A Critical Study*, 63 *ff.*

29. Arnold Weinstein, *Speech, Self, and Place in American Fiction from Hawthorne to DeLillo*, 16. I take this phrase somewhat out of context, for Weinstein is one of the few recent critics to focus on the character of Wakefield himself rather than the storyteller's presentation of the tale.
30. Alexander Gelley, *Narrative Crossings: Theory and Pragmatics of Prose Fiction*, 169. Subsequent references will be cited parenthetically.
31. Ralph Waldo Emerson, *The Journals of Ralph Waldo Emerson*, ed. William H. Gilman, et al. (Cambridge: Belknap Press, 1960—), IX: 405.
32. Lawrence Buell, *New England Literary Culture: From Revolution through Renaissance*, 157–65.
33. See John G. Bayer, "Narrative Techniques and Oral Tradition in *The Scarlet Letter*," *American Literature* 52 (May 1980): 250–63; David S. Reynolds, *Beneath the American Renaissance*, 225–42; Michael P. Kramer, *Imagining Language in America: From Revolution to Civil War*, 162–97.
34. Edwin P. Whipple, "Nathaniel Hawthorne," in *Hawthorne: The Critical Heritage*, ed. J. Donald Crowley, 342–43. See also earlier reviews by Whipple (156) and Duyckinck (78).
35. See C. S. B. Swann, "The Practice and Theory of Storytelling: Nathaniel Hawthorne and Walter Benjamin," *Journal of American Studies* 12 (1978): 185–202. Exactly why *The Story Teller* went unpublished remains a mystery. After failing to find a book publisher for the project, Hawthorne (through an intermediary, Samuel G. Goodrich) placed it with the *New-England Magazine* for serialization. "The Story Teller. No. 1" and "The Story Teller. No. 2" (now titled "Passages") appeared in November and December 1834, but the succeeding fifteen pieces appeared without the intended storytelling frame. Most readings of the probable contents are based on Nelson F. Adkins's "The Early Projected Works of Nathaniel Hawthorne," *Papers of the Bibliographical Society of America* 39 (1945): 119–55. Because the narrator speaks of writing "Wakefield" while *The Story Teller* tales were to have been orally performed, some critics have argued against its inclusion in the cycle, yet they

overlook the point that, as "Passages" reveals, the narrator is writing the tales some time after they were performed. What is missing is the scene of the story's performance, the contextual link, that would have incorporated the tale into the frame.

36. David Leverenz, *Manhood and the American Renaissance*, 231–32.
37. Louis O. Mink, "History and Fiction as Modes of Comprehension," in *Historical Understanding*, ed. Brian Fay, Eugene O. Golub, and Richard T. Cann (Ithaca: Cornell University Press, 1987), 56.
38. Robert L. Chibka, "Hawthorne's Tale Told Twice: A Reading of 'Wakefield,'" *Emerson Society Quarterly* 28 (fall 1982): 226. Subsequent references will be cited parenthetically.
39. David S. Reynolds, "From Doctrine to Narrative: The Rise of Pulpit Storytelling in America," *American Quarterly* 33 (1981): 479–98. See also Charles Grandison Finney, *Lectures on Revivals of Religion*, 208–9.
40. Richard Brodhead, *The School of Hawthorne*, 28.
41. Herman Melville, "Bartleby, the Scrivener: A Story of Wall Street," in *The Writings of Herman Melville, Vol. IX:* The Piazza Tales *and Other Prose Pieces, 1839–1860*, ed. Harrison Hayford, Alma A. MacDougall, G. Thomas Tanselle, et. al. (Evanston and Chicago: Northwestern University Press, 1987), 14, 19. Subsequent references will be cited parenthetically.
42. Dan McCall, *The Silence of Bartleby*, 116–20.
43. Gregory S. Jay, *America the Scrivener: Deconstruction and the Subject of Literary History*, 25–26.
44. Hershel Parker, "The Sequel in 'Bartleby,'" in *Bartleby the Inscrutable: A Collection of Commentary on Herman Melville's Tale "Bartleby the Scrivener,"* ed. Thomas M. Inge (Hamden, Conn.: Archon Books, 1979), 161.
45. Walter J. Ong, *Orality and Literacy: The Technologizing of the Word*, 52–53.
46. Charles G. Hoffman, "The Shorter Fictions of Herman Melville," *South Atlantic Quarterly* 52 (July 1953): 420.
47. Jean-Nöel Kapferer, *Rumors: Uses, Interpretations and Images*, 183.
48. W. L. Symonds, "The Carnival of the Romantic," *Atlantic Monthly* 6 (August 1860): 129–41.
49. William Dean Howells, *Criticism and Fiction*, 104.

Notes to Part 2

1. Quoted in Rebecca Harding Davis, *Life in the Iron Mills and Other Stories*, ed. Tillie Olsen (New York: Feminist Press, 1985), 153. All parenthetical references to the story itself refer to this edition.
2. Elizabeth Stuart Phelps, "Stories that Stay," *Century* 81 (1910): 120.
3. Robyn R. Warhol, *Gendered Interventions: Narrative Discourse in the Victorian Novel*, 205. Subsequent references will be cited parenthetically.
4. Henry James, "The Jolly Corner," in *Eight Tales from the Major Phase:* In the Cage *and Others*, ed. Morton Dauwen Zabel (New York: W. W. Norton, 1958), 337.
5. As Christopher Wilson has noted, genteel publications like the *Atlantic, Harper's, The Century*, and other pivotal promoters of realism endorsed the idea of a "companionate readership" in which the audience could "pause, reconsider, and even collaborate in the meaning of the text" only *after* mass-market competitors like *McClure's, The World's Work*, and *Ladies' Home Journal* absorbed the burgeoning rhetoric of the progressive era's consumer culture and transformed reading from a leisurely exchange into an aggressive "embrace of 'real life.'" By 1900, the *Atlantic* was lamenting the disappearance of addresses to the "gentle reader" in stories—barely forty years after actively campaigning against them. See Christopher Wilson, "The Rhetoric of Consumption: Mass Market Magazines and the Demise of the Gentle Reader, 1880–1920," in *The Culture of Consumption: Critical Essays in American History, 1880–1980*, ed. Richard Wightman Fox and T. J. Jackson Lears (New York: Pantheon, 1984), 41–42.
6. Alice B. Neal Haven, "American Female Authorship," *Godey's Lady's Book* 44 (1852): 145–48.
7. See Robert F. Marler, "From Tale to Short Story: The Emergence of a New Genre in the 1850s," in *New Short Story Theories*, 153–69.
8. The "banging" quotation appears in Edwin H. Cady's *The Realist at War: The Mature Years, 1885–1920, of William Dean Howells*, 1. The reference to Jewett and Freeman appears in Howells' *Criticism and Fiction*, 29.
9. Rose Terry Cooke, "Miss Muffett and the Spider," *Harper's New Monthly Magazine* 20 (1860): 764.

10. See T. S. Perry, "Ivan Turgenieff," *Atlantic Monthly* 33 (May 1874): 569; Henry James, Review of *Around a Spring*, by Gustave Droz, *Atlantic Monthly* 28 (August 1871): 248; James, Review of *Waiting for the Verdict*, by Rebecca Harding Davis, *The Nation* 21 November 1867: 410; and James, Review of *Dallas Gallbraith* by Davis, *The Nation* 22 October 1868: 330–31.
11. Fields's request is indicative of the compulsory femininity to which women writers were expected to subscribe. See Jean Fagan Yellin, "The 'Feminization' of Rebecca Harding Davis," *American Literary History* 2 (1990): 203–19. Gilman quotes Scudder's rejection in her autobiography, *The Living of Charlotte Perkins Gilman*, 119. For the "chords of feeling" comment, see Review of *The Foe in the Household*, by Caroline Chesebro' *Atlantic Monthly* 28 (July 1871): 126.
12. Amy Kaplan, *The Social Construction of Realism*, 28. For other gender-oriented studies of the rise of realism, see Alfred Habegger, *Gender, Fantasy, and Realism in American Literature*, 103–12; Josephine Donovan, *New England Local Color Literature: A Woman's Tradition*; Susan Coultrap-McQuin, *Doing Literary Business: American Women Writers in the Nineteenth Century*; Christopher Wilson, *The Labor of Words: Literary Professionalism in the Progressive Era*, 1–62; Michael Davitt Bell, *The Problem of American Realism: Studies in the Cultural History of a Literary Idea*.
13. William Dean Howells, "Novel-Writing and Novel-Reading," in *Howells and James: A Double Billing* (New York: New York Public Library Pamphlets, 1958), 6.
14. Frank Norris, "Why Women Should Write the Best Novels and Why They Don't," in *The Complete Works of Frank Norris*, Volume 7 (Garden City: Doubleday, 1928), 177–78.
15. Karl Kroeber, *Retelling/Rereading: The Fate of Storytelling in Modern Times*, 99.
16. Elaine Sargent Apthorp, "Sentiment, Naturalism, and the Female Regionalist." *Legacy* 7 (spring 1990): 6.
17. Maribel W. Molyneaux, for example, argues that Davis conveys autobiographical frustrations with limited opportunities for women's work through the "intrusive narrative voice of a self-announcing woman writer"—though at no point does the narrator actually announce her womanhood. By contrast, Jane

Atteridge Rose claims that Davis assumes a specifically masculine voice because "she could not have told a story of sordid life in the iron mills without pulling the focus away from the story to explain her knowledge of it," though, again, nothing in the text reveals the narrator's sex. See, Molyneaux, "Sculpture in the Iron Mills: Rebecca Harding Davis's Korl Woman." *Women's Studies* 17 (1990): 163, and Rose, "Reading 'Life in the Iron-Mills' Contextually: A Key to Rebecca Harding Davis's Fiction," in *Conversations: Contemporary Critical Theory and the Teaching of Literature*, eds. Charles Moran and Elizabeth F. Penfield (Urbana: NCTE, 1989), 191.

18. Patricia Yaeger, *Honey-Mad Women: Emancipatory Strategies in Women's Writing*, 268. Subsequent references will be cited parenthetically.
19. Robert F. Marler, "From Tale to Short Story," 169; Arthur Lubow, *The Reporter Who Would Be King: A Biography of Richard Harding Davis*, 15–16; Sharon M. Harris, *Rebecca Harding Davis and American Realism*, 28–57.
20. Judith Fetterley, for example, dismisses Deborah as an artistic failure because her presence suggests that "women's hunger for love may be denied or fed, but whether their life turns tragic or joyous bears no relation to their class." See *Provisions: A Reader of Nineteenth-Century Women Writers*, 312.
21. Dillon defines footings as a complex register of linguistic markers, including interrogatives, modals, and pronouns, that convey varying degrees of "engagement" ranging from romance to combat between a speaker and addressee. See Dillion, *Rhetoric as Social Imagination: Explorations in the Interpersonal Function of Language*, 14–34.
22. Sacvan Bercovitch, *The American Jeremiad*, xi. Subsequent references will be cited parenthetically.
23. Jane Tompkins, *Sensational Designs: The Cultural Work of American Fiction, 1790–1865*, 143. In her chapter on *Uncle Tom's Cabin* in *Gendered Interventions,* Warhol defines the sermonic direct addresses as part of the engaging narrative strategy because the invocation of "you," "thou," and "ye" make a "general appeal to the reader's presumed experience of emotions, in order to render more immediately present the feelings" of the characters. What makes Stowe's novel a

"cross-gendered" text are more specific addresses to readers that reveal the narrator staging the text (101–15). I have redefined Warhol's categories to better illustrate the split between gendered narrative and gendered style in "Life in the Iron Mills." Unlike Stowe, Davis does not distance her real-life audience to signal irony. I associate the jeremiad with the distancing strategy because the scripted role of the "you" encourages the audience to identify with the storyteller's "we." While distanced from the fictional reader, we are incorporated in the narrator's ideal community.

24. The passage ends with an odd, ironic aphorism that illustrates how swiftly the storyteller switches between the distancing and engaging strategies: "Man cannot live by work alone." Speaking an aphorism about "man" that sounds suspiciously like something Dr. May might declare, the narrator dramatizes how authoritarian speech acts distance an audience by predicating a reality rather than negotiating it. By doing so, however, she/he would seem to distance the audience as well at the very moment that she/he seems most interested in engaging it.
25. Nina Baym, *Novels, Readers, and Reviewers*, 257.
26. The term first appears in Kate Field's article "English Authors in Florence," *Atlantic Monthly* 14 (December 1864): 666.
27. Horace Scudder, "New England in the Short Story," *Atlantic Monthly* 63 (June 1891): 845–46. Subsequent references will be cited parenthetically.
28. Horace Scudder, "Stockton's Stories," *Atlantic Monthly* 59 (January 1887): 131.
29. Horace Scudder, "Miss Jewett," *Atlantic Monthly* 73 (January 1894): 133.
30. See Ann Douglas Wood, "The Literature of Impoverishment: The Women Local Colorists in America 1865–1914," *Women's Studies* 1 (1972): 3–45, perhaps the most controversial critique of local-color writing, which argues that women regionalists, unlike the generation of sentimentalists before them, retreated from the literary marketplace and reconciled themselves to the marginality created for them by the publishing industry. In *The Problem of American Realism: Studies in the Cultural History of a Literary Idea*, Michael Davitt Bell flirts with a similar thesis, though he ultimately decides that "assumptions at the heart of

realist thinking . . . prohibited women from full participation in the realist program" (177). For arguments that specifically define local color as a woman's literary tradition, see Josephine Donovan, *New England Local Color Literature*; Elizabeth Ammons, *Conflicting Stories: American Women Writers at the Turn into the Twentieth Century*; Anne Romines, *The Home Plot: Women, Writing, and Domestic Ritual.*

31. Horace Scudder, Review of *Old Friends and New*, by Sarah Orne Jewett, *Atlantic Monthly* 45 (May 1880): 685.
32. Elizabeth Ammons, "The Shape of Violence in Jewett's 'A White Heron,'" *Colby Library Quarterly* 22 (March 1986): 6–16.
33. Terry Heller, "The Rhetoric of Communion in Jewett's 'A White Heron,'" *Colby Library Quarterly* 26 (September 1990): 187.
34. Louis A. Renza, *"A White Heron" and the Question of Minor Literature*, 110. Subsequent references will be cited parenthetically.
35. Sarah Orne Jewett, *Letters of Sarah Orne Jewett*, ed. Annie Fields (Boston: Houghton Mifflin, 1911), 100. Subsequent references will be cited as Fields. References to *Sarah Orne Jewett Letters*, ed. Richard Cary (Waterville: Colby College Press, 1967) will be cited as Cary. Though vital resources for Jewett biographers, neither edition is definitive, for both are seriously crippled by expurgations and omissions. Cary's edition is a vast improvement but excludes numerous letters not owned by Colby College.
36. William Dean Howells, *Editor's Study, by William Dean Howells*, ed. James W. Simpson (Troy: Whitson Publishing Co., 1983), 1. The quotation originally appeared in Howells' debut "Editor's Study" column in *Harper's* in January 1886.
37. This style of interaction takes shape in the same sociocultural context that Caroll Smith-Rosenberg describes as the "female world of love and ritual," an intimate yet highly formal realm of mutual support and exchange through which many nineteenth-century women cultivated their writing and education. Jewett engaged in a number of such affectionate, often romantic correspondences, most famously with James T. Fields's widow, Annie, after his death in 1881. See "The Female World of Love and Ritual," in *Disorderly Conduct: Visions of Gender in Victorian America* (New York: Knopf, 1985), 53–76.

38. The phrase "canine servitude" is borrowed from Annis Pratt's "Women and Nature in Modern Fiction," *Contemporary Literature* 13 (autumn 1972): 479. Margaret Roman suggests that, for Jewett, the image was not derogatory: "This comparison . . . speaks of a person's longing to find an emotionally supportive relationship." See Magaret Roman, *Sarah Orne Jewett: Reconstructing Gender*, 199–200. Quotations from "A White Heron" refer to *Best Short Stories of Sarah Orne Jewett, Volume II*, ed. Willa Cather (Gloucester: Peter Smith, 1965), 1–22.
39. Emily Dickinson, Poem 754, *The Complete Poems of Emily Dickinson*, ed. Thomas H. Johnson (New York: Little, Brown, 1988), 369. Carol J. Singley explores the similarities between the two works through the paradigm of initiation rather than style. See Carol J. Singley, "Sarah Orne Jewett, Emily Dickinson and Female Initiation," *Colby Library Quarterly* 22 (March 1986): 36–47.
40. I refer here to a long debate over whether women employ rhetorical hedges more frequently than men or whether this "voluble" tendency is a social stereotype. Otto Jesperson argues that female speakers use adverbs of intensity like "so" because "women much more often than men break off without finishing their sentences, because they start talking without having thought out what they are going to say." See Otto Jesperson, *Language: Its Nature, Development and Origin* (London: Allen & Unwin, 1922), 215. The obvious sexism of such an assertion only points out the paucity of its own logic. Yet many linguists with a specifically feminist perspective have committed similar errors of generalization. Robin Lakoff, for example, is routinely criticized for suggesting that women indulge in "empty" adjectives because of a socialized inferiority complex. See Robin Lakoff, *Language and Woman's Place*, 54.
41. F. O. Matthiessen, *Sarah Orne Jewett*, 82, 102.
42. Roland Barthes, "The Reality Effect," in *The Rustle of Language*, trans. Richard Howard (New York: Hill and Wang, 1986), 141–48.
43. Quoted in Ann J. Lane, *To* Herland *and Beyond: The Life and Work of Charlotte Perkins Gilman*, 155.
44. Quoted in Charlotte Perkins Gilman, *The Living of Charlotte Perkins Gilman*, 96.

45. Citations from the story refer to Catherine Golden, ed., *The Captive Imagination: A Casebook on "The Yellow Wallpaper"* (New York: Feminist Press, 1992), 24–42.
46. Julia Bates Dock has recently challenged the critical commonplace that "The Yellow Wallpaper" was originally read as a Poe-styled horror story instead of a critique of sexual politics. Unearthing three long-ignored reviews, she shows how "the story's first readers did recognize its indictments of marriage and of the treatment of women." See Julia Bates Dock, "'But One Expects That': Charlotte Perkins Gilman's 'The Yellow Wallpaper' and the Shifting Light of Scholarship," *PMLA* 111 (January 1996): 59–60. For a representative example, see Henry B. Blackwell's review in *Woman's Journal* (17 June 1899): 187.
47. Charlotte Perkins Gilman, "Why I Wrote 'The Yellow Wallpaper,'" in *The Captive Imagination*, 53.
48. Charlotte Perkins Gilman, "Thoughts and Figgerings," quoted in Polly Wynn Allen, *Building Domestic Liberty: Charlotte Perkins Gilman's Architectural Feminism* (Amherst: University of Massachusetts Press, 1988), 145.
49. Wai Chee Dimock, "Feminism, New Historicism, and the Reader," in *Readers in History: Nineteenth-Century American Literature and the Contexts of Response*, 92, 94.
50. Annette Kolodny, "A Map for Misreading: Gender and the Interpretation of Literary Texts," in *The Captive Imagination*, 155–56.
51. Frank Norris, "Story-tellers vs. Novelists," in *The Complete Novels and Essays of Frank Norris*, ed. Donald Pizer (New York: Library of America, 1986), 1192.
52. Quoted in Bent Priesler, *Linguistic Sex Roles in Conversation*, 181.
53. Karen Ford, "'The Yellow Wallpaper' and Women's Discourse," *Tulsa Studies in Women's Literature* 4 (fall 1985): 311.
54. See Paula Treichler, "Escaping the Sentence: Diagnosis and Discourse in 'The Yellow Wallpaper'" and Richard Feldstein, "Reader, Text, and Ambiguous Referentiality in 'The Yellow Wallpaper,'" in *The Captive Imagination*, 204–5 and 315–16, respectively.
55. The manuscript is housed in Folder 221 of the Charlotte Perkins Gilman Collection at the Schlesinger Library, Radcliffe College.

56. Quoted in James R. Mellow, *Charmed Circle: Gertrude Stein & Company* (Boston: Houghton Mifflin, 1973), 172.

Notes to Part 3

1. Fredric Jameson, *Marxism and Form: Twentieth Century Dialectical Theories of Literature*, 334.
2. Herbert Ellsworth Cory, "The Senility of the Short Story," *The Dial* 62 (3 May 1917): 379–81.
3. Christopher Wilson, "Rhetoric of Consumption," 39–64; Munsey's quote appears in Theodore Peterson's *Magazines in the Twentieth Century*, 15.
4. Henry Seidel Canby, "Free Fiction," *Atlantic Monthly* 116 (July 1915): 60–68.
5. Fred Lewis Pattee, "The Present Stage of the Short Story," *English Journal* 12 (September 1923): 447.
6. Edward J. O'Brien, *The Dance of the Machines: The Short Story in the Industrial Age*, 124–25, 152–53, 138.
7. Austin Wright, *The American Short Story in the 1920s*, 326. Subsequent references will be cited parenthetically. Suzanne Ferguson, "Defining the Short Story: Impressionism and Form," in *The New Short Story Theories*, 219–20; Dominic Head, *The Modernist Short Story*, 1.
8. Karl Kroeber, *Retelling/Rereading*, 106.
9. Michel Foucault, "What Is an Author?" ed. Paul Rabinow, trans. Josué V. Harari, in *The Foucault Reader* (New York: Pantheon Books, 1984), 101–20.
10. Gertrude Stein, "The King or Something (The Public is Invited to Dance)," *Geography and Plays* (Boston: Four Seas, 1922), 132. References to "Miss Furr and Miss Skeene" refer to this edition as well. See also the reprint in *Vanity Fair* (July 1923): 55.
11. Gertrude Stein, *Narration: Four Lectures*, ed. Thornton Wilder (Chicago: University of Chicago Press, 1969), 52. Subsequent references will be cited parenthetically.
12. James R. Mellow, *Charmed Circle*, 331; Wendy Steiner, *Exact Resemblance to Exact Resemblance: The Literary Portraiture of Gertrude Stein*, 16.

13. For accounts of Stein's early years in Paris, see Mellow, *Charmed Circle*, 50–78. For an account of the Stein-Toklas relationship and its influence on Stein's writing, see Shari Benstock, *Women of the Left Bank: Paris 1900–1940*, 143–93.
14. Marjorie Perloff, "Ninety-Percent Rotarian: Gertrude Stein's Hemingway," *American Literature* 62 (December 1990): 676. Subsequent references will be cited parenthetically.
15. It remains unclear whether Stein knew of the homosexual connotations of "gay" when she composed the piece. Perloff has traced the word's etymology, showing that in the early 1900s its most subversive meaning was synonymous with "lascivious." The homosexual meaning first arose among Parisian gays in the 1920s, but did not become widely known until the late 1960s. See "Ninety-Percent Rotarian," note 14 (675–76). As *Vanity Fair's* parody of "Miss Furr and Miss Skeene" implies, the erotic connotations of "gay" may have been more widely recognized (at least by New York magazine editors) than previously assumed.
16. Richard Bridgman, *Gertrude Stein in Pieces*, 158. For an examination of how women modernists, including Stein, create a private, resolutely non-heterosexist language of their own, see Shari Benstock, "Expatriate Sapphic Modernism: Entering Literary History," in *Lesbian Texts and Contexts: Radical Revisions*, ed. Karla Jay and Joanne Glasglow (New York: New York University Press, 1990), 183–203.
17. I quote the definition of *heteroglossia* offered in the glossary of Mikhail Bakhtin's *The Dialogic Imagination: Four Essays*, ed. Michael Holquist, trans. Michael Holquist and Caryl Emerson (Austin: University of Texas Press, 1981), 428.
18. Harriet Scott Chessman, *The Public is Invited to Dance: Representation, the Body, and Dialogue in Gertrude Stein*, 148.
19. V. N. Volosinov, *Marxism and the Philosophy of Language*, trans. Ladislav Matejka and I. R. Titunik (Cambridge: Harvard University Press, 1986), 130. Subsequent references will be cited parenthetically. While Bakhtin is generally assumed to be the author, I retain the original attribution.
20. Edmund Wilson, *Axel's Castle: A Study in the Imaginative Literature of 1870–1930*, 194–95.
21. K.D., "When Helen Furr Got Gay With Harold Moos: A Narra-

tive Written in the Now Popular Manner of Gertrude Stein," *Vanity Fair* (October 1923): 37.

22. The two are "The Undefeated" and "Banal Story," written respectively in late 1924 and early 1925, between the composition of "Big Two-Hearted River" and "The Battler," the last two stories completed for *In Our Time*. The pieces that rely predominantly on dialogue, including "The Killers," "Hills," "A Simple Enquiry," and "Ten Indians" were completed from mid-1926 to spring 1927, more than a year and a half later. See Paul Smith, *A Reader's Guide to the Short Stories of Ernest Hemingway*.
23. K.S. Review of *Men Without Women*, by Ernest Hemingway, *Boston Evening Transcript Book Section* 7 January 1928: 4.
24. Virginia Woolf. "An Essay in Criticism," in *Hemingway: The Critical Heritage*, ed. Jeffrey Meyers (London: Routledge and Kegan Paul, 1982), 101–6.
25. For the original comment, see Ernest Hemingway, *Ernest Hemingway: Selected Letters*, 245.
26. Mikhail Bakhtin, *Problems of Dostoevsky's Poetics*, ed. and trans. Caryl Emerson (Minneapolis: University of Minnesota Press, 1984), 189–90.
27. Nina Baym, "Actually, I Felt Sorry for the Lion," in *New Critical Approaches to the Short Stories of Ernest Hemingway*, ed. Jackson J. Benson (Durham: Duke University Press, 1991), 112.
28. Madeline Kahn, *Narrative Transvestism*, 6.
29. Pamela Smiley, "Gender-Linked Miscommunication in 'Hills Like White Elephants,'" in *New Critical Approaches to the Short Stories of Ernest Hemingway*, 291–92. Smiley is referring to Robin Lakoff's *Language and Woman's Place* (54), but see also Lakoff's revision of her theory of tag questions in *Talking Power: The Politics of Language in Our Lives*, 247.
30. Deborah Tannen, *That's Not What I Meant! How Conversation Makes or Breaks Your Relations With Others*, 62. See also Tannen, *Talking Voices: Repetition, Dialogue, and Imagery in Conversational Discourse*, 47–53.
31. Wyndham Lewis, "The Dumb Ox: A Study of Ernest Hemingway," in *Hemingway: The Critical Heritage*, ed. Jeffrey Meyers, (London: Routledge and Kegan Paul, 1982), 195. Subsequent references will be cited parenthetically.
32. See Douglas Messerli, *Djuna Barnes: A Bibliography*, 91–92, 118. For a rare essay devoted to Barnes's short fiction, see

Suzanne Ferguson, "Djuna Barnes's Short Stories: An Estrangement of the Heart," *Southern Review* 5 (January 1969): 26–41.

33. Julian Symons, *Makers of the New: The Revolution in Literature 1912–1939*, 192–93.
34. Quoted in Andrew Field, *Djuna: The Life and Times of Djuna Barnes*, 108. Subsequent references to this biography will be cited parenthetically. Field quotes a 1922 *Chicago Literary Times* description of Barnes's face as "white as a signal of terror, save for the scarlet martyrdom of full lips that have never become accustomed to life." As he suggests, the description turns Barnes into "a semblance of one of her own merciless sketches" by parodying her style (119).
35. Karen Kaivola, *All Contraries Confounded: The Lyrical Fiction of Virginia Woolf, Djuna Barnes, and Marguerite Duras*, 63.
36. Djuna Barnes, "Run Girls, Run," in *Vagaries Malicieux: Two Stories by Djuna Barnes* (New York: Frank Hallman, 1974), 39. Subsequent references will be cited parenthetically.
37. Hank O'Neal, *Life is painful, nasty, and short—in my case it has only been painful and nasty: Djuna Barnes, 1978–1981: An Informal Memoir* (New York: Paragon House, 1990), 21. The Barnes collection housed at the McKeldin Library at the University of Maryland includes a typescript of the story that clearly identifies it as a "fragment" of the novel. See the folder in Series II, Box 5 entitled "Fragment 'Run Girls, Run!'" The piece is marked "Bow Down," the original title of *Nightwood*, in the upper right corner and includes a handwritten note on page 3: "from something published, I think in New Orleans (?) or was it Majorica [*sic*]." Barnes was thinking of New Orleans' *The Double Dealer*, which published "Vagaries Malicieux." See also Barnes's 1970–72 correspondence with Coby Britton, an editor at *Poetry Magazine*. Series I, Box 15 includes a rare copy of the 1936 version of the story, including Barnes's subsequent editorial comments.
38. Charles Jones, "Varieties of Speech Representation in Conrad's *The Secret Agent*," *Lingua* 20 (1968): 173.
39. Susan Snaider Lanser, "Speaking in Tongues: *Ladies Almanack* and the Discourse of Desire," in *Silence and Power: A Reevaluation of Djuna Barnes*, ed. Mary Lynn Broe (Carbondale: Southern Illinois University Press, 1991), 162.
40. For a reading of the Rabelais-influenced imagery of the female

grotesque in Barnes's work, see Marie Ponsot, "A Reader's *Ryder*," in *Silence and Power: A Reevaluation of Djuna Barnes*, 94–136.

41. Originally conceived as a chapter of an unpublished novel entitled *Tarbaby's Sunrise*, "Almos' a Man" was briefly considered for inclusion in *Uncle Tom's Children* (1939), Wright's first story collection. But instead it only appeared in *Harper's Bazaar* two months before *Native Son* was published when editor George Davis solicited a contribution in the fall of 1939. Wright was so busy completing his novel that he asked a friend, Marie Mencken, to cull a finished story from the *Tarbaby* manuscript. (The extent of Mencken's editorial emendations has yet to be catalogued). See Michel Fabre, *The Ordeal of Richard Wright*, trans. Isabel Barzun (New York: Morrow, 1973), 194. Quotations from the original version of "Almos' a Man" refer to Richard Wright, *Best Short Stories of 1940*, ed. Edward J. O'Brien (Boston: Houghton Mifflin, 1941), 356–70.
42. Edward Margolies, "Wright's Craft: The Short Stories," in *Richard Wright: Critical Perspectives Past and Present*, ed. Henry Louis Gates and K. A. Appiah (New York: Amistad, 1993), 87.
43. Richard Wright, "Gertrude Stein's Story is Drenched in Hitler's Horrors," in *Richard Wright Reader*, eds. Ellen Wright and Michel Fabre (New York: Harper and Row, 1978), 75. In a longer, unpublished version of the same essay, entitled "Memories of My Grandmother," he carries this line of thinking even further, linking Stein's vernacular to rhythms in jazz and scat, thus bridging modernist surrealism with African-American oral traditions. Several other writers of color have found in "Melanctha" echoes of what Gayl Jones calls "the incremental repetition and syntactical details of blues balladry, and in the fragmentations and juxtapositions the effect of African American jazz." See Gayl Jones, *Liberating Voices: Oral Tradition in African American Literature*, 75.
44. John McCluskey, Jr., "Two Steppin': Richard Wright's Encounter with Blue-Jazz," *American Literature* 55 (October 1983): 333.
45. Richard Wright, "How 'Bigger' Was Born," in *Richard Wright: The Early Works:* Lawd Today!, Uncle Tom's Children, Native

Son, ed. Arnold Rampersad (New York: Library of America, 1990), 862. Subsequent references will be cited parenthetically.

46. Richard Wright, "Between Laughter and Tears," *New Masses* 5 October 1937: 22, 25; and "Blueprint for Negro Writing," in the *Richard Wright Reader*, 45–46.
47. Henry Louis Gates, *The Signifying Monkey: A Theory of Afro-American Literary Criticism*, 182–86.
48. Wright added an even more acidic sign of Dave's status in the community in his 1960 revision. In the original story, his mother spies Joe's catalogue and says, "We kin use it around the house" (358). In the rewrite, she says "We kin use it in the outhouse." See Richard Wright, *Eight Men*, 11. Subsequent references to this edition will be cited parenthetically.
49. Houston A. Baker, Jr., *Blues, Ideology, and Afro-American Literature: A Vernacular Theory*, 139–72. Subsequent references will be cited parenthetically.
50. James Baldwin, "Alas, Poor Richard," in *Nobody Knows My Name: More Notes from a Native Son* (New York: Dial Press, 1963), 148; Vanessa Haley, *Instructor's Manual to Accompany* Fictions, *Second Edition by Joseph F. Trimmer and C. Wade Jennings*, 191–92 (emphasis added).
51. Roland Barthes, *Writing Degree Zero*, trans. Annette Lavers and Colin Smith (New York: Noonday Press, 1968) 78.
52. John Barth, "The Literature of Exhaustion," *Atlantic Monthly* 220 (August 1967): 32.

Notes to Part 4

1. Martha Bayles, "The *New Yorker* Story," *Harper's* (July 1984): 69–71.
2. Madison Smartt Bell, "Less is Less: The Diminishing Landscape of the American Short Story," *Harper's* (April 1986): 64–69. To recognize how unoriginal the "less is less" jibe is in attacks on minimalism, see similarly titled essays by James Atlas (*Atlantic Monthly* 247 [June 1981]: 96–98) and Joshua Gilder (*New Criterion* 1 [February 1983]: 78–82).
3. John W. Aldridge, *Talents and Technicians: Literary Chic and*

the New Assembly-Line Fiction (New York: Scribner's, 1991), 51, 81. Subsequent references will be cited parenthetically.

4. Bob Shacochis, "Style Wars in Fiction & Oceanfront Real Estate: Rednecks in Leotards," *AWP Chronicle* 25 (May 1993): 1–5. For a response, see Eve Shelnutt, "Macro-Minimalist Fiction: The Trickle-Down Effect," in the same issue, 1, 13–18.
5. William O'Rourke, "Morphological Metaphors for the Short Story: Matters of Production, Reproduction, and Consumption," in *Short Story Theory at a Crossroads*, 193–205.
6. See Marshall Bruce Gentry and William L. Stull, eds. *Conversations with Raymond Carver*, 153; and Bonnie Lyons and Bill Oliver, "An Interview with Bobbie Ann Mason," *Contemporary Literature* 32 (fall 1991): 458. Subsequent references to both texts will be cited parenthetically. See also John Barth, "A Few Words About Minimalism," The *New York Times Book Review* 28 December 1986: 25; and Frederick Barthleme, "On Being Wrong: Convicted Minimalist Spills Bean," The *New York Times* 3 April 1988, sec. 7:1: 25–27.
7. Kim A. Herzinger, "Minimalism as Postmodernism," *New Orleans Review* 16 (fall 1989): 73–77.
8. Philip E. Simmons, "Minimalist Fiction as 'Low' Postmodernism: Mass Culture and the Search for History," *Genre* 24 (spring 1991): 51, 53.
9. See Walter Benjamin, "The Storyteller," 89; Karl Kroeber, *Retelling/Rereading*, 67.
10. Stephen Kern, *The Culture of Time and Space 1880–1918*, 68.
11. Fredric Jameson, "Postmodernism and Consumer Society," in *The Anti-Aesthetic*, ed. Hal Foster (Port Townsend, Wash.: Bay Press, 1983), 125. Subsequent references will be cited parenthetically.
12. Bobbie Ann Mason, "Shiloh," in *Shiloh and Other Stories* (New York: Harper and Row, 1982), 1. Subsequent references will be cited parenthetically.
13. Raymond Williams, *Television: Technology and Cultural Form* (New York: Schocken, 1975), 86–90.
14. William H. Gass, "A Failing Grade for the Present Tense," The *New York Times Book Review* 11 October 1987: 35.
15. Elizabeth Deeds Ermath has explored how traditional narrators draw their authority from linear temporality by "threading together into one system and one act of attention a whole series

of moments and perspectives. Thus the continuums of time and of consciousness literally appear inseparable, functioning together as the medium of events even though this particular mutuality is rarely mentioned because to do so would be to compromise the whole effect and to locate a vulnerability in the presentation of objectivity . . . [the omniscient narrator] maintains the communication between past, present, and future, and thus the possibility of causal sequences from one to another. Any realistic, that is, representational and historical narrative, has as its primary cultural effect the inscription of a single, homogeneous time stretching to infinity." As she shows, postmodern writers exploit the separability of time and consciousness by flaunting the very vulnerability in presentation that typical narrators try to obscure; tense is a central device in this project. See Elizabeth Deeds Ermath, *Sequel to History: Postmodernism and the Crisis of Representational Time*, 27–28.

16. See Suzanne Fleischman, *Tense and Narrativity: From Medieval Performance to Modern Fiction*, 170. Subsequent references will be cited parenthetically.
17. Bob Perelman, "Parataxis and Narrative: The New Sentence in Theory and Practice," *American Literature* 65 (June 1993): 313, 318. Subsequent references will be cited parenthetically.
18. See Julia Kristeva's "Women's Time," ed. Toril Moi, trans. Alice Jardine and Harry Blake, in *The Kristeva Reader* (London: Basil Blackwell, 1986), 187–213. Subsequent references will be cited parenthetically.
19. Many readers argue that the final glimpse of Norma Jean on a cliff above the Tennessee River is an image of suicide. My own reading has been influenced by Mason's explicit denial: "You can imagine my surprise when I hear that some students think Norma Jean is going to jump because she's standing on the edge of a cliff at the end of the story. That's so weird. Maybe *Leroy* would jump but not Norma Jean. She's a survivor." See Lyons and Oliver, "An Interview with Bobbie Ann Mason," 56.
20. Quoted in Fleischman, *Tense and Narrativity*, 37.
21. Gérard Genette, *Narrative Discourse: An Essay in Method*, trans. Janet E. Lewin (Ithaca: Cornell University Press, 1980), 116.
22. Alexander Gelley, *Narrative Crossings: Theory and Pragmatics of Prose Fiction*, 171.

23. The lines are from "Gazebo," "So Much Water So Close to Home," and "Where I'm Calling From," in Carver's *Where I'm Calling From: New and Selected Stories* (New York: Atlantic Monthly Press, 1988), 139, 213, and 291–92 respectively. All references to Carver's stories are cited from this edition. My reading here ignores how often Carver rewrote these stories from collection to collection; for an example of his revision, see Thomas J. Haslam, "'Where I'm Calling From': A Textual and Critical Study," *Studies in Short Fiction* 29 (winter 1992): 57–65.
24. William L. Stull, "Beyond Hopelessville: Another Side of Raymond Carver," *Philological Quarterly* 64 (winter 1985): 1. For the "barren idiom" quote, see Atlas, "Less is Less," 96; for "stunning inarticulateness," see Robert Houston, "A Stunning Inarticulateness," *Nation* 4 July 1981: 23–25.
25. Quoted in Kay Bonetti, Interview with Raymond Carver. *Saturday Review* September–October 1983: 23.
26. Kirk Nesset, *The Stories of Raymond Carver: A Critical Study*, 97. Subsequent references will be cited parenthetically.
27. Roland Barthes, "From Speech to Writing," in *The Grain of the Voice*, trans. Richard Howard (New York: Noonday Press, 1968), 4. In a similar vein, Marc Chénetier describes Carver's interpersonal cues as his "WH factor." This "insistent use of interrogations, interrogative structures, and indefinite centers" encourages readers "to look among the blanks and negations for answers feeding on transcended literal meaning." See "Living On/Off the 'Reserve': Performance, Interrogation, and Negativity in the Works of Raymond Carver," in *Critical Angles: European Views of Contemporary American Literature*, ed. Marc Chénetier (Carbondale: Southern Illinois University Press, 1990), 178.
28. Rick Altman, "Television/Sound," in *Studies in Entertainment*, ed. Tania Modleski, 46.
29. John Updike, "Bech in Czech," The *New Yorker* 20 April 1987: 44.

Notes to Postscript

1. Richard Fusco, *Maupassant and the American Short Story: The Influence of Form at the Turn of the Century*, 217.

2. Dan Pope, "The Post-Minimalist American Story or What Comes After Carver?" *Gettysburg Review* 1 (spring 1988): 331–42; Sven Birkerts, "David Foster Wallace," in *American Energies: Essays on Fiction* (New York: Morrow, 1992), 386–92.
3. Robert Shapard, introduction to *Sudden Fiction: American Short-Short Stories*, eds. Robert Shapard and James Thomas (Salt Lake City: Penegrine Press, 1986), xiii–xvi.
4. Charles Baxter, introduction to *Sudden Fiction International: Sixty Short-Short Stories*, ed. Robert Shapard and James Thomas (New York: Norton, 1990), 21.
5. "Flat Prose," *Atlantic Monthly* 114 (October 1914): 432. For the first short-short story fad, see Andrew Levy, *The Culture and Commerce of the American Short Story*, 9.
6. David Foster Wallace, "Westward the Course of Empire Takes its Way," in *Girl with Curious Hair* (New York: Norton, 1990), 238; Tim O'Brien, "How to Tell a True War Story," in *The Things They Carried* (New York: Houghton Mifflin, 1990), 76; Sandra Cisneros, "Anguiano Religious Articles . . . ," in *Woman Hollering Creek* (New York: Viking, 1992), 114; Robert Olen Butler, "A Ghost Story," in *A Good Scent from a Strange Mountain* (New York: Henry Holt, 1992), 111; Pam Houston, "How to Talk to a Hunter," in *Cowboys are My Weakness* (New York: Norton, 1993), 13.

Bibliography

Adkins, Nelson F. "The Early Projected Works of Nathaniel Hawthorne." *Papers of the Bibliographical Society of America* 39 (1945): 119–55.

Aldridge, John W. *Talents and Technicians: Literary Chic and the New Assembly-Line Fiction*. New York: Scribner's, 1991.

Allen, Polly Wynn. *Building Domestic Liberty: Charlotte Perkins Gilman's Architectural Feminism*. Amherst: University of Massachusetts Press, 1988.

Altman, Rick. "Television/Sound." In *Studies in Entertainment*, edited by Tania Modleski, 39–45. Bloomington: Indiana University Press, 1986.

Ammons, Elizabeth. *Conflicting Stories: American Women Writers at the Turn into the Twentieth Century*. New York: Oxford University Press, 1991.

———. "The Shape of Violence in Jewett's 'A White Heron.'" *Colby Library Quarterly* 22 (March 1986): 6–16.

Apthorp, Elaine Sargent. "Sentiment, Naturalism, and the Female Regionalist." *Legacy* 7 (spring 1990): 3–22.

"The Art of Story-Telling." *The American Magazine and Historical Chronicle* (1744): 469–71.

Atlas, James. "Less is Less." *Atlantic Monthly* 247 (June 1981): 96–98.

Baker, Houston, A., Jr. *Blues, Ideology, and Afro-American Literature: A Vernacular Theory*. Chicago: University of Chicago Press, 1984.

Bakhtin, Mikhail. *The Dialogic Imagination: Four Essays*, edited by Michael Holquist, translated by Michael Holquist and Caryl Emerson. Austin: University of Texas Press, 1981.

———. *Problems of Dostoevsky's Poetics*, edited and translated by Caryl Emerson. Minneapolis: University of Minnesota Press, 1984.

Baldeshwiler, Eileen. "The Lyric Short Story: The Sketch of a History." In *The New Short Story Theories*, edited by Charles E. May, 231–41. Athens: Ohio University Press, 1994. First published in *Studies in Short Fiction* 6.4 (1969): 443–53.

Baldwin, James. *Nobody Knows My Name: More Notes from a Native Son*. New York: Dial Press, 1963.

Barnes, Djuna. "Run Girls, Run." In *Vagaries Malicieux: Two Stories by Djuna Barnes*, 31–41. New York: Frank Hallman, 1974. First published in *Caravel* 1 (March 1936): 1–7.

Barth, John. "A Few Words About Minimalism." The *New York Times Book Review* 28 December 1986: 1, 25.

———. "It's a Long Story." *Harper's* (June 1990): 71–78.

———. "The Literature of Exhaustion." *Atlantic Monthly* 220 (August 1967): 29–34.

Barthes, Roland. "From Speech to Writing." In *The Grain of the Voice*, translated by Richard Howard, 3–7. New York: Noonday Press, 1968.

———. "The Reality Effect." In *The Rustle of Language*, translated by Richard Howard, 141–48. New York: Hill and Wang, 1986.

———. *Writing Degree Zero*, translated by Annette Lavers and Colin Smith. 1953. Reprint, New York: Noonday Press, 1968.

Barthleme, Frederick. "On Being Wrong: Convicted Minimalist Spills Bean." The *New York Times* 3 April 1988, sec. 7:1, 25–27.

Baxter, Charles. Introduction to *Sudden Fiction International: Sixty Short-Short Stories*, edited by Robert Shapard and James Thomas. New York: Norton, 1990.

Bayer, John G. "Narrative Techniques and Oral Tradition in *The Scarlet Letter*," *American Literature* 52 (May 1980): 250–63.

Bayles, Martha. "The *New Yorker* Story." *Harper's* (July 1984): 69–71.

Baym, Nina. "Actually, I Felt Sorry for the Lion." In *New Critical Approaches to the Short Stories of Ernest Hemingway*, edited by Jackson J. Benson, 112–20. Durham: Duke University Press, 1991.

———. *Novels, Readers, and Reviewers: Responses to Fiction in Antebellum America*. Ithaca: Cornell University Press, 1984.

Beegel, Susan F. *Hemingway's Craft of Omission: Four Manuscript Examples*. Ann Arbor: UMI Research Press, 1988.

Bell, Madison Smartt. "Less is Less: The Diminishing Landscape of the American Short Story." *Harper's* (April 1986): 64–69.

Bell, Michael Davitt. *The Problem of American Realism: Studies in the Cultural History of a Literary Idea*. Chicago: University of Chicago Press, 1993.

Benjamin, Walter. "The Storyteller." In *Illuminations*, edited by Hannah Arendt, translated by Harry Zohn, 83–109. New York: Schocken, 1969.

Benstock, Shari. "Expatriate Sapphic Modernism: Entering Literary History." In *Lesbian Texts and Contexts: Radical Revisions*, edited by Karla Jay and Joanne Glasglow, 183–203. New York: New York University Press, 1990.

———. *Women of the Left Bank: Paris 1900–1940*. Austin: University of Texas Press, 1986.

Bercovitch, Sacvan. *The American Jeremiad*. Madison: University of Wisconsin Press, 1978.

Birkerts, Sven. "David Foster Wallace." In *American Energies: Essays on Fiction*, 386–92. New York: Morrow, 1992.

Bissell, Champion. "Serials and Continuations." *Sartain's Union Magazine* 8 (1851) 270–78.

Blackwell, Henry B. Review of "The Yellow Wallpaper" by Charlotte Perkins Gilman. *Woman's Journal* 17 June 1899: 187.

Bonetti, Kay. Interview with Raymond Carver. *Saturday Review* September–October 1983: 20–23.

Bonheim, Helmut. *The Narrative Modes: Techniques of the Short Story*. London: Cambridge University Press, 1982.

Booth, Wayne C. *The Rhetoric of Fiction*. Chicago: University of Chicago Press, 1961.

Borges, Jorge Luis. "Nathaniel Hawthorne." In *Borges: A Reader*, edited by Emir Rodriguez Monegal and Alastair Reid, 217–30. 1949. Reprint, New York: E. P. Dutton, 1981.

Bridgman, Richard. *The Colloquial Style in America*. New York: Oxford University Press, 1966.

———. *Gertrude Stein in Pieces*. New York: Oxford University Press, 1970.

Brodhead, Richard. *The School of Hawthorne*. New York: Oxford University Press, 1986.

Broughton, T. Alan. "How Short is Short?" *The Writer* 106 (July 1993): 15–16.

Buell, Lawrence. *New England Literary Culture: From Revolution through Renaissance*. New York: Cambridge University Press, 1986.

Butler, Robert Olen. *A Good Scent from a Strange Mountain*. New York: Henry Holt, 1992.

Cady, Edwin H. *The Realist at War: The Mature Years, 1885–1920, of William Dean Howells*. Syracuse: Syracuse University Press, 1958.

Canby, Henry Seidel. "Free Fiction." *Atlantic Monthly* 116 (July 1915): 60–68.

Carver, Raymond. "On Writing." In *Fires: Essays, Poems, Stories*, 16–18. Santa Barbara: Capra Press, 1983.

———. *Where I'm Calling From: New and Selected Stories*. New York: Atlantic Monthly Press, 1988.

Chambers, Ross. *Story and Situation: Narrative Seduction and the Power of Fiction*. Minneapolis: University of Minnesota Press, 1984.

Chénetier, Marc. "Living On/Off the 'Reserve': Performance, Interrogation, and Negativity in the Works of Raymond Carver." In *Critical Angles: European Views of Contemporary American Literature*, edited by Marc Chénetier, 164–91. Carbondale: Southern Illinois University Press, 1990.

Chessman, Harriet Scott. *The Public is Invited to Dance: Representation, the Body, and Dialogue in Gertrude Stein*. Palo Alto: Stanford University Press, 1989.

Chibka, Robert L. "Hawthorne's Tale Told Twice: A Reading of 'Wakefield.'" *Emerson Society Quarterly* 28 (fall 1982): 220–32.

Cisneros, Sandra. *Woman Hollering Creek*. New York: Viking, 1992.

Cooke, Rose Terry. "Miss Muffett and the Spider." *Harper's New Monthly Magazine* 20 (1860): 764–71.

Cory, Herbert Ellsworth. "The Senility of the Short Story." *The Dial* 62 3 May 1917: 379–81.

Coultrap-McQuin, Susan. *Doing Literary Business: American Women Writers in the Nineteenth Century*. Chapel Hill: University of North Carolina Press, 1989.

Crowley, J. Donald, ed. *The American Short Story, 1850–1900*. Boston: Twayne, 1984.

———, ed. *Hawthorne: The Critical Heritage*. New York: Barnes and Noble, 1970.

Current-Garcia, Eugene. *The American Short Story, Before 1850* Vol. 1. Boston: Twayne, 1985.

Davis, Rebecca Harding. *Life in the Iron Mills and Other Stories*, edited by Tillie Olsen. New York: Feminist Press, 1985.

Dickinson, Emily. *The Complete Poems of Emily Dickinson*, edited by Thomas H. Johnson. New York: Little, Brown, 1988.

Dillon, George. *Rhetoric as Social Imagination: Explorations in the Interpersonal Function of Language*. Bloomington: Indiana University Press, 1986.

Dimock, Wai Chee. "Feminism, New Historicism, and the Reader." In *Readers in History: Nineteenth-Century American Literature and the Contexts of Response*, edited by James L. Machor, 85–106. Baltimore: Johns Hopkins University Press, 1993.

D., K. "When Helen Furr Got Gay With Harold Moos: A Narrative Written in the Now Popular Manner of Gertrude Stein." *Vanity Fair* (October 1923): 37.

Dock, Julia Bates. "'But One Expects That': Charlotte Perkins Gilman's 'The Yellow Wallpaper' and the Shifting Light of Scholarship." *PMLA* 111 (January 1996): 52–65.

Donovan, Josephine. *New England Local Color Literature: A Woman's Tradition*. New York: Ungar, 1983.

Douglas, Ann. *The Feminization of American Culture*. New York: Knopf, 1977.

Douglas Wood, Ann. "The Literature of Impoverishment: The Women Local Colorists in America 1865–1914." *Women's Studies* 1 (1972): 3–45.

Emerson, Ralph Waldo. *The Journals of Ralph Waldo Emerson*, edited by William H. Gilman et al. Cambridge: Belknap Press, 1960–.

Ermath, Elizabeth Deeds. *Sequel to History: Postmodernism and the Crisis of Representational Time*. Princeton: Princeton University Press, 1992.

Evans, Walter. "Nineteenth-Century American Theory of the Short Story: The Dual Tradition." *Orbis Litterarum* 34 (1979): 314–30.

Fabre, Michel. *The Ordeal of Richard Wright*, translated by Isabel Barzun. New York: Morrow, 1973.

Feldstein, Richard. "Text, Reader and Ambiguous Referentiality in 'The Yellow Wallpaper.'" In *The Captive Imagination: A Casebook on "The Yellow Wallpaper,"* edited by Catherine Golden, 307–18. New York: Feminist Press, 1992.

Ferguson, Suzanne. "Defining the Short Story: Impressionism and Form." In *The New Short Story Theories*, edited by Charles E. May, 218–30. Athens: Ohio University Press, 1994. First published in *Modern Fiction Studies* 28 (spring 1982): 13–24.

———. "Djuna Barnes's Short Stories: An Estrangement of the Heart." *Southern Review* 5 (January 1969): 26–41.

Fetterley, Judith. *Provisions: A Reader of Nineteenth-Century Women Writers*. Bloomington: Indiana University Press, 1984.

———. *The Resisting Reader: A Feminist Approach to American Fiction*. Bloomington: Indiana University Press, 1978.

Field, Andrew. *Djuna: The Life and Times of Djuna Barnes*. New York: Putnam's, 1983.

Field, Kate. "English Authors in Florence." *Atlantic Monthly* 14 (December 1864): 660–71.

Finney, Charles Grandison. *Lectures on Revivals of Religion*. 1835. Reprint, Cambridge: Harvard University Press, 1980.

Fish, Stanley. *Self-Consuming Artifacts: The Experience of Seventeenth-Century Literature*. Berkeley and Los Angeles: University of California Press, 1972.

———. *Surprised by Sin: The Reader in "Paradise Lost."* London: St. Martin's Press, 1967.

"Flat Prose." *Atlantic Monthly* 114 (October 1914): 430–32.

Fleischman, Suzanne. *Tense and Narrativity: From Medieval Performance to Modern Fiction*. Austin: University of Texas Press, 1990.

Ford, Karen. "'The Yellow Wallpaper' and Women's Discourse." *Tulsa Studies in Women's Literature* 4 (fall 1985): 309–14.

Foucault, Michel. "What Is an Author?" In *The Foucault Reader*, edited by Paul Rabinow, translated by Josué V. Harari, 101–20. New York: Pantheon Books, 1984.

Friedman, Norman. "Recent Short Story Theories: Problems in Definition." In *Short Story Theory at a Crossroads*, edited by Susan Lohafer and Jo Ellyn Clarey, 13–31. Baton Rogue: Louisiana State Press, 1989.

———. "What Makes a Short Story Short?" In *Essentials of the Theory of Fiction*, edited by Michael J. Hoffman and Patrick D. Murphy, 152–69. Durham: Duke University Press, 1990.

Fusco, Richard. *Maupassant and the American Short Story: The Influence of Form at the Turn of the Century*. University Park: Pennsylvania State University Press, 1994.

Gass, William H. "A Failing Grade for the Present Tense." The *New York Times Book Review* 11 October 1987: 1, 32, 34–35, 38.

Gates, Henry Louis. *The Signifying Monkey: A Theory of Afro-American Literary Criticism*. New York: Oxford University Press, 1988.

Gelley, Alexander. *Narrative Crossings: Theory and Pragmatics of Prose Fiction*. Baltimore: Johns Hopkins University Press, 1981.

Genette, Gérard. *Narrative Discourse: An Essay in Method*, translated by Janet E. Lewin. Ithaca: Cornell University Press, 1980.

Gentry, Marshall Bruce and William L. Stull, eds. *Conversations with Raymond Carver*. Jackson: University Press of Mississippi, 1990.

Gerlach, John. *Toward the End: Closure in the American Short Story*. Tuscaloosa: University of Alabama Press, 1985.

Gilder, Joshua. "Less is Less." *New Criterion* 1 (February 1983): 78–82.

Gilman, Charlotte Perkins. *The Living of Charlotte Perkins Gilman*. 1935. Reprint, New York: Arno Press, 1972.

———. "Why I Wrote 'The Yellow Wallpaper.'" In *The Captive Imagination: A Casebook on "The Yellow Wallpaper,"* edited by Catherine Golden, 51–53. New York: Feminist Press, 1992.

Golden, Catherine, ed. *The Captive Imagination: A Casebook on "The Yellow Wallpaper."* New York: Feminist Press, 1992.

Griswold, Rufus. *The Prose Writers of America*. Philadelphia: Carey and Hart, 1847.

Habegger, Alfred. *Gender, Fantasy, and Realism in American Literature*. New York: Columbia University Press, 1982.

Haley, Vanessa. *Instructor's Manual to Accompany* Fictions, Second Edition by Joseph F. Trimmer and C. Wade Jennings. New York: Harcourt Brace Jovanovich, 1989.

Hall, David D. "The Uses of Literacy in New England, 1600–1850." In *Printing and Society in Early America*, edited by William L. Joyce, et al., 1–47. Worcester: American Antiquarian Society, 1983.

Hamilton, Kristie. "Toward a Cultural Theory of the Antebellum Literary Sketch." *Genre* 23 (winter 1990): 297–323.

Hanson, Clare. *Short Stories and Short Fictions, 1880–1980*. London: Macmillan, 1985.

———. "'Things out of Words': Towards a Poetics of Short Fiction." In *Re-reading the Short Story*, edited by Clare Hanson, 22–33. London: Methuen, 1990.

Harris, Sharon M. *Rebecca Harding Davis and American Realism*. Philadelphia: University of Pennsylvania Press, 1991.

Harte, Bret. "The Rise of the 'Short Story.'" In *Discussions of the Short Story*, edited by Hollis Summers, 5–9. Boston: D. C. Heath, 1963. First published in *Cornhill Magazine* 7 (1899): 1–8.

Haslam, Thomas J. "'Where I'm Calling From': A Textual and Critical Study." *Studies in Short Fiction* 29 (winter 1992): 57–65.

Haven, Alice B. Neal. "American Female Authorship." *Godey's Lady's Book* 44 (1852): 145–48.

Hawthorne, Nathaniel. *The Centenary Edition of the Works of Nathaniel Hawthorne*, edited by William Charvat, et al. 16 vols. Columbus: Ohio University Press, 1962–85.

Head, Dominic. *The Modernist Short Story: A Study in Theory and Practice*. London: Cambridge University Press, 1992.

Hedges, William. *Washington Irving: An American Study, 1802–1832*. Baltimore: Johns Hopkins University Press, 1965.

Heller, Terry. "The Rhetoric of Communion in Jewett's 'A White Heron.'" *Colby Library Quarterly* 26 (September 1990): 182–94.

Hemingway, Ernest. "The Art of the Short Story." In *Essays on the*

Short Stories of Ernest Hemingway, edited by Jackson J. Benson, 1–13. Durham: Duke University Press, 1991.

———. *The Complete Short Stories of Ernest Hemingway: The Finca Vigía Edition*, edited by John, Patrick, and Gregory Hemingway. New York: Scribner's, 1987.

———. *Death in the Afternoon*. New York: Scribner's, 1932.

———. *Ernest Hemingway: Selected Letters, 1917–1961*, edited by Carlos Baker. New York: Scribner's, 1981.

———. *A Moveable Feast*. New York: Scribner's, 1964.

Herzinger, Kim A. "Minimalism as Postmodernism." *New Orleans Review* 16 (fall 1989): 73–81.

Hills, Rust. *Writing in General and the Short Story in Particular: An Informal Textbook*. Boston: Houghton Mifflin, 1977.

Hocks, Richard A. *Henry James: A Study of the Short Fiction*. Boston: Twayne, 1990.

Hodges, Graham. *New York City Cartmen, 1667–1850*. New York: New York University Press, 1986.

Hoffman, Charles G. "The Shorter Fictions of Herman Melville." *South Atlantic Quarterly* 52 (July 1953): 414–30.

Houston, Pam. *Cowboys are My Weakness*. New York: Norton, 1993.

Houston, Robert. "A Stunning Inarticulateness." *Nation* 4 July 1981: 23–25.

Howells, William Dean. *Criticism and Fiction*. 1891. Reprint, New York: Hill and Wang, 1967.

———. *Editor's Study, by William Dean Howells*, edited by James W. Simpson. Troy: Whitson Publishing Co., 1983.

———. "Novel-Writing and Novel-Reading." In *Howells and James: A Double Billing*, 1–15. New York: New York Public Library Pamphlets, 1958.

Irving, Washington. *The Complete Writings of Washington Irving*, edited by Richard Dilworth Rust, et al. 30 vols. Boston: Twayne Publishers, 1978–89.

Iser, Wolfgang. *The Implied Reader: Patterns of Communication in Prose Fiction from Bunyan to Beckett*. Baltimore: Johns Hopkins University Press, 1974.

James, Henry. *The Art of the Novel*, edited by Richard P. Blackmur. New York: Scribner's, 1932.

———. "The Jolly Corner." In *Eight Tales from the Major Phase:* In the Cage *and Others,* edited by Morton Dauwen Zabel, 314–50. New York: W. W. Norton, 1958.

———. Review of *Around a Spring* by Gustave Droz. *Atlantic Monthly* 28 (August 1871): 248–51.

———. Review of *Dallas Gallbraith* by Rebecca Harding Davis. *The Nation* 22 October 1868: 330–31.

———. Review of *Waiting for the Verdict* by Rebecca Harding Davis. *The Nation* 21 November 1867: 410–11.

———. "The Storyteller at Large: Mr. Henry Harland." In *The American Essays of Henry James,* edited by Leon Edel, 186–93. Princeton: Princeton University Press, 1989.

Jameson, Fredic. *Marxism and Form: Twentieth Century Dialectical Theories of Literature.* Princeton: Princeton University Press, 1971.

———. "Postmodernism and Consumer Society." In *The Anti-Aesthetic,* edited by Hal Foster, 111–25. Port Townsend, Wash.: Bay Press, 1983.

Jay, Gregory S. *America the Scrivener: Deconstruction and the Subject of Literary History.* Ithaca: Cornell University Press, 1990.

Jesperson, Otto. *Language: Its Nature, Development and Origin.* London: Allen and Unwin, 1922.

Jewett, Sarah Orne. *Letters of Sarah Orne Jewett,* edited by Annie Fields. Boston: Houghton Mifflin, 1911.

———. *Sarah Orne Jewett Letters,* edited by Richard Cary. Waterville: Colby College Press, 1967.

———. "A White Heron." *Best Short Stories of Sarah Orne Jewett, Volume II,* edited by Willa Cather, 1–22. 1920. Reprint, Gloucester: Peter Smith, 1965.

Jones, Charles. "Varieties of Speech Representation in Conrad's *The Secret Agent.*" *Lingua* 20 (1968): 162–76.

Jones, Gayl. *Liberating Voices: Oral Tradition in African American Literature.* Cambridge: Harvard University Press, 1991.

Kahn, Madeline. *Narrative Transvestism.* Ithaca: Cornell University Press, 1989.

Kaivola, Karen. *All Contraries Confounded: The Lyrical Fiction of Virginia Woolf, Djuna Barnes, and Marguerite Duras.* Iowa City: University of Iowa Press, 1991.

Kapferer, Jean-Nöel. *Rumors: Uses, Interpretations and Images.* New Brunswick: Transaction Publishers, 1990.

Kaplan, Amy. *The Social Construction of Realism*. Chicago: University of Chicago Press, 1988.

Kern, Stephen. *The Culture of Time and Space 1880–1918*. Cambridge: Harvard University Press, 1983.

Kolodny, Annette. "A Map for Misreading: Gender and the Interpretation of Literary Texts." In *The Captive Imagination: A Casebook on "The Yellow Wallpaper,"* edited by Catherine Golden, 149–67. New York: Feminist Press, 1992.

Kristeva, Julia. "Women's Time." In *The Kristeva Reader*, edited by Toril Moi, translated by Alice Jardine and Harry Blake, 187–213. London: Basil Blackwell, 1986.

Kroeber, Karl. *Retelling/Rereading: The Fate of Storytelling in Modern Times*. New Brunswick: Rutgers University Press, 1992.

Lakoff, Robin. *Language and Woman's Place*. New York: Harper and Row, 1975.

———. *Talking Power: The Politics of Language in Our Lives*. New York: Basic Books, 1991.

Landor, William. "Washington Irving: His Works, Genius, and Character." *Sartain's Union Magazine* 7 (1850): 288–98.

Lane, Ann J. *To* Herland *and Beyond: The Life and Work of Charlotte Perkins Gilman*. New York: Pantheon, 1990.

Lanser, Susan Snaider. *The Narrative Act: Point of View in Prose Fiction*. Princeton: Princeton University Press, 1981.

———. "Speaking in Tongues: *Ladies Almanack* and the Discourse of Desire." In *Silence and Power: A Reevaluation of Djuna Barnes*, edited by Mary Lynn Broe, 156–69. Carbondale: Southern Illinois University Press, 1991.

Lawrence, James Cooper. "A Theory of the Short Story." In *Short Story Theories*, edited by Charles E. May, 60–71. Athens: Ohio University Press, 1976.

Leitch, Thomas M. *What Stories Are: Narrative Theory and Interpretation*. University City: Pennsylvania State University Press, 1986.

Leverenz, David. *Manhood and the American Renaissance*. Ithaca: Cornell University Press, 1989.

Levy, Andrew. *The Culture and Commerce of the American Short Story*. New York: Cambridge University Press, 1993.

Lewis, Wyndham. "The Dumb Ox: A Study of Ernest Hemingway."

In *Hemingway: The Critical Heritage*, edited by Jeffrey Meyers, 186–209. London: Routledge and Kegan Paul, 1982.

Lohafer, Susan. "A Cognitive Approach to Storyness." In *The New Short Story Theories*, edited by Charles E. May, 301–11. Athens: Ohio University Press, 1994.

———. *Coming to Terms with the Short Story*. Baton Rouge: Louisiana State University Press, 1983.

———. "Preclosure and Story Processing." In *Short Story Theory at a Crossroads*, edited by Susan Lohafer and Jo Ellyn Clarey, 249–75. Baton Rogue: Louisiana State Press, 1989.

——— and Jo Ellyn Clarey, eds. *Short Story Theory at a Crossroads*. Baton Rogue: Louisiana State University Press, 1989.

Lubow, Arthur. *The Reporter Who Would Be King: A Biography of Richard Harding Davis*. New York: Scribner's, 1991.

Lyons, Bonnie and Bill Oliver. "An Interview with Bobbie Ann Mason." *Contemporary Literature* 32 (fall 1991): 449–70.

Machor, James L. "Historical Hermeneutics and Antebellum Fiction." In *Readers in History: Nineteenth-Century American Literature and the Contexts of Response*, edited by James L. Machor, 54–84. Baltimore: Johns Hopkins University Press, 1992.

Margolies, Edward. "Wright's Craft: The Short Stories." In *Richard Wright: Critical Perspectives Past and Present*, edited by Henry Louis Gates and K. A. Appiah, 75–97. New York: Amistad, 1993.

Marler, Robert F. "From Tale to Short Story: The Emergence of a New Genre in the 1850s." In *The New Short Story Theories*, edited by Charles E. May, 165–81. Athens: Ohio University Press, 1994. First published in *American Literature* 44 (1974): 152–69.

Martin, Terence. "Rip, Ichabod, and the American Imagination." *American Literature* 31 (May 1959): 137–49.

Marx, Leo. *The Pilot and the Passenger: Essays on Literature, Technology, and Culture in the United States*. New York: Oxford University Press, 1988.

Mason, Bobbie Ann. *Shiloh and Other Stories*. New York: Harper and Row, 1982.

Matthews, Brander. "The Philosophy of the Short-Story." In *The New Short Story Theories*, edited by Charles E. May, 73–80. Athens: Ohio University Press, 1994. First published in *Lippincott's* 36 (October 1885): 366–74.

Matthiessen, F. O. *Sarah Orne Jewett*. Boston: Houghton Mifflin, 1929.

May, Charles E. "The Nature of Knowledge in Short Fiction." In *The New Short Story Theories*, edited by Charles E. May, 131–46. Athens: Ohio University Press, 1994. First published in *Studies in Short Fiction* 21 (1984): 327–38.

———, ed. *The New Short Story Theories*. Athens: Ohio University Press, 1994.

———, ed. *Short Story Theories*. Athens: Ohio University Press, 1976.

———. "The Unique Effect of the Short Story: A Reconsideration and an Example." *Studies in Short Fiction* 13 (summer 1976): 289–97.

McCall, Dan. *The Silence of Bartleby*. Ithaca: Cornell University Press, 1988.

McCluskey, John Jr. "Two Steppin': Richard Wright's Encounter with Blue-Jazz." *American Literature* 55 (October 1983): 332–44.

Mellow, James R. *Charmed Circle: Gertrude Stein & Company*. Boston: Houghton Mifflin, 1973.

Melville, Herman. "Bartleby, the Scrivener: A Story of Wall Street." In *The Writings of Herman Melville, Vol IX:* The Piazza Tales *and Other Prose Pieces, 1839–1860*, edited by Harrison Hayford, Alma A. MacDougall, G. Thomas Tanselle, et. al, 13–45. Evanston and Chicago: Northwestern University Press, 1987.

Messerli, Douglas. *Djuna Barnes: A Bibliography*. New York: David Lewis, 1975.

Mink, Louis O. "History and Fiction as Modes of Comprehension." In *Historical Understanding*, edited by Brian Fay, Eugene O. Golub, and Richard T. Cann, 42–60. Ithaca: Cornell University Press, 1987.

Molyneaux, Maribel W. "Sculpture in the Iron Mills: Rebecca Harding Davis's Korl Woman." *Women's Studies* 17 (1990): 157–77.

Monagham, E. Jennifer and E. Wendy Saal. "The Reader, the Scribe, the Thinker." In *Formation of School Subjects: The Struggle for Creating an American Institution*, edited by Thomas S. Popkewitz, 85–122. New York: Falmer, 1987.

Myers, Andrew B., ed. *A Century of Commentary on the Works of Washington Irving*. Tarrytown: Sleepy Hollow, 1976.

Neal, John. "Story-Telling." The *New-England Magazine* (January 1835): 1–8.

Nesset, Kirk. *The Stories of Raymond Carver: A Critical Study.* Athens: Ohio University Press, 1995.

"The New Copyright Law." The *American Monthly Magazine* 11 (February 1838): 105–20.

Norris, Frank. "Story-tellers vs. Novelists." In *The Complete Novels and Essays of Frank Norris*, edited by Donald Pizer, 1191–95. New York: Library of America, 1986.

———. "Why Women Should Write the Best Novels." In *The Complete Works of Frank Norris*. Vol. 7, 177–81. Garden City: Doubleday, 1928.

O'Brien, Edward J. *The Advance of the American Short Story*. 1926. New York: Dodd, Mead, 1976.

———. *The Dance of the Machines: The Short Story in the Industrial Age*. New York: Macaulay, 1929.

O'Brien, Tim. *The Things They Carried.* New York: Houghton Mifflin, 1990.

O'Connor, Flannery. "Writing Short Stories." In *Mysteries and Manners: Occasional Prose*, edited by Sally and Robert Fitzgerald, 87–106. New York: Farrar Straus Giroux, 1969.

O'Connor, Frank. *The Lonely Voice: A Sketch of the Short Story.* Cleveland: World Publishing, 1962.

O'Neal, Hank. *Life is painful, nasty, and short—in my case it has only been painful and nasty: Djuna Barnes, 1978–1981: An Informal Memoir*. New York: Paragon House, 1990.

Ong, Walter J. *Orality and Literacy: The Technologizing of the Word.* London and New York: Methuen, 1982.

O'Rourke, William. "Morphological Metaphors for the Short Story: Matters of Production, Reproduction, and Consumption." In *Short Story Theory at a Crossroads*, edited by Susan Lohafer and Jo Ellyn Clarey, 193–208. Baton Rogue: Louisiana State University Press, 1989.

Parker, Hershel. "The Sequel in 'Bartleby.'" In *Bartleby the Inscrutable: A Collection of Commentary on Herman Melville's Tale "Bartleby the Scrivener,"* edited by Thomas M. Inge, 159–65. Hamden: Archon Books, 1979.

Pasco, Allan H. "On Defining Short Stories." In *The New Short Story Theories*, edited by Charles E. May, 114–30. Athens: Ohio University Press, 1994. First published in *New Literary History* 22 (spring 1991): 407–22.

———. "The Short Story: The Short of It." *Style* 27 (fall 1993): 442–63.

Pattee, Fred Lewis. *The Development of the American Short Story: An Historical Sketch*. New York: Harper, 1923.

———. "The Present Stage of the Short Story." *English Journal* 12 (September 1923): 439–49.

Peden, William. *The American Short Story: Front Line in the National Defense of Literature*. Boston: Houghton Mifflin, 1964.

Penn, W. S. "The Tale as Genre in Short Fiction." In *The New Short Story Theories*, edited by Charles E. May, 44–55. Athens: Ohio University Press, 1994. First published in *Southern Humanities Review* 15 (1981): 234–35.

Perelman, Bob. "Parataxis and Narrative: The New Sentence in Theory and Practice." *American Literature* 65 (June 1993): 312–24.

Perloff, Marjorie. "Ninety-Percent Rotarian: Gertrude Stein's Hemingway." *American Literature* 62 (December 1990): 668–83.

Perry, Bliss. *A Study of Prose Fiction*. Boston: Houghton Mifflin, 1902.

Perry, T. S. "Ivan Turgenieff." *Atlantic Monthly* 33 (May 1874): 569.

Peterson, Theodore. *Magazines in the Twentieth Century*. Urbana: University of Illinois Press, 1964.

Phelps, Elizabeth Stuart. "Stories that Stay." *Century* 81 (1910): 118–24.

Plimpton, George, ed. *Writers at Work: The Paris Review Interviews*. New York: Penguin, 1977.

Poe, Edgar Allan. "Review of *Twice-Told Tales* and *Mosses from an Old Manse*." *Edgar Allan Poe: Essays and Reviews*, edited by G. R. Thompson, 568–88. New York: Library of America, 1984.

Ponsot, Marie. "A Reader's *Ryder*." In *Silence and Power: A Reevaluation of Djuna Barnes*, edited by Mary Lynn Broe, 94–136. Carbondale: Southern Illinois University Press, 1991.

Pope, Dan. "The Post-Minimalist American Story or What Comes After Carver?" *Gettysburg Review* 1 (spring 1988): 331–42.

Portelli, Alessandro. *The Text and the Voice: Writing, Speech, and Democracy in American Literature*. New York: Columbia University Press, 1994.

Pratt, Annis. "Women and Nature in Modern Fiction." *Contemporary Literature* 13 (autumn 1972): 476–90.

Pratt, Mary Louise. "The Short Story: The Long and Short of It." In *The New Short Story Theories*, edited by Charles E. May, 91–113. Athens: Ohio University Press, 1994. First published in *Poetics* 10 (1981): 179–80.

Priesler, Bent. *Linguistic Sex Roles in Conversation*. Berlin: Moutin de Gruyter, 1986.

Prescott, William H. "Essay Writing." *North American Review* 14 (April 1822): 319–50.

Reid, Ian. "Destabilizing Frames for Story." In *Short Story Theory at a Crossroads*, edited by Susan Lohafer and Jo Ellyn Clarey, 299–310. Baton Rogue: Louisiana State University Press, 1989.

Renza, Louis A. *"A White Heron" and the Question of Minor Literature*. Madison: University of Wisconsin Press, 1984.

Review of *The Foe in the Household* by Caroline Chesebro' *Atlantic Monthly* 28 (July 1871): 126.

"Review of New Books." *Graham's Magazine* 40 (1852): 443.

Review of *The Sketch Book of Geoffrey Crayon, Gent.* by Washington Irving. The *New York Post* 26 June 1819: 1.

Reynolds, David S. "From Doctrine to Narrative: The Rise of Pulpit Storytelling in America." *American Quarterly* 33 (1981): 479–98.

Rohrberger, Mary. *Hawthorne and the Modern Short Story: A Study in the Genre*. The Hague: Mouton, 1966.

——— and Dan E. Burns. "Short Fiction and the Numinous Realm: Another Attempt at Definition." *Modern Fiction Studies* 28 (spring 1982): 5–12.

Roman, Margaret. *Sarah Orne Jewett: Reconstructing Gender*. Tuscaloosa: University of Alabama Press, 1992.

Romines, Anne. *The Home Plot: Women, Writing, and Domestic Ritual*. Amherst: University of Massachusetts Press, 1992.

Rose, Jane Atteridge. "Reading 'Life in the Iron Mills' Contextually: A Key to Rebecca Harding Davis's Fiction." In *Conversations: Contemporary Critical Theory and the Teaching of Literature*, edited by Charles Moran and Elizabeth F. Penfield, 187–99. Urbana: NCTE, 1989.

Rubin-Dorsky, Jeffrey. *Adrift in the Old World: The Psychological Pilgrimage of Washington Irving*. Chicago: University of Chicago Press, 1988.

Scudder, Horace. "Miss Jewett." *Atlantic Monthly* 73 (January 1894): 130–33.

———. "New England in the Short Story." *Atlantic Monthly* 63 (June 1891): 845–50.

———. Review of *Old Friends and New* by Sarah Orne Jewett. *Atlantic Monthly* 45 (May 1880): 685–86.

———. "Stockton's Stories." *Atlantic Monthly* 59 (January 1887): 130–32.

Shacochis, Bob. "Style Wars in Fiction & Oceanfront Real Estate: Rednecks in Leotards." *AWP Chronicle* 25 (May 1993): 1–5.

Shapard, Robert. Introduction to *Sudden Fiction: American Short-Short Stories*, edited by Robert Shapard and James Thomas, xiii–xvi. Salt Lake City: Peregrine Press, 1986.

Shaw, Valerie. *The Short Story: A Critical Introduction*. London: Longman, 1983.

Shelnutt, Eve. "Macro-Minimalist Fiction: The Trickle-Down Effect." *AWP Chronicle* 25 (May 1993): 1, 13–18.

Simmons, Philip E. "Minimalist Fiction as 'Low' Postmodernism: Mass Culture and the Search for History." *Genre* 24 (spring 1991): 45–62.

Singley, Carol J. "Sarah Orne Jewett, Emily Dickinson and Female Initiation." *Colby Library Quarterly* 22 (March 1986): 36–47.

S., K. Review of *Men Without Women* by Ernest Hemingway. *Boston Evening Transcript Book Section* 7 January 1928: 4.

Smiley, Pamela. "Gender-Linked Miscommunication in 'Hills Like White Elephants.'" In *New Critical Approaches to the Short Stories of Ernest Hemingway*, edited by Jackson J. Benson, 288–99. Durham: Duke University Press, 1991.

Smith, Nina Banton. *American Reading Instruction: Its development and significance in gaining a perspective on current practices in reading*. Newark: International Reading Association, 1965.

Smith, Paul. "Hemingway's Early Manuscripts: The Theory and Practice of Omission." *The Journal of Modern Literature* 10 (June 1983): 268–88.

———. *A Reader's Guide to the Short Stories of Ernest Hemingway*. Boston: G. K. Hall, 1989.

Smith-Rosenberg, Caroll. "The Female World of Love and Ritual." In *Disorderly Conduct: Visions of Gender in Victorian America*, 53–76. New York: Knopf, 1985.

Stein, Gertrude. "Miss Furr and Miss Skeene." In *Geography and Plays*, 16–22. Boston: Four Seas, 1922.

———. "Miss Furr and Miss Skeene." *Vanity Fair* (July 1923): 55.

———. *Narration: Four Lectures*, edited by Thornton Wilder. 1935. Reprint, Chicago: University of Chicago Press, 1969.

Steiner, Wendy. *Exact Resemblance to Exact Resemblance: The Literary Portraiture of Gertrude Stein*. New Haven: Yale University Press, 1978.

Stevick, Philip, ed. *The American Short Story, 1900–1945*. Boston: Twayne, 1983.

Stull, William L. "Beyond Hopelessville: Another Side of Raymond Carver." *Philological Quarterly* 64 (winter 1985): 1–15.

Suleiman, Susan R. and Inge Crosman, eds. *The Reader in the Text: Essays on Audience and Interpretation*. Princeton: Princeton University Press, 1980.

Swann, C. S. B. "The Practice and Theory of Storytelling: Nathaniel Hawthorne and Walter Benjamin." *Journal of American Studies* 12 (1978): 185–202.

Symonds, W. L. "The Carnival of the Romantic." *Atlantic Monthly* 6 (August 1860): 129–41.

Symons, Julian. *Makers of the New: The Revolution in Literature 1912–1939*. New York: Random House, 1987.

Tallack, Douglas. *The Nineteenth-Century American Short Story: Language, Form, and Ideology*. London: Routledge, 1993.

Tannen, Deborah. *Talking Voices: Repetition, Dialogue, and Imagery in Conversational Discourse*. Cambridge: Cambridge University Press, 1989.

———. *That's Not What I Meant! How Conversation Makes or Breaks Your Relations With Others*. New York: Morrow, 1986.

Thompson, G. R. *The Art of Authorial Presence: Hawthorne's Provincial Tales*. Durham: Duke University Press, 1993.

———. "Literary Politics and the 'Legitimate Sphere': Poe, Hawthorne, and the 'Tale Proper.'" *Nineteenth-Century Fiction* 49 (fall 1994): 167–97.

Tichi, Cecelia. *Shifting Gears: Technology, Literature, Culture in Modernist America*. Chapel Hill: University of North Carolina Press, 1987.

Tompkins, Jane P., ed. *Reader-Response Criticism: From Formalism to Post-Structuralism.* Baltimore: Johns Hopkins University Press, 1980.

———. *Sensational Designs: The Cultural Work of American Fiction, 1790–1865.* New York: Oxford University Press, 1985.

Treichler, Paula. "Escaping the Sentence: Diagnosis and Discourse in 'The Yellow Wallpaper.'" In *The Captive Imagination: A Casebook on "The Yellow Wallpaper,"* edited by Catherine Golden, 191–210. New York: Feminist Press, 1992.

Tuckerman, Henry T. "Nathaniel Hawthorne." In *The Recognition of Nathaniel Hawthorne: Selected Criticism Since 1828,* edited by B. Bernard Cohen, 55–63. Ann Arbor: University of Michigan Press, 1969. First published in *Southern Literary Messenger* (1851): 344–49.

Twain, Mark. "How to Tell a Story." In *The Complete Essays of Mark Twain,* edited by Charles Neider. Garden City: Hanover, 1956.

Updike, John. "Bech in Czech." The *New Yorker* 20 April 1987: 32–45.

Volosinov, V. N. *Marxism and the Philosophy of Language,* translated by Ladislav Matejka and I. R. Titunik. 1929. Reprint, Cambridge: Harvard University Press, 1986.

Voss, Arthur. *The American Short Story: A Critical Survey.* Norman: University of Oklahoma Press, 1973.

Waggoner, Hyatt. *Hawthorne: A Critical Study.* Cambridge: Harvard University Press, 1955.

Walker, Warren S. "From Raconteur to Writer: Oral Roots and Printed Leaves of Short Fiction." In *The Teller and the Tale: Aspects of the Short Story,* edited by Wendell M. Aycock, 13–26. Lubbock: Texas Tech Press, 1982.

Wallace, David Foster. *Girl with Curious Hair.* New York: Norton, 1990.

Wallace, Henry Bissell. *Literary Criticisms and Other Papers.* Philadelphia: Parry and McMillan, 1856.

Warhol, Robyn R. *Gendered Interventions: Narrative Discourse in the Victorian Novel.* New Brunswick: Rutgers University Press, 1989.

Weaver, Gordon, ed. *The American Short Story, 1945–1980.* Boston: Twayne, 1984.

Weinstein, Arnold. *Speech, Self, and Place in American Fiction from*

Hawthorne to DeLillo. New York: Oxford University Press, 1993.

Welty, Eudora. "Looking at Short Stories." In *The Eye of the Story: Selected Essays and Reviews*, 97–118. New York: Random House, 1978.

———. "The Writing and Reading of Short Stories." In *Short Story Theories*, edited by Charles E. May, 159–77. Athens: Ohio University Press, 1976.

Williams, Raymond. *Television: Technology and Cultural Form*. New York: Schocken, 1975.

Wilson, Christopher. *The Labor of Words: Literary Professionalism in the Progressive Era*. Athens: University of Georgia Press, 1985.

———. "The Rhetoric of Consumption: Mass Market Magazines and the Demise of the Gentle Reader, 1880–1920." In *The Culture of Consumption: Critical Essays in American History, 1880–1980*, edited by Richard Wightman Fox and T. J. Jackson Lears, 39–64. New York: Pantheon, 1984.

Wilson, Edmund. *Axel's Castle: A Study in the Imaginative Literature of 1870–1930*. New York: Scribner's, 1931.

Wilson, R. Jackson. *Figures of Speech: American Writers and the Literary Marketplace, from Benjamin Franklin to Emily Dickinson*. Baltimore: Johns Hopkins University Press, 1990.

Woolf, Virginia. "An Essay in Criticism." In *Hemingway: The Critical Heritage*, edited by Jeffrey Meyers, 101–6. London: Routledge and Kegan Paul, 1982. First published in *The New York Herald Tribune Books* 9 October 1927: 1, 8.

Wright, Austin. *The American Short Story in the 1920s*. Chicago: University of Chicago Press, 1962.

Wright Richard. "Almos' a Man." In *Best Short Stories of 1940*, edited by Edward J. O'Brien, 356–70. Boston: Houghton Mifflin, 1941.

———. "Between Laughter and Tears." *New Masses* 5 October 1937: 22, 25.

———. "Blueprint for Negro Writing." In *Richard Wright Reader*, edited by Ellen Wright and Michel Fabre, 36–50. New York: Harper and Row, 1978.

———. *Eight Men*. New York: World Publishing, 1961.

———. "Gertrude Stein's Story is Drenched in Hitler's Horrors." In

Richard Wright Reader, edited by Ellen Wright and Michel Fabre, 75–78. New York: Harper and Row, 1978.

———. "How 'Bigger' Was Born." In *Richard Wright: The Early Works:* Lawd Today!, Uncle Tom's Children, Native Son, edited by Arnold Rampersad, 853–81. New York: Library of America, 1990.

Yaeger, Patricia. *Honey-Mad Women: Emancipatory Strategies in Women's Writing*. New York: Columbia University Press, 1988.

Yellin, Jean Fagan. "The 'Feminization' of Rebecca Harding Davis." *American Literary History* 2 (1990): 203–19.

Zagarell, Sandra A. "Narrative of Community: The Identification of a Genre." *Signs* 13 (spring 1988): 498–527.

Index

G

H

I

J

K

ISBN 0-89301-202-5

90000>

EAN

9 780893 012021